Y0-CBD-670

Events and Sustainability

Increasing concerns over climate and environmental change, the global economic and financial crisis and impacts on host communities, audiences, participants and destinations have reinforced the need for more sustainable approaches to events. Sustainability now features as part of the bid process for many mega-events, such as the Olympic Games, as well as significant regional and local events, where the event organisers are required by funding bodies and governments to generate broader outcomes for the locality.

This book is the first to offer students a comprehensive introduction to the full range of issues and topics relevant to event sustainability including impacts, operating and policy environments, stimulating urban regeneration and creating lasting legacies, as well as practical knowledge on how to achieve a sustainable event. Taking a holistic approach drawing on multidisciplinary theory it offers insight into the economic, socio-cultural and environmental impacts and how these can be adapted or mitigated. Theory and practice are linked through integrated case studies based on a wide range of event types from mega events to community festivals to show impacts, best practice and how better sustainable practice can be achieved in the future. Learning objectives, discussion questions and further reading suggestions are included to aid understanding and further knowledge; additional resources for lecturers and students including power point slides, video and web links are available online.

Events and Sustainability is essential reading for all events management students and future managers.

Kirsten Holmes is an Associate Professor in Tourism at Curtin University, Western Australia. She has 14 years' experience of teaching event management and event sustainability in the UK and Australia. Her research examines volunteerism in tourism and leisure settings, with a focus on events.

Michael Hughes is a Senior Lecturer in Environmental Management at Murdoch University, Perth, Western Australia. He has a keen interest in environmental management, policy and sustainability. Michael has published on perceptions of nature, industrial development in remote natural areas and the value of wildlife tourism.

Judith Mair is a Senior Lecturer in Event Management in the UQ Business School, University of Queensland, Australia. She is author of *Conferences and Conventions: A Research Perspective*. Her research interests include events, tourism and sustainability and she has published many journal articles on these topics in international journals.

Jack Carlsen has 30 years of academic experience and is currently an Adjunct Professor at Curtin University, Western Australia. He has an extensive research track record, which has produced more than 150 career publications on various topics related to sustainable tourism planning, markets, development and evaluation.

'As sustainability is now a key driver of most activity, *Events and Sustainability* is a "must read" text for event management students. It is a well structured text that comprehensively addresses all of the key dimensions of sustainable events in a highly accessible fashion. Each chapter sets clear learning outcomes and provides highly relevant case studies and thought provoking discussion questions. *Events and Sustainability* will also make a valuable reference for event practitioners.' – Leo Jago, Professor in Hospitality and Events, University of Surrey, UK

'Against an environment of increased commoditisation and competition, austerity in the west and abundance in emerging economies, never has an understanding of the role of sustainability to today's economy and society been more important. This text offers a pragmatic, enlightened and realistic insight into the increasing challenges and opportunities that are facing festivals and events in order to develop and deliver more sustainable events. The combined use of context setting, key theory, international case studies, public and private sector examples and activities and discussion makes this a must read for any student or practitioner studying or interested in the future sustainability of events.' – Dr Jane Ali-Knight, Director of Edinburgh Institute: Festivals, Events and Tourism, Edinburgh Napier University, UK

Events and Sustainability

Kirsten Holmes, Michael Hughes, Judith Mair and Jack Carlsen

Routledge
Taylor & Francis Group

LONDON AND NEW YORK

First published 2015
by Routledge
2 Park Square, Milton Park, Abingdon, Oxon OX14 4RN

and by Routledge
711 Third Avenue, New York, NY 10017

Routledge is an imprint of the Taylor & Francis Group, an informa business

© 2015 Kirsten Holmes, Michael Hughes, Judith Mair and Jack Carlsen

The right of Kirsten Holmes, Michael Hughes, Judith Mair and Jack Carlsen to be identified as the authors of this work has been asserted by them in accordance with sections 77 and 78 of the Copyright, Designs and Patents Act 1988.

All rights reserved. No part of this book may be reprinted or reproduced or utilised in any form or by any electronic, mechanical, or other means, now known or hereafter invented, including photocopying and recording, or in any information storage or retrieval system, without permission in writing from the publishers.

Trademark notice: Product or corporate names may be trademarks or registered trademarks, and are used only for identification and explanation without intent to infringe.

British Library Cataloguing in Publication Data
A catalogue record for this book is available from the British Library

Library of Congress Cataloging in Publication Data
Holmes, Kirsten.
Events and sustainability / Kirsten Holmes, Michael Hughes, Judith Mair and Jack Carlsen.
    pages cm
    Includes bibliographical references and index.
    1. Special events–Management. 2. Special events–Planning. 3. Special events industry–Environmental aspects. 4. Sustainability. I. Hughes, Michael, 1971- II. Mair, Judith. III. Carlsen, Jack. IV. Title.
GT3405.H65 2015
394.2–dc23   2014038135

ISBN: 978-0-415-74449-2 (hbk)
ISBN: 978-0-415-74450-8 (pbk)
ISBN: 978-1-315-81301-1 (ebk)

Typeset in Frutiger
by Sunrise Setting Ltd, Paignton, UK

Printed and bound in the United States of America by Publishers Graphics, LLC on sustainably sourced paper.

Dedication

Kirsten – To Steven, Gwenllian and Roslyn
Michael – To Mary, Elisabeth and Samuel and my Dad, Tony
Judith – To Douglas, Stewart, Scott and my Dad
Jack – To my parents, Yvonne and Jack

Contents

List of figures xi
List of tables xii
List of boxes xiii
About the authors xiv
Preface xvi

1 Introduction to sustainable events 1

Why develop sustainable events? 2
What is sustainable development? 2
What is sustainability? 3
Sustainable events 5
Events and economic, social and environmental impacts 5
Event impact standards and guides 6
Sustainable event stakeholders 6
The structure of this book 8
Chapter summary 9
Case study: Greening a music festival 10

Part I The events context 15

2 The internal and external environment for sustainable event organisers 17

Introduction 18
The internal environment of an event 18
Scope of the event 21
Understanding the internal and external environment of an event 21
Event stakeholders 24
Constraints on event sustainability 26
Chapter summary 28
Case study: The International Sailing Federation World Championships, Fremantle 2011 29

Contents

3   Sustainable events and public policy   **32**

Introduction   33
Why do governments get involved in events?   34
Government approaches to involvement in events   36
Events and government policy domains   39
Sustainable events policy   41
The role of politics within events   41
Chapter summary   42
Case study: Subvention in Malaysia's convention industry   43

4   Sustainable events and urban regeneration   **48**

Introduction   49
Why do governments use events for regeneration?   49
Event-led and event-themed regeneration   50
Outside physical regeneration   52
Sustainable event regeneration   53
The dark side of event-led regeneration   55
Chapter summary   56
Case study: The impacts of urban regeneration for the
    XIX Commonwealth Games, Delhi 2010   57

Part II   Impacts of sustainable events   **61**

5   Economic impacts of events   **63**

Introduction   64
Positive and negative economic impacts of events   65
Estimating economic impact of events   66
Towards sustainable events economic evaluation   72
Chapter summary   73
Case study: Meta-analysis of 18 major events in New Zealand   74

6   Environmental impacts of events   **78**

Introduction   79
What is 'the environment'?   79
What does 'environmental impact' mean?   80
Types of impact   82
Measuring environmental impacts   90
Managing environmental impacts   92
Chapter summary   92
Case study: Peats Ridge Festival, Glenworth Valley, Australia   93

7   Socio-cultural impacts of events   **98**

Introduction   99
Measuring socio-cultural impacts   101
Social capital   103
Community perceptions of events   104
What do events mean to communities?   106
Chapter summary   108
Case study: Community relevance at Bluesfest Blues and
  Roots Festival, Byron Bay   108

8   Delivering the sustainable event   **113**

Introduction   114
Delivering economic sustainability   114
Delivering socio-cultural sustainability   117
Delivering environmental sustainability   119
Delivering a holistically sustainable event   122
Systems thinking   123
Key attributes of systems thinking   124
Chapter summary   126
Case study: London 2012 Olympic Games – delivering
  a sustainable event   127

Part III   Logistics of sustainable events   **133**

9   Employment, volunteering and sustainable events   **135**

Introduction   136
Issues in sustainable event staffing   136
Challenges for community events   138
Volunteers and sustainable events   138
Management of event volunteer programmes   139
The employment and employability legacies   142
Chapter summary   143
Case study: Manchester Event Volunteers   144

10   Risk and crisis management for sustainable events   **148**

Introduction   149
Risks and event sustainability   151
Risk management process   154
Crisis and disaster management for events   156
Chapter summary   157
Case study: Risk management at Edinburgh's Hogmanay   157

Contents

11   The challenge of creating sustainable event legacies   **162**

Introduction   163
The challenges (or politics) of legacy planning   163
What happens when legacy plans fail?   165
Why do event legacies fail to deliver?   165
Legacy planning to avoid failure   168
Chapter summary   169
Case study: The 2004 Athens Olympic Games legacy   170

12   Creating sustainable legacies from events   **174**

Introduction   175
Different types of legacy   175
The hard legacy   177
The inspirational (or soft) legacy   178
Different types of events, different legacy opportunities   179
Sustainable legacy planning   180
Chapter summary   182
Case study: Legacy planning for Brazil 2016   184

Part IV   Conclusion   **189**

13   Developing sustainable events: summary and future directions **191**

Introduction   192
Summary and review   192
The future of sustainable events   194
Final thoughts   197

Glossary   **199**
Index   **202**

List of figures

1.1 Common diagrams used to represent the sustainability concept 3
2.1 The internal environment for sustainable events 18
2.2 Strategic SWOT analytical framework 23
2.3 Stakeholders of the London 2012 Olympics 25
7.1 Social Impact Perception scale (sample question) 101
8.1 A generalised events environmental management system framework 120
8.2 Engineering resilience 126
8.3 Ecological resilience 126
10.1 Risk matrix for events 155
12.1 The legacy opportunity matrix 179
12.2 The sustainable legacy timeline 183
13.1 Summary of economic, environmental and social impacts described in this book 194

List of tables

1.1	Example definitions of sustainable development since 1987	4
1.2	Examples of sustainable event guides, toolkits and standards	7
5.1	Value-added multiplier effects of a AU$10 million event	67
5.2	Methodology for post-event estimation of the national cost and benefits	76
6.1	Example of some potential environmental impacts of different types of planned event held in natural area locations	83
6.2	Examples of standardised average estimated CO_2 emissions from different event-related sources	91
7.1	Positive and negative socio-cultural impacts of events	100
8.1	Examples of how events can support sustainable economies	116
8.2	Attributes of systems thinking	125
10.1	Areas of event risk	150
10.2	Events and festivals cancelled due to severe weather	153
11.1	Cost overrun of the summer Olympic Games	169

List of boxes

2.1	The Moscone Centre, San Francisco	20
2.2	Bidding for the FIFA World Cup	27
3.1	Government major events policy: the case of VMEC	36
3.2	Events strategies – the case of the Singapore F1 Grand Prix	38
3.3	Politics and the Olympics	42
4.1	Fremantle and the America's Cup	50
4.2	Post-event use of Olympic villages	52
4.3	Principles for sustainable event regeneration	54
5.1	Reported economic impacts of the Indy 500	64
5.2	FIFA World Cup 2022 cost–benefit analysis guidelines	69
6.1	The Event Impacts Project	82
7.1	FIFA World Cup 2010, South Africa	102
7.2	Using social capital to assess socio-cultural impacts of events	104
7.3	Contested meanings at the Parkes Elvis Festival	107
8.1	Infrastructure gains from events	115
8.2	Coachella	118
8.3	The 'green' ticket at Splendour in the Grass	121
9.1	Staffing at the Vancouver Winter Olympics	137
9.2	Establishing a volunteer programme for the Commonwealth Heads of Government Meeting, Perth 2011	140
9.3	Glasgow 2014's employability legacy	143
10.1	Economic risks: the collapse of Peats Ridge Festival	151
10.2	Death and injury at festivals and events	152
10.3	Risk of disaster: the Boston Marathon bombing	156
11.1	Constraints for creating an employment legacy	164
11.2	The Sydney Olympic Park	167
11.3	A tourism legacy for the European Capital of Culture (ECoC)	168
12.1	Social legacies of Manchester 2002 Commonwealth Games	176
12.2	The Barcelona model	177
12.3	The FIFA World Cup 2010 and reconciliation in South Africa	178
13.1	Global challenges for the events sector	195

About the authors

Kirsten Holmes is an Associate Professor in Tourism at Curtin University, Western Australia. She has previously worked at the Universities of Sheffield and Surrey and has 14 years' experience of teaching event management and event sustainability in the UK and Australia. Her research focusses on volunteerism in tourism and leisure settings and she is the author of *Managing volunteers in tourism: attractions, destinations and events* (with Karen Smith, published by Elsevier) and editor of *Event volunteering: international perspectives on the event volunteering experience* (with Karen Smith, Leonie Lockstone-Binney and Tom Baum, published by Routledge).

Michael Hughes is a Senior Lecturer in Environmental Management at Murdoch University, Perth, Western Australia. Michael has researched in the areas of tourism, recreation and environmental management for the past 20 years. He has a keen interest in sustainable development and sustainability as well as environmental sociology. Michael has published on regional development, nature based tourism, natural area policy and management, environmental attitudes, perceptions and visitor behaviour management. He enjoys picnics, bushwalking and camping with his family in the Australian Bush.

Judith Mair is a Senior Lecturer in Event Management in the UQ Business School, University of Queensland, Australia. Her research interests include pro-environmental behaviour and resilience both in tourism and events; the impacts of events on community and society; consumer behaviour in events and tourism; the relationship between events and climate change; and business and major events. Her PhD investigated decision-making in the events context and was completed at the University of Strathclyde. Judith is working on a number of projects including investigating the potential for events to act as a catalyst for encouraging pro-environmental behaviour change; researching the links between events and social capital; and assessing the potential impacts of climate change on the tourism and events sector.

Jack Carlsen has 30 years of academic experience and is currently an Adjunct Professor at Curtin University, Western Australia where he founded the Curtin Sustainable Tourism Centre in 2002. He has an excellent research track record, which has produced more than 150 scholarly publications on various topics related to sustainable tourism planning, markets, development and evaluation. He has successfully collaborated with more than 50 colleagues in Australia and internationally and almost 90 per cent of his publications have been co-authored with other leading international researchers. He is on the editorial board of a number of international journals and established the *International Journal of Event and Festival Management,* first published in 2010. Jack is also Director of Tourism Research Services, a consulting firm he established in 1991 to complete timely and accurate reporting on all aspects of tourism planning, marketing management and evaluation for public and private agencies across Australia and internationally. He is based near Margaret River, Western Australia, where he enjoys the ocean, forests, wineries and hospitality of the region.

Preface

The role of sustainability in events and festivals is becoming increasingly important and now features as part of the bid process for many mega-events, such as the Olympic Games. However, it is also significant for regional and local events, where the event organisers are required by funding bodies and governments to generate broader outcomes for the locality. Frequently, event audiences are demanding that the events and festivals they attend adopt more sustainable practice, for example through water use or waste management. This growth in the events sector is reflected in academic programmes where the impacts of events, their legacies and sustainability issues increasingly form a key part of event management education. Yet, there are to date few textbooks which consider sustainability as a holistic part of events management. This has proved a constraint to the authorship team in our own events management classes, as there is currently no student-friendly textbook available which addresses the broad remit of event sustainability.

This textbook seeks to address this gap in the market by adopting a holistic approach to event sustainability and to take this further by introducing the contemporary ecological systems approach to sustainability as a means to integrate the different components (economic, environmental and socio-cultural). The textbook uses a consistent structure within each chapter, an accessible style for students, including up-to-date and classic case studies, and provides support for instructors and further study for students. We hope it will add value to Event Management programmes globally.

Kirsten Holmes
Michael Hughes
Judith Mair
Jack Carlsen

Chapter 1

Introduction to sustainable events

Learning outcomes

After studying this chapter you should be able to:

- Understand the importance of creating more sustainable events
- Define the terms 'sustainable development' and 'sustainability'
- Understand the three dimensions of sustainability: economic, environmental and social
- Relate these concepts to sustainable planned events
- Identify sustainability guidelines for event organisers

Why develop sustainable events?

Events and festivals have an important role in our lives. They help us to celebrate and commemorate personal and public landmark occasions, they bring communities together and they provide opportunities for entertainment. Governments are keen to host and organise events that will bring publicity, create jobs and attract tourism. Businesses and governments use events to promote their product, build relationships with their clients and to generally conduct their business. Events and festivals offer destinations, governments and businesses the opportunity to deliver something unique and ever-changing.

Events take place in specific political, economic, environmental and social contexts and all events create impacts, both positive and negative. An event that results in more negative impacts than positive is undesirable, may lose support from the local community or generate negative publicity and is ultimately not sustainable. Support for events relies on maximising the positive impacts (benefits) and minimising negative impacts. This book examines how event organisers can ensure events contribute positively in the short and long term. Making a positive contribution can contribute towards the sustainability of the event as well as ensure it benefits communities associated with the event.

Developing sustainable events is a way of approaching event management from a more holistic perspective that can benefit event key stakeholders as well as communities affected by the event. There are pragmatic and altruistic motivations for sustainable development of events. Sustainable development and sustainability has gained global recognition as an important issue associated with the continued survival of human society. The idea of sustainability has permeated all aspects of society and is therefore an important consideration in event development. However, events also need support from communities, governments and the media and adhering to the sustainable development agenda is an effective way of gathering that support.

What is sustainable development?

Sustainable development is a process that results in the goal of sustainability. The term 'sustainable' means to exist in perpetuity without depleting the resources necessary for continuation into the future. Development refers to change over time, but not necessarily growth. Sustainable development therefore refers to a process of transformation (Liburd and Edwards, 2010). Drawing on the original United Nations definition (WCED, 1987), sustainable development is commonly based on the notion of human progress towards maintaining or improving standards of living without compromising the natural systems on which all life depends for survival.

There is a significant body of knowledge on this topic stretching back at least two centuries. Earlier writers such as Thomas Malthus (1798) wrote about the limits to growth in what were then agricultural societies where human population expansion could outstrip the ability of farms to grow adequate food supplies. This was due to the limited ability to supply food to the increasing number of people as urban expansion reduced the amount of land available for food production. In the mid to late twentieth century authors such as Paul R. Ehrlich (1968) and Rachel Carson (1962) popularised the environmental movement when writing on the potential consequences of the modern industrialised era and mass consumerism, although their arguments were from a similar basis to those of Thomas Malthus two hundred years earlier.

   The fundamental issue remains the same, that is, the increasing rate of resource consumption by humans in a world with finite resources and limits to productivity. The issue became more globally prominent and entered mainstream thought with a series of UN sponsored meetings of national leaders and scientists during the 1970s. This culminated in the 1983 UN summit on the environment and the subsequent report *Our Common Future* by Gro Harlem Brundtland (WCED, 1987). The original summit has been followed by subsequent summits each decade (e.g. 1992, 2002 and 2012) at which national leaders discuss the complex and ongoing process of sustainable development.

What is sustainability?

Sustainability is the goal of sustainable development. Sustainability suggests an equilibrium or condition of stability in which consumption and renewal of resources are in a balance that maintains conditions for human survival that can continue for ever. This is usually illustrated using images such as three pillars, a Venn diagram, or even nested ovals representing the three main elements underpinning human society, namely, the economic, environment and social domains (Figure 1.1).

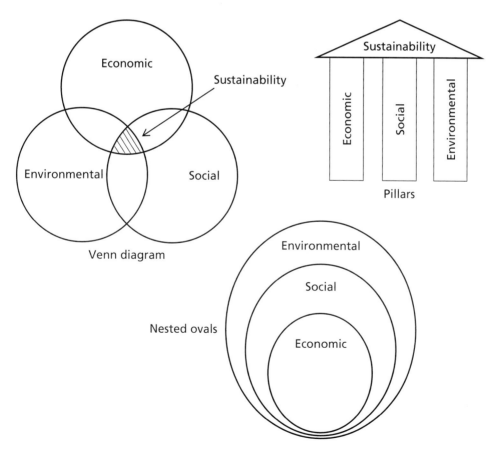

Figure 1.1 Common diagrams used to represent the sustainability concept

That is, the traditional notion of sustainability is based on simultaneous achievement of:

1 *Economic sustainability* in the form of viable enterprises and related economic activity that can be maintained in the long term
2 *Social sustainability* where society is based on ethical and equitable principles in terms of equal opportunity and human rights, maintaining and strengthening local communities and their social support systems and the absence of exploitation
3 *Environmental sustainability* where natural resources are conserved and responsibly managed, especially those that are non-renewable and/or vital for life support, by minimising pollution, conserving biological diversity and protecting natural heritage

There is a wide range of definitions for sustainable development and sustainability that depend on whom is doing the defining and the reason it is being defined. Table 1.1 provides some examples of the hundreds that may exist.

While some definitions may be more human focussed while others are more ecologically focussed, there are some common themes among these various definitions. These common elements include maintaining or enhancing human wellbeing and natural resources in relation to the term 'sustainable' and notions of change over time, or dynamic shifts, in relation to the term 'development'.

Table 1.1 Example definitions of sustainable development since 1987

Definition – Sustainable development is:	Source
'... a process of change in which the exploitation of resources, the direction of investments, the orientation of technological development, and institutional change are all in harmony and enhance both current and future potential to meet human needs and aspirations.'	WCED (1987: 46)
'... [a] strategy that manages all assets, natural resources and human resources, as well as financial and physical assets, for increasing long-term wealth and wellbeing.'	Repetto, cited in Pearce et al. (1990: 4)
'... a dynamic process in which communities anticipate and accommodate the needs of current and future generations in ways that reproduce and balance local social, economic and ecological systems, and link local actions to global concerns.'	Berke and Conroy (2000: 23)
Where human development goals are achieved based on society metabolising natural resources into waste no faster than nature can convert the waste back into resources.	Moran et al. (2008)
Where human production and consumption systems, such as agriculture, transport and energy generation, function within ecological boundaries.	Meadowcroft (2009)
'... development that promotes the capabilities of present people without compromising capabilities of future generations.'	Leßmann and Rauschmayer (2013: 97)

Sustainable events

By their nature, any planned event will usually result in a range of positive and negative impacts at the local and wider scale, depending on the type and size of the event. According to Schlenker, Foley and Getz (2010), the initial focus of event impact measurement and management was on economics. This is because the success of an event or festival was commonly considered to relate primarily to its economic contribution to event stakeholders and the region where the event occurs. While economics are obviously important, event organisers and managers as well as event goers have become more aware of the wider impacts of events and the need to ensure negative impacts are minimised while any benefits are maximised across social, economic and environmental issues.

Although event impact assessment began with a focus on economics, there was also an almost counter approach focussed on the 'Green Event' which was designed to minimise negative environmental impacts and potentially contribute some environmental benefits. A Green Event is defined as an event that has a sustainability policy and/or implements sustainable management practices (Laing and Frost, 2010). The 'Green Event' idea began with a focus on environmental issues but has since expanded to include social and economic concerns.

Events and economic, social and environmental impacts

Drawing on the United Nations definitions, in order to be sustainable, events need to address the three aspects that include environmental, economic and social issues. For example:

1 *Economic issues*: Depending on size and scale, the event itself is economically viable and contributes to the development of viable enterprises in the region in which it occurs and also triggers related economic activity that can be maintained in the long term. The measurement and monitoring of the positive and negative economic impacts of events is discussed in Chapter 5.
2 *Environmental issues*: Event planning and operation focusses on conservation of natural resources by minimising pollution and other negative impacts, actively working to conserve natural and built environments where the event takes place and perhaps more broadly. The measurement and monitoring of the positive and negative environmental impacts of events is discussed in Chapter 6.
3 *Social issues*: The event is based on socially ethical and equitable principles, for example, equal opportunity employment and reasonable working conditions with an absence of exploitation. Events may also contribute to maintaining and strengthening local communities through local employment and promotion of aspects such as social and cultural pride, conservation of cultural heritage and strengthening community networks. The measurement and monitoring of the positive and negative social impacts of events is discussed in Chapter 7.

Event planners can seek to ensure that the impacts of an event stay within acceptable limits that do not contribute to economic adversity, social disadvantage or environmental degradation for the region in which it occurs. That is, the region in which the event occurs is able to absorb any negative impacts and maintain or improve its economic, social and/or environmental condition. Chapter 4 discusses the idea of events and regeneration and Chapter 8 provides an overview of delivering the sustainable event. Regeneration refers to revitalising or improving economic, social and environmental conditions in a region as a result of preparing for and staging a mega-event, such as an Olympics or Commonwealth Games event or World Cup or Expo event. The long-term legacies of events are discussed in Chapters 11 and 12, on event legacies and why they fail or succeed.

Event impact standards and guides

To help event planners and managers develop sustainable events, numerous guides, standards and certification programmes have been developed in recent years. These generally include all three issues of environmental, economic and social impacts. Some are designed for events of any type and scale, others have a specific focus. Some guides are government-led, some have been developed by not-for-profit organisations and others are industry driven. Table 1.2 outlines some examples of standards, guidelines and certification programmes designed to assist in sustainable event development.

For example, ISO20121 is a set of international standards published in 2012 detailing requirements for a high quality event sustainability management system for any type of event. This includes social, economic and environmental issues (www.iso.org). ISO20121 was based on the British Standards Institute BS8901 for sustainable event management (first published in 2007). The first official use of ISO20121 was for the London Olympic Games in 2012.

These guides and certification programmes offer a great deal of information and advice on how to plan and implement a sustainable event. However, although an event organiser may be keen to implement sustainable management practices, not all stakeholders share their goal.

Sustainable event stakeholders

In order for an event to be successful, a range of past research highlights the importance of a shared vision and understanding amongst key stakeholders. This is especially the case when event planners wish to implement specific management actions to achieve that vision. It is important to communicate the importance and need to all key stakeholders, and gain their support, for an event to effectively implement sustainable practices (Laing and Frost, 2010).

Key stakeholders in sustainable events may include:

- Sponsors
- Government agencies
- Venue owners and managers
- Land owners and managers
- Community groups
- Volunteers
- Media

Table 1.2 Examples of sustainable event guides, toolkits and standards

Document	Publisher	Focus
ISO20121	International Standards Organisation (ISO)	Detailed guide on all aspects of event management for all types of planned event.
BS8901 Sustainability in Event Management	British Standards Institute	Standards designed for the events industry for all aspects of sustainability in events.
Sustainable Events Guide	UK Department for Environment, Food and Rural Affairs (DEFRA)	A guide to assist government departments to plan sustainable events.
Event Impacts Toolkit	UK Sport, Visit Britain, Event Scotland, London Development Agency, Northwest Development Agency, Yorkshire Forward, Glasgow City Marketing Bureau	A toolkit for event planners with good practice guidelines and resources for measuring and monitoring economic, environmental and social impacts.
Encore Festival and Event Evaluation Toolkit	Sustainable Tourism Cooperative Research Centre, Australia	A toolkit for measuring the economic impact of any type and size of event. Also includes environmental and social impact modules.
Sustainable Events Guidelines	Tasmanian Environmental Protection Authority, Events Tasmania	Some key points and a check list relating to managing negative environmental and social impacts.
A Greener Festival	A Greener Festival: a not-for-profit company aimed at assisting arts and music festivals becoming more sustainable	Awards and good practice guides for sustainable arts and music festivals, focusing on green-field festivals.
Yourope Clean'n'Green Award	Yourope – a European festival association	Environmental guidelines for music festivals.

Sources: www.iso.org; http://www.bsigroup.com/; http://archive.defra.gov.uk/sustainable/government/advice/sustainable-events-guide.htm; http://www.eventimpacts.com/; http://epa.tas.gov.au/sustainability/sustainable-event-guidelines; http://www.agreenerfestival.com/; http://www.yourope.org/ [accessed 12 November, 2014]; Schlenker et al., 2010

Each stakeholder is likely to have a different priority according to their vested interests. Achieving agreement between these groups and managing them effectively can be a challenge. It is also important to ensure that staff and volunteers associated with the event understand their role in implementing sustainability practices with clear responsibilities and lines of communication. These issues are covered in Chapter 2 of this book on the internal and external environment for events and event public policy in Chapter 3.

The structure of this book

This chapter has outlined that sustainability applied to events is complex and multifaceted. As sustainability has grown as a global concern, a number of books have been published on the various aspects of sustainability, for example Jones (2014), which examines the environmental sustainability and events or Smith (2012), which examines how events are used in urban regeneration projects. This book adopts a holistic approach to event sustainability, combining theory with practical implications supported by boxed examples and detailed case studies.

The book is divided into four parts. Part I sets the context for event sustainability with an overview of the environment within which events take place. Chapter 2 examines the internal and external environment for sustainable events; the context within which events and festivals operate that is the social, economic and political environment; and the relevant stakeholders, including those immediate to the event as well as the broader context of government, the media and funding bodies. This analysis leads to identification of the constraints and limitations to creating sustainable events including those both within and outside the event manager's control.

Chapter 3 investigates why governments support events; different policy approaches towards events; and the role of national and international politics within events, for example, how mega-events have become the focus for national and international protest. Chapter 4 reviews the broader role of events within urban planning and renewal; compares and contrasts event-led and event-themed approaches to urban regeneration; evaluates the physical, economic and social benefits that can be gained from regeneration; and identifies possible negative consequences of event-led regeneration including displacement of local populations; breakdown of communities and the creation of exclusionary cities.

Part II focusses on the impacts of events. Chapter 5 describes the economic impacts of events and analyses the ways in which economic impacts can be estimated. Chapter 6 analyses how events impact on the environment, including the natural environment and built environment; identifies what impacts are within the event manager's locus of control and how best to influence impacts which are outside of this. The chapter reviews methods for measuring the environmental impact of events and identifies ways of minimising the negative environmental impact of events and provides examples of good environmental practice in events and festival management.

Chapter 7 presents the social, cultural and psychological impacts of events; examines the value of events for local communities, how events shape communal identities and how the management of events for tourism can alter this; and identifies ways of assessing the social impacts of events. Chapter 8 introduces the application of ecological systems thinking for sustainable events. This chapter also reviews ways in which event managers can integrate sustainability into event planning and goes through the practicalities of sustainability for an event, including waste, recycling, water conservation, using sustainable products, social and economic elements – such as using locally sourced goods and services, volunteers, employment.

Part III examines how event managers can develop sustainable events in practice. Chapter 9 presents different staffing issues for events; outlines the role of volunteers in events and identifies how events can contribute towards an employability legacy for the host destination. Chapter 10 reviews the role of risk, crisis and disaster management in delivering sustainable events and how event managers can plan and prevent these potential problems. Chapter 11 investigates why event legacies fail and identifies challenges in planning and delivering event legacies. Chapter 12 aims to detect reasons why event legacies are successful and present examples of good practice. In Part IV, Chapter 13 summarises the key themes of the book and speculates about the future of event sustainability.

How to use this book

Each chapter provides an overview of the topic, supported by relevant academic and industry research. This is illustrated by examples from events and festivals globally. Readers will find that some examples have been used repeatedly. This is a deliberate decision to emphasise the multi-faceted nature of events. At the end of the chapter are discussion questions and learning activities which can be used in class or for independent study and each chapter includes an extended case study, with further discussion questions. The references are supplied at the end of the relevant chapter, to make it easier for the reader to find the original source and the references are supplemented with additional academic, government and industry resources including web links and further readings.

Chapter summary

This chapter introduced the importance of the transformation towards sustainable events. Contemporary understanding of the concept of sustainability has evolved from the 1987 Brundtland report, *Our Common Future* (WCED, 1987), completed for the United Nations and is concerned with ensuring that human development does not overwhelm the ability of resources to renew themselves. Sustainable development is usually separated into economic, environmental and social dimensions although genuine sustainable development integrates these three 'pillars' of sustainability.

Sustainability does not necessarily mean that development must remain static, rather the development must not exceed the ability of the social-economic-environmental system to absorb the changes. From an events perspective the focus is on minimising negative impacts and maximising positive impacts. Initially, event organisers were primarily concerned with the economic impacts of events but increasingly the environmental and social impacts have become important. In response to this, governments, industry groups and not-for-profit organisations have devised a series of guidelines to help event organisers create more sustainable events.

Learning activities

1   Thinking about the last event you attended, how much consideration do you give to sustainability issues?
2   Download two of the sustainable event guides from the 'Further resources' section. Compare the two guides with each other – what are the differences and the similarities?
3   Can any event be sustainable? Conduct an online search to identify a range of events that claim to be sustainable or undertake sustainable practices. Categorise the events based on type. Are there any types of event that are obviously missing from your list? If so, what types are missing?

4 From Activity 3, identify the general sustainable practices each event claims to undertake. Are certain types of event more comprehensive and/or convincing in their sustainable management practices?

Case study: Greening a music festival

There is a proliferation of guides on how to create a more sustainable event. Some of these are government led (such as the UK's DEFRA or Tasmania's EPA guidelines), some are industry-driven (for example, Yourope's Clean'n'Green Award), others developed by event venues or not-for-profit organisations (A Greener Festival). Generally sustainability guides address the following issues:

- Environmental sustainability
- The well-being of stakeholders
- Management sustainability
- Transparency and ethical practice
- Sharing of good practice

There has been a particular focus on creating sustainability guidelines for green-field music festivals. There are various reasons for this drive:

- *Green-field festivals require that everything is brought into the site.* This can generate substantial waste. Anyone who has been at a music festival as the audience pack up and go home will have seen the mess they can leave behind: rubbish, forgotten food and camping equipment.
- A further factor may be that *music festivals often target younger audiences,* who may be more concerned with environmental issues, although the mess left at these festivals suggests otherwise.
- Another issue is that *sustainable practice states that humans should leave no trace of their visit.* This is clearly not possible at a purpose built venue but is desirable at a green-field site.

Live Earth was a series of music events in 2007 (in London, Sydney, Johannesburg, Tokyo, Rio, New York, Shanghai and Hamburg), which were designed to use entertainment to increase environmental awareness, with a particular focus on climate change. It was extremely important that the events themselves adhered to sustainability good practice and the event organisers produced their own sustainable event guidelines. Live Earth presents the following arguments for why events should try to be more sustainable:

1 The event may inspire the audience to take some of these ideas home with them.
2 Sustainable events will lead to a reduction in carbon emissions, helping to combat climate change.
3 The concerts can protect the environments within which they take place.

4 Sustainable practice will generate positive media attention, attract sponsors and lead to cost savings.
5 Adopting sustainable practice now will prepare the event organisers for forthcoming legislative requirements.
6 Sustainable achievements such as percentage of waste recycled, provides measureable results, which can be used to set future goals.

The focus of the guidelines is primarily on environmental impacts and measures but there are also some social and marketing considerations. Marketing concerns are focussed on using the event to promote sustainability to all relevant stakeholders including suppliers, staff and volunteers with support from the artists. Social concerns are focussed around sourcing products locally to benefit the host community or using fair trade products to make sure that the workers who produced these had appropriate working conditions.
    The guidelines advise on achieving sustainability across the following areas:

- Event production
    o Use eco-labelled and locally-produced materials
    o Use chemical free cleaning products
    o Use recycled paper

- Catering
    o Use local produce to reduce food miles
    o Supply refillable water cups or bottles
    o Use compostable containers for food

- Marketing and merchandising
    o Use recycled paper and vegetable inks
    o Select merchandise made from sustainable materials
    o Use fair trade materials where possible
    o Avoid wrapping programmes or merchandise individually in plastic bags

- Waste management
    o Use paperless tickets
    o Place recycling bins in highly visible and busy places
    o Provide the appropriate materials to assist food traders in recycling, such as a separate bin for food scraps

- Energy
    o Use energy efficient equipment, such as LED lights
    o Turn off equipment when not in use
    o Audit all power consumption to identify high users

- Water use
    o Use compost or dry toilets
    o Use low-flow showerheads and taps
    o Supply water-free sanitiser

(Continued)

Case study (continued)

- Transport
  - o Use shuttle buses to bring people to the site
  - o Allocate car parking quotas for each group of stakeholders
  - o Use bicycles to move around the site

The irony of the London Live Earth concert was that it generated considerable carbon emissions from the artists who were flown from around the world to play at the event. The event's carbon footprint was calculated at 31,500 tons, over 3,000 times the footprint of the average UK resident (Smith, 2007). In contrast, the Live Earth (2009) Green Event Guidelines report that the event organisers were able to recycle or compost 79 out of the 97 tons of waste generated by the event and by holding the concerts during daylight hours, the event reduced the potential carbon emissions.

Discussion questions

1 What are the benefits for event organisers for making their events more sustainable?
2 Look at the website for the Roskilde Festival, a huge annual green-field music festival in Denmark, http://roskilde-festival.dk/. How sustainable is the event currently? How could this event be made more sustainable?
3 How can a music festival be used to promote more sustainable behaviour in everyday life?

Further reading and online resources

A Greener Festival. Available online at http://www.agreenerfestival.com/ [accessed 10 November, 2014].

Events Impacts Toolkit. Available online at http://www.eventimpacts.com/ [accessed 10 November, 2014].

Roskilde Festival, green-field music festival in Denmark. Available online at http://roskilde-festival.dk/ [accessed 20 November, 2014].

Tasmania Environment Protection Authority guidelines, available online at http://epa.tas.gov.au/sustainability/sustainable-event-guidelines [accessed 10 November, 2014].

Yourope Clean'n'Green award. Available online at http://www.yourope.org/en/gointroduction [accessed 10 November, 2014].

References

Berke, P. and Conroy, M. (2000). Are we planning for sustainable development? *Journal of the American Planning Association*. 66 (1), 21–33.

Carson, R. (1962). *Silent spring*. Boston: Houghton Mifflin Harcourt.

Ehrlich, P. R. and Ehrlich, A. (1968). *The population bomb.* New York: Ballantine Books.

Jones, M. (2014). *Sustainable events.* London: Routledge.

Laing, J. and Frost, W. (2010). How green was my festival: exploring challenges and opportunities associated with staging green events. *International Journal of Hospitality Management*, 29 (2), 261–7.

Leßmann, O. and Rauschmayer, F. (2013). Re-conceptualizing sustainable development on the basis of the capability approach: a model and its difficulties. *Journal of Human Development and Capabilities*, 14 (1), 95–114.

Liburd, J. and Edwards, D. (2010) *Understanding the sustainable development of tourism.* Oxford: Goodfellows Publishers.

Live Earth (2009). *Green event guidelines.* Live Earth, available at http://www.greeneventbook.com/wp-content/uploads/2012/05/liveearthgreenguidelines.pdf [accessed 10 November, 2014].

Malthus, T. (1798). *An essay on the principle of population, as it affects the future improvement of society.* London: J. Johnson.

Meadowcroft, J. (2009). What about the politics? Sustainable development, transition management, and long-term energy transitions. *Policy Sciences*, 42 (4), 323–40.

Moran, D. D., Wackernagel, M., Kitzes, J. A., Goldfinger, S. H. and Boutaud, A. (2008). Measuring sustainable development – nation by nation. *Ecological economics*, 64 (3), 470–4.

Pearce, D., Barbier, E. and Markandya, A. (1990) *Sustainable development: economics and environment in the Third World.* Cheltenham: Edward Elgar Publishing.

Schlenker, K., Foley, C. and Getz, D. (2010). *ENCORE festival and event evaluation kit: review and redevelopment.* Gold Coast, Queensland: Sustainable Tourism CRC.

Smith, D. (2007). Rockin' all over the world (but just watch your carbon footprint). *The Observer*, http://www.theguardian.com/media/2007/jul/08/musicnews.broadcasting.

Smith, A. (2012). *Events and urban regeneration.* London: Routledge.

WCED (World Commission on Environment and Development). (1987). *Our common future.* Oxford: Oxford University Press.

PART I

The events context

Chapter 2

The internal and external environment for sustainable event organisers

Learning outcomes

After studying this chapter you should be able to:

- Understand the complex environment within which event organisation takes place
- Analyse the internal and external environments for event organisers
- Identify tools for analysing the contexts within which event organisation takes place
- Conduct a stakeholder analysis for use by event organisers
- Identify the constraints and limits to organising sustainable events

Introduction

Chapter 1 sets out the definition of what is a planned event. Planned events operate in complex economic, environmental and social realities which involve a range of stakeholders beyond the event organisers, the performers or participants and the audience. These stakeholders can include the host community, the media, local, regional and national governments and special interest groups. Smith-Christensen describes a sustainable event as being 'managed as an autonomous cyclical process through the interaction between event management, host community and event-goers' (2009: 23).

This chapter examines the range of stakeholders involved in organising a planned event, the different environments involved in managing a planned event and the challenges these present to achieving sustainability within the events context.

The internal environment of an event

To begin with, however, we will examine the *internal environment* for managing an event and how this relates to sustainability issues. A planned event needs to be organised and the internal environment is constructed by the people who are organising this event. The people and the way they are organised will depend on the nature and scale of the event. For example, is the event a small, community event such as a school fete which is being organised by a committee of volunteers from the local area? Or is it a major international meeting of Heads of State, such as the Commonwealth Heads of Government Meeting (CHOGM), which requires substantial professional organisation, not to mention security measures? While these two very different events will have quite different stakeholders, the internal environment will actually be similar, but on a completely different scale. The internal environment for any planned event is summarised in Figure 2.1.

Organising any event involves the following elements:

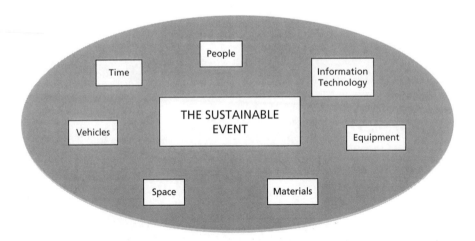

Figure 2.1 The internal environment for sustainable events

People

Who will be involved in organising the event? Will it be paid, professional event organisers? Will it be a local sports club? Who will be staffing the event? Paid staff, hired for the event, paid staff redeployed from another event or function and/or volunteers? If the event is being organised by volunteers, is this sustainable? Can these individuals dedicate sufficient time to the event alongside their day to day paid jobs, families and other commitments? If the event is going to rely on volunteers, how will they be recruited, trained and managed to ensure that the event is delivered as required? Note that different staffing models are presented in Chapter 9.

Information technology

What information technology (IT) equipment will be required and sourced by the event organisers? Will any project management software be procured or can simple spreadsheets in programs such as Excel be used? How will the events team communicate with each other and other stakeholders? A major conference, exhibition, music festival or sports competition will each have specialist IT requirements. Have the costs for IT, IT support and power supplies for the equipment been included in the budget? Can power be sourced from a more sustainable supplier? See Chapter 6 for more details on the environmental impacts of events.

Equipment

What equipment will be needed for the event? If this is a one-off or occasional event, can the equipment be hired or borrowed? How will the equipment be powered? Again, can a more sustainable power supplier be sourced? Sourcing equipment from local suppliers, for example, will reduce carbon emissions from transporting it to the event site and LED lighting is a more energy-efficient option.

Materials

What materials will be needed both in the events office and for the event itself? Can materials such as advertising or set dressing be reused? Do physical flyers and tickets need to be provided? At the end of the event, what happens to the material? Are they stored away for future events or recycled where possible? The Sage Gateshead, an arts venue in the UK, provides a guide to making events more sustainable, which includes advice for minimising waste, such as using potted plants rather than cut flowers or avoiding one-use materials, including stage felting or carpets (http://www.sagegateshead.com/).

Space

Space refers to both the event organisers' office environment (if there is one) and the setting. The appropriate venue is crucial to the staging of an event and will depend on the event theme and size. Different settings present different sustainability challenges. Increasingly, purpose-built venues are taking into account the environmental impact of their construction and operation. Newer venues can incorporate measures such as sensor lighting to limit electricity consumption or a moisture sensor system for watering the pitch as at Wembley Stadium, London (Harvey, 2009). Green-field venues offer alternative challenges. While there are fewer negative impacts associated with constructing a temporary venue, these sites can have limited public transport options and require temporary generators and toilets, which limits the sustainability measures that can be implemented (for some examples, see the case study of Peats Ridge Festival, Chapter 6). Of course some events require that the natural environment becomes the venue – for example a surfing competition must take place by the sea and event organisers need to give careful consideration for minimising the impact of the event on the fragile coastal environment.

Box 2.1 The Moscone Centre, San Francisco

The Moscone Centre, an exhibitions and conventions centre developed and owned by the City and County of San Francisco but managed privately, sets the standard for sustainable performance within the events sector. Some of their programmes include:

1   The centre began recycling material in 1998 and now recycles nearly 2 million pounds of material annually.
2   Their exclusive caterer, SAVOR, composts all organic waste from their kitchens and donates unused food to local not-for-profit organisations and also uses biodiesel fuel in their delivery vans.
3   Moscone West, an extension to the complex completed in 2003, features low emission glass to reduce energy loss.
4   The Moscone Centre employs a full-time air quality technician to continually monitor air quality.
5   In 2004, the centre installed solar panels on the roof which generate enough power for 500 homes.
6   The centre also installed energy efficient lighting and lightbulbs, which reduced energy consumption from lighting in the first year by up to 20 per cent.
7   Contractors of major projects are required to track and report their recycling and disposal of waste generated by the project.
8   The centre is located in the centre of San Francisco, close to local and regional transport and within walking distance of 20,000 hotel rooms, which enables event planners to minimise transport emissions generated by their event.

Source: http://www.moscone.com/mtgplanners/green_meetings.html

Vehicles

What vehicles will be needed to transport equipment and performers to the event site? Again, can these be borrowed or hired or can transport be outsourced? Given that transport is often one of the biggest contributors to carbon emissions associated with an event (see Chapter 6), there are ways to minimise travel for the event organisers and performers by using other forms of transportation and/or choosing a venue with good public transport. For example, at the 1994 Winter Olympics in Lillehammer, the Olympic Village constructed a temporary train system for transport of accommodation modules as well as people.

Time

The schedule for the event and lead-in time needs to allow for sustainability concerns to be taken into account. For example, it may take longer to source suppliers of compostable food containers or to conduct consultation with the local community. Business Events Sydney, the convention bureau for Sydney and New South Wales provides advice for event organisers on managing their timeline here: http://www.businesseventssydney.com.au/plan-an-event/event-planning-toolkit/preparation/creating-a-timeline.cfm [accessed 12 November, 2014].

Scope of the event

Closely associated with the human, physical, resource, temporal and information scale of an event is the scope of an event, which requires parameters to be set around the following four variables:

1 *Demographic scope.* Who is associated with the event in terms of visitor profiles, business community members, staff and volunteers, competitors and performers, stakeholders, sponsors and partners? Should non-attendees within the event host destination be considered by the event organisers, or only those directly involved in the event?
2 *Geographic scope.* What are the spatial boundaries of the event and the associated economic impacts? Mobile events pose a particular challenge in this regard, whereas the boundaries for static events are more easily established. Do event destination and tourism destination boundaries coincide?
3 *Temporal scope.* Over what time frame will event impacts be generated? Again, events with a defined duration (such as sporting competitions and music festivals) are more easily assessed than those occurring over longer periods (such as art exhibitions). Similarly, visitor profiles can vary greatly between weekends and weekdays, so not all event days can be expected to generate the same impacts and outcomes. Some major events can also have a legacy that encourages increased numbers of people to visit the destination long after the event ends. The legacy that events leave behind is discussed in detail in Chapter 12.
4 *Economic scope.* Visitors', organisers' and stakeholders' expenditure at events can vary greatly in terms of incidence and impact, depending on the extent to which event inputs are sourced locally or imported and the extent to which regional, state or territorial, or national economies are affected by the event.

Understanding the internal and external environment of an event

If the internal environment is about the event organisation, the external environment is about the political, economic, social, technological, legal and ecological context within which the event operates. Various tools can be used by event organisers to assess the environment within which they are operating and identify the potential challenges to achieving sustainability. One framework used in strategic management of the broader environment within which a company operates is Political, Economic,

Social, Technological, Legal and Ecological (PESTLE) analysis. In an events context, PESTLE analysis involves examining what factors in the external environment may have an impact on the event and therefore what action event organisers should take and what factors need to be monitored. The different components of a PESTLE analysis in relation to events are:

- *Political* – To what extent do the local, regional and/or national governments support and influence the event?
- *Economic* – What economic factors affect the costs and revenues of the event, such as the inflation, interest and exchange rates?
- *Social* – What are the different cultural and ethnic groups within the host population and what relationships do the event organisers need to foster with these groups?
- *Technological* – What technologies are available for organising, managing, staging, monitoring and evaluating events? Does the local area have suitable equipment and power systems for the event?
- *Legal* – What health, policing, planning, environmental and transportation legislation has an impact on the event? For example, traffic restrictions, food and water quality protection and pollution controls.
- *Ecological* – How will the natural and built environment be impacted by the event?

Any such analysis will also need to take into account the relevant scope and scale for the event. A mega-event will involve far more people and places, have a longer lead time and a larger budget and leave longer lasting legacies than a smaller festival or event. However, PESTLE analysis can be applied across the broad range of events in order to understand the organisational and operational environment.

Another approach to analysing and understanding the event organisation is strategic Strengths, Weaknesses, Opportunities and Threats (SWOT) analysis. A strategic SWOT analysis involves three stages, as follows:

Stage One – Situation analysis using SWOT

In order for the appropriate strategies to be identified, a candid and current process of identification of the Strengths, Weaknesses, Opportunities and Threats (SWOT) relevant to organisations or destinations is needed (Carlsen and Andersson, 2011). The SWOT must be phrased in such a way that they will lead to specific strategies that can be identified and implemented. Positive, rather than normative statements of SWOT are required, that clearly describe the situation. Strengths and weaknesses should be considered as INTERNAL to the organisation, that is, it is within the ambit, power and resources of management and executive to control the strengths and weaknesses that exist. Opportunities and threats should be considered as EXTERNAL to the organisation, that is, beyond the control of management and part of the general operating environment (see Figure 2.2).

The situation analysis stage of the strategic SWOT analysis involves the following first four steps:

1 Identification of the INTERNAL strengths of the organisation
2 Identification of the INTERNAL weaknesses of the organisation
3 Identification of the EXTERNAL opportunities for the organisation
4 Identification of the EXTERNAL threats to the organisation

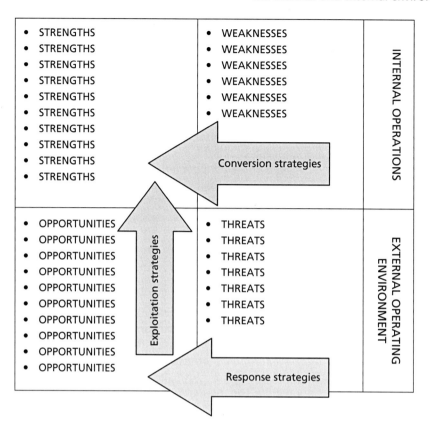

Figure 2.2 Strategic SWOT analytical framework

Stage Two – Strategy development

The internal strengths and weaknesses identified should all be within the ambit and control of the organisation. Strategies for converting weaknesses to strengths should be the first to be developed and implemented. They could be considered as the 'low hanging fruit' within the organisation, that is, things that it is not doing well, but that could benefit from the right strategies, resources and effort.

Once strategies for creating a stronger organisation through addressing weaknesses have been identified, it will then be in a position to develop strategies to exploit external opportunities and respond to threats. A stronger organisation that has exploited all opportunities will have the structure, ability and resources to be better able to anticipate and respond to the identified and anticipated threats that will emerge over time.

Hence, the final strategic steps in SWOT analysis are to:

5   Develop and implement strategies for CONVERTING weaknesses to strengths
6   Develop and implement strategies to EXPLOIT opportunities, and
7   Prepare strategies to RESPOND to threats to the organisation

Note that the process of exploitation of opportunities can also result in creation of strengths. Likewise, every threat can also be considered as an opportunity, which could then, if exploited, create another strength. Figure 2.2 describes the strategic SWOT approach and the processes for converting, exploiting and responding identified weaknesses, opportunities and threats with a view to building stronger organisations in the future.

Stage Three – Strategic scenarios

The final stage in the strategic SWOT analysis is the creation of scenarios based on the identified conversion, exploitation and response strategies developed in stage two. Basically, all strategies are considered in light of how they will shape the organisation in the future and any potential conflicts or problems with them can be identified. The scenario will also aid in identifying the resources required for implementation and implications for budgets and funding. Finally, the scenario can be used to develop a time frame for strategy implementation, in other words, a means of prioritising and sequencing the implementation of strategies.

Event stakeholders

The external environment for an event is also concerned with the event stakeholders. An event stakeholder can be defined as 'Groups or individuals who are affected or could be affected by an event's existence' (Reid and Arcodia, 2002: 346). Stakeholders can be divided into primary stakeholders – people and organisations without whose support the event would not take place – and secondary stakeholders – groups or individuals not directly involved in the event but nonetheless can still have a significant impact on its success. Ideally, the aims and objectives of all stakeholders in an event will coincide so that the success of an event will reflect directly and favourably on all stakeholders, both primary and secondary, involved with the event. If the values that underpin stakeholders' aims and objectives include sustainability and this is an integral component of event organisation, the event has a much better opportunity to move towards sustainability in the future. This second group also includes people who may be affected by the event although they are not directly involved in it. The stakeholders for each event will vary substantially but are likely to include:

- The event organisation
- The venue or host location
- The client (if the event is being organised by a contractor)
- The performers or participants
- The event audience/attendees
- Organisation management, staff and volunteers
- The host community
- Local businesses suppliers and contractors
- Local, regional and/or national governments
- Sponsors, partners and contributors
- Media and public relations organisations
- Other interested groups, such as cultural, ethnic and environmental groups

Figure 2.3 shows the different stakeholders of the London 2012 Olympics. The Olympic Games is an international event, organised by a national committee on behalf of the International Olympic Committee. In the case of the 2012 Olympic Games, this was the

Figure 2.3 Stakeholders of the London 2012 Olympics
Source: Adapted from Theodoraki, 2007, Figure 6.1

London Organising Committee of the Olympic Games or LOCOG. The Olympic Games are an international event and are of great interest to participating countries' governments and international sporting associations as well as attracting international sponsors and media. Other stakeholders include the various communities in London and around the UK, many of whom contributed financially to the event through their taxes, volunteers and lobbyists, wanting to get their special interest included in the Olympic programme. Managing all of these stakeholders would be impossible but that does not mean that their concerns should not be considered in the run up to the event.

Understanding stakeholders

Stakeholder theory identifies three characteristics of stakeholders in an organisation (Mitchell et al., 1997):

1 *Power* – the ability of the stakeholder to impose their will
2 *Legitimacy* – the perception that the stakeholder's actions are appropriate
3 *Urgency* – the immediacy of the stakeholder's concerns

Stakeholder theory was developed as a means to identify the most important (or salient) stakeholders for an organisation from a management perspective, that is, which stakeholders should managers concern themselves with most. The most salient stakeholders are those that combine all three elements of power, legitimacy and urgency. In an events context, the most powerful stakeholders could be the client, government and the media but that does not necessarily make them the most urgent – that could be a rare species of birds that happen to nest at the event site.

Getz, Andersson and Larson (2007) provide an alternative, generic classification of event stakeholders, which defines them by their relationship to the event rather than their function:

- Allies and collaborators, e.g. partners
- Co-producers, e.g. other organisations involved in the event
- Facilitators, e.g. sponsors
- Suppliers and venues
- The impacted, e.g. the audience, local residents
- Regulators, e.g. government

Once an event organiser has generated a list of all the relevant stakeholders, these can be classified according to Getz, Andersson and Larson's (2007) framework to identify an appropriate stakeholder management strategy. It is important to recognise that one stakeholder may have several roles within this framework. Getz (2012) gives the example of government, which could act as a facilitator by giving grants, could hire out the venue and is also likely to have a regulatory role.

Constraints on event sustainability

The external environment presents even more constraints on developing a sustainable event compared to the internal environment. This is because the external environment includes many more stakeholders and variables, which are frequently outside the event organiser's control. These constraints include:

Bid process

There is substantial international pressure for mega-events, costing destinations billions of dollars for what might be a one-off two week event, to become more sustainable. This is also supported by the client organisations, on whose behalf the events are organised. However, the competitive bid process for these events often prevents this. For a start, it is expensive to put together a bid to host a major international event, for example, Football Federation Australia admitted to spending AU$45 million on the unsuccessful bid to host the 2018 FIFA World Cup, not to mention the time that goes into preparing bid applications. The bid for a mega-event also needs to 'wow' the judges and this can encourage blue-sky bids proposing dramatic opening and closing ceremonies and spectacular new venues. Bids can also make grand claims about the potential benefits of the event such as environmental improvements to the event site or over-promising affordable housing after the event, without thinking through the realities of actually having to deliver on these.

Funding

The funding of an event from public and private sources is always a potential limitation as event budgets are usually tight and event organisers can be compelled to

Box 2.2 Bidding for the FIFA World Cup

FIFA relatively recently introduced compulsory sustainability considerations to their bid process. While Brazil has taken steps to minimise the environmental impact of the event and evaluated the tournament's carbon footprint, the first tournaments that have been required to include social and environmental chapters within their bid documents are 2018 (Russia) and 2022 (Qatar). Green building certification will be mandatory for all stadia built for these tournaments and going forward into the future. Previously, such initiatives were voluntary.

It will be interesting to see how Qatar – where temperatures regularly rise above 38 degrees Celsius in the summer, when the tournament will take place – will manage its carbon footprint, given the need to keep both players and fans cool. The local organising committee claims it will have the technology to create carbon-neutral and cool stadia. However, FIFA have debated whether to move the tournament to the winter months, where the temperature is much more hospitable. Any change in the timing of the event could cause substantial disruption for European domestic leagues and the European Champions League. European teams include players from around the world, who will be recalled to play for their national team. Given the huge earnings these clubs make from seat tickets and media coverage, such disruption could be extremely expensive.

Sources: FIFA announces sustainability strategy (http://www.stadia-magazine.com/news.php?NewsID=40508); FIFA meets to debate moving 2022 World Cup to winter (http://america.aljazeera.com/articles/2013/10/3/fifa-meets-to-debatemoving2022worldcuptowinter.html) [accessed November, 2014].

make savings by using cheaper suppliers who do not meet sustainability requirements. For example, good practice says that food should ideally be sourced locally but this may be more expensive than buying food from a national supplier. For a mega-event, the impacts of funding shortfalls can be enormous, with whole schemes planned in the bid document being abandoned as the event deadline approaches. Plus, the costs of a mega-event do not end at the event, with venues needing to be managed and maintained long after the event has been staged. A failure to budget for their upkeep means that venues can be left unused to decay, leaving no positive legacy for the destination. See Chapter 11 for examples of this negative legacy.

Political support

Achieving a sustainable event may depend on gaining sufficient support from local, regional or national governments. Event organisers may depend on political support for public transport options to the event venue, or for help with recycling materials from the event. Politicians are often focussed primarily on economic outcomes and the politicians involved may need to be persuaded of the benefits of sustainability and managing the events' impacts, particularly when bidding for a major event. Governments change and the new government may have a different policy towards events. The relationship between events, policy and sustainability is explored further in Chapter 3.

Infrastructure

The event organisers may be constrained by the location of the event in terms of the infrastructure. Venues may not conform to environmental standards or be connected to public transport. There may be no public transport to the destination at all. Power supplies may be limited and only available from fossil fuel sources. The event theme may demand that the event takes place in a fragile environment, such as the extreme marathon movement, which runs long distance races in harsh and remote environments. In these cases it is important to assess whether the benefits of holding the event outweigh the drawbacks. For example, the Addo Elephant Run, which takes place in Addo Elephant National Park in South Africa has the potential to bring economic benefits to this region of South Africa, providing accommodation to participants before and after the race. However, the event takes place within a national park. The course predominantly uses existing trails and gravel roads within the park and checkpoints do not provide sustenance contained in cups or sachets to minimise littering as a result of the event (see http://www.extrememarathons.com/ADDO/Overview.html [accessed 12 November, 2014]).

Audience

The event organiser may develop the most sustainable event ever planned, but how do they ensure that the audience buy into their plans? Choosing a venue that is close to public transport options only benefits the environment if the event audience makes use of this transport and do not instead choose to use private transport. Event organisers can use different methods to encourage their audience to support their initiatives, such as communicating their information via social media or providing incentives such as discounted travel passes. However, event organisers can only communicate with, but not control the actions of their audience.

Chapter summary

This chapter provides an overview of the internal and external environment within which events and festivals operate. Analysing the internal and external environment is the first step to being able to take action towards developing more sustainable events. Compared to a regular business, event organisers face a number of constraints which create challenges for achieving sustainability. The finite timescale for events is a particular challenge as this can rarely be changed. As this chapter has demonstrated, events and festivals do not take place in a vacuum and depending on the theme of the event there are many primary and secondary stakeholders who may be affected by, or want to influence, the event. Identifying and managing these stakeholders is a further challenge. These themes are followed up in subsequent chapters.

Learning activities

1   Imagine you are an event organiser. How would you run your office to ensure that you practice sustainability yourself?
2   Choose an event which has featured recently in the news. List all the relevant stakeholders for this event. Now organise the stakeholders using Getz, Andersson and

Larson's (2007) categorisation. Which stakeholders are the most important for the event organisers?

3 Using the internet, research your local or nearest exhibition and convention centre. How does it compare in terms of sustainability to the Moscone Centre? What does it do well and where could it improve?

4 Conduct a strategic SWOT analysis of an organisation involved in a forthcoming event in your city or country. What are the organisation's strengths, weaknesses, opportunities and threats in relation to the event? What conversion, exploitation and response strategies would you recommend for this event organisation?

Case study: The International Sailing Federation World Championships, Fremantle 2011

The International World Sailing Championships were hosted by Fremantle, Western Australia 3–18 December 2011 at a cost of AU$17.6 million to the Australian tax payer. This was the third ISAF World Championships tournament and involved 789 competitors from 76 nations. The event sought to leverage on Fremantle's sailing heritage as the site for the 1987 defence of the America's Cup, which has involved a regeneration project that has transformed Fremantle. The event was organised on behalf of the International Sailing Federation and as a qualifying event for 75 per cent of the quota for the London 2012 Olympics this was a major international event.

The event took over the port city of Fremantle with venues including the sailing clubs, the Italian Club, which served as the hub for the event volunteer programme and other sites around the city were used by the media, the race time-keeping team, transport and the World's Festival, which was a temporary village built on Esplanade Park, a grassed area close to the harbourside.

Although the event was hosted in Fremantle, a separate city to Perth and the main port, the event was branded as being hosted in Perth. This included having a large 'Perth' sign erected next to the harbour at Bathers Beach. Media coverage therefore left audiences unclear as to whether they were watching the event in Fremantle or Perth, and Fremantle may have missed out on a valuable marketing opportunity. The Mayor of Fremantle commented that the mixed branding of the event would be confusing to sailors, who are used to Fremantle's waters and noted that Fremantle and Perth have different identities. In contrast, the head of the Western Australian State Government's event agency, Eventcorp stated that the Perth branding would reinforce the state capital's global marketing strategy. Fremantle City Council responded with their own 'guerrilla' branding strategy, which placed Fremantle signage on various vantage points around the city (see http://www.abc.net.au/news/2011-12-07/fremantle-publicises-itself-feature/3718102 [accessed 11 November, 2014]).

The World's Festival featured various cultural and food events and was designed to provide an on-land attraction for visitors to Fremantle. The event organisers were contractually obliged to stage the World's Festival as part of the event.

(Continued)

Case study (continued)

A problem with sailing races is that they take place on the water and it can be difficult to view the action from the land. The World's Festival was designed to provide spectators with something else to do between races. While the event organisers hailed the event as a success, the event received substantial criticism from businesses involved in the World's Festival and elsewhere in Fremantle that the event did not bring them any benefits in spite of the enormous cost of staging the event. This was not helped by unseasonal stormy weather which had disrupted the sailing, which meant that both casual visitors and sailing enthusiasts were deterred from visiting. The media had also talked about potential parking problems during the event and anticipated crowding from spectators which may have also put off tourists from visiting the port city.

The event was sponsored by both the Western Australian State Government and the Australian Federal Government for a range of reasons including international profile and sports promotion and increased tourism, with the Federal Government stating 'With the Championships doubling as a qualifying event for the 2012 London Olympic Games Sailing Competition, Australia will be in the international spotlight. The successful staging of the Championships will enhance our reputation as a world-class host of major sporting events and will showcase Australia as an attractive destination for international travellers.'

Fremantle is known for hosting regular events and festivals throughout the year and local residents are used to sharing their home with visitors. During the championships, a number of additional bars were opened in non-traditional venues such as Kidogo Art Gallery, next to Bathers Beach and Fremantle's liquor licensing laws were relaxed, which was welcomed by local residents. Residents were also able to enjoy free entertainment at the World's Festival including an open air concert by the Perth Symphony Orchestra.

Vendors at the World's Festival and local businesses were, however, unimpressed by the economic returns from the event. The owner of an award-winning pizza restaurant which had a stall as part of the World's Festival closed this down after losing 'probably four or five thousand dollars'. 'They promised us 200,000 to 250,000 people over the 16 days,' he said. 'Where are they?' In contrast, the WA Minister for Tourism reported that more than 7,800 people attended the event (including participants, their families and support teams), which generated an economic benefit of AU$38.6 million. According to the Minister, their average length of stay was 21 days, which calculates to 197,000 visitor nights for tourism and hospitality businesses (http://www.sailing.org/news/27412.php [accessed 12 November, 2014]).

The event organisers remained positive about the event, commenting:

> In the end, the most important thing is how WA and Australia performed on the world stage running a very significant international event. The only people who complained were those who tried to make money out of the event. I had 1100 volunteers, every one of them had a great time.
>
> John Longley, event director

Discussion questions

1 List the stakeholders for ISAF 2011.
2 Put them into a table and compare their aims. Do any stakeholder groups have conflicting aims?
3 Which stakeholders achieved their aims and which did not?
4 What could the organisers of ISAF 2011 have done differently in order to manage the stakeholders better?

Further reading and online resources

Freeman, R. (1984). *Strategic management: a stakeholder approach*. Boston, MA: Pitman.

The Moscone Centre. Available online at http://www.moscone.com/mtgplanners/green_meetings.html [accessed 20 November, 2014].

'World sailing championship boosts state's coffers'. Available online at http://www.tourism.wa.gov.au/Latest_news/Previous_news_stories/2012_previous_news_stories/June_2012/Pages/World_Sailing_Champs_boost_State_coffers.aspx [accessed 11 November, 2014].

References

Carlsen, J. and Andersson, T. (2011). Strategic SWOT analysis for public, private and not-for-profit festival organisations. *International Journal of Event and Festival Management*, 2 (1), 83–97.

Getz, D. (2012). *Event studies: theory, research and policy for planned events*. London: Routledge.

Getz, D., Andersson, T. and Larson, M. (2007). Festival stakeholder roles: concepts and case studies, *Event Management*, 10 (2/3), 103–22.

Harvey, E. (2009). Greening Live Earth, In Raj, R. and J. Musgrave (Eds) *Event management and sustainability*. Wallingford: CABI, pp. 195–205.

Mitchell, R., Agle, B. and Wood, D. (1997). Towards a theory of stakeholder identification and salience: defining the principle of who and what really counts. *Academy of Management Review*, 22 (4), 853–66.

Reid, S. and Arcodia, C. (2002). Understanding the role of the stakeholder in event management. In Jago, L., Deery, R. and Hede, A. (Eds) *Events and place making*. Sydney: The Australian Centre for Event Management, UTS.

Smith-Christensen, C. (2009). Sustainability as a concept within events. In Raj, R. and Musgrave, J. (Eds) *Event management and sustainability*. Wallingford: CABI, pp. 22–31.

Theodoraki, E. (2007). *Olympic event organization*. London: Routledge.

Chapter 3

Sustainable events and public policy

Learning outcomes

After studying this chapter you should be able to:

- Discuss the reasons why governments get involved in events
- Identify the various approaches for government involvement with events
- Explain the links between events and a range of public policy domains (including economic development, social, cultural and environmental)
- Examine the role of national and international politics in mega-events

Introduction

Public policy consists of a goal-directed process by governments and their agencies, with the aim of addressing specific problems or areas of public concern (Getz, 2012). Public policy takes the form of laws, regulations, decisions and intentions, or promises of governments. Policy is the focal activity of governments. The most straightforward definition is probably that put forward by Dye (1992: 2): 'public policy is whatever governments choose to do or not to do'. There are strong links between policy and power, as it is usually those in power (democratic governments, or alternative ruling bodies) which make policy and therefore make decisions as to how a country will deal with a particular problem or issue. Public policy in any given country is a consequence of the political environment, the values and ideologies of those in power, the institutional frameworks in place and its decision-making processes (Whitford, 2009). Each of these will be discussed in this chapter.

It is important to understand public policy for three main reasons (Hall and Rusher, 2004). According to Hall and Rusher, firstly, as researchers, it is helpful to gain an understanding of why policy decisions are made, as well as what the consequences of various policy decisions are. Secondly, for professionals, it is useful to understand the policy-making process, so that they can ascertain where and when they might have input into policy decisions. Finally, they suggest that the political dimension of policy should be studied so that it is easier to understand why particular political parties make particular policy decisions, and to work out how to influence these political parties to make 'good' decisions.

In the events context, the links between public policy and events are not well studied or understood (Getz, 2009). In addition, events policies are often inconsistently applied, so for example, a national events policy may not be applicable to regional or local areas (Whitford, 2009). Expanding on the definition of public policy given earlier (Dye, 1992), event policy could be considered to be whatever governments choose to do or not to do in relation to events.

In order to understand public policy and events, it is important to be aware of the various actors and institutions that shape policy. Governments do get involved directly with events and event policy, but there are other bodies that also play a role. Getz (2012) suggests the following are the key political stakeholders:

- *Legislators* – in democratic countries these are elected representatives, but in other systems, these are the people in power who make the laws
- *Government agencies* – those departments and agencies responsible for issues that are related to events, such as economic development, tourism, sports and cultural agencies
- *Law enforcement agencies* – since events need to operate within the law
- *Public-private partnerships* – as events are often funded this way
- *Quasi-governmental organisations* – such as event development corporations, or national event or sport associations
- *Regulators* – health and safety, hygiene, security etc.

Other stakeholders may include large corporations, business leaders, investors and local residents (Foley et al., 2012). Some of the stakeholders are in the position of making policy decisions, but the majority are interested in influencing policy decisions, through lobbying and other public relations activities.

For the most part, event (and tourism) policies are often decided at a national level and tend to be 'top down' (Getz, 2009), meaning that decisions on strategies for events are made by governments without a great deal of consultation with event organisers, producers and other local and regional stakeholders (Whitford, 2004). There are many reasons for governments to get involved in events, and these will be covered in the next section.

Why do governments get involved in events?

As Whitford (2009) points out, many governments use events as a vehicle for economic development, as the economic benefits for hosting events can be clearly demonstrated (see Chapter 5 for further discussion on the economic impact of events). There are legitimate reasons for government involvement in events, particularly given the links between events and tourism. However, Stokes and Jago (2007) note that when it comes to government involvement in events, the economic and tourism priorities are dominant, despite the other benefits that hosting events may bring. Getz (2009: 65) adds to this, explaining that the value of events is often calculated in terms of their monetary success leading to events being seen as 'economic tools' in the minds of the public. Naturally, governments want to see a return on investment from any public money that they invest in hosting or staging events. In countries with alternative systems of power, the imperatives to stage events for their financial value may be equally strong, but the rationale for government intervention may be different. Additionally, different levels of government will have different policy objectives with regard to events, and sometimes the policies of local or regional governments may be in opposition to national policy priorities (Hall and Rusher, 2004).

There are in fact a range of reasons for government involvement in events, and these include the concepts of the public good, social equity, political ideology, the free market system, and other intangible social benefits.

Public good

Events have a range of tangible and intangible benefits to society and the community (for further discussion on this, see Chapter 7). Where these benefits are seen to accrue to everyone (e.g. where events contribute to the economy, this should be good for everyone, and when events promote a healthier more sustainable environment, this should be good for everyone), this is known as a public good – something that is good for everyone. If government can demonstrate that investment in such events with public money will result in public good, then this is a powerful argument in favour of government intervention in events (Getz, 2009). However, it has been argued that viewing events as public goods, and therefore funding them through public money, has led to exaggerations of the socio-economic value of events (Solberg and Preuss, 2007).

Social equity

The concept of social equity is closely linked to the public good argument, but refers to equality of access to events. As Veal (2010) points out, not all events have a benefit for everyone, and some events may be seen as exclusive, either because of the high costs of attending, or the exclusive nature of their contents (high art and culture for example, that may not appeal to the majority). In these cases, while funding the event may be a public good, it is unlikely to be equally accessible to all members of society. Therefore, government support for such events would violate the concept of social equity (Getz, 2009). Government event policy should recognise the question of equity and give it due consideration when a decision is made as to whether to support an event or not.

Ideology

The ideology of a political party relates to the fundamental philosophies that guide them. These can be related to values, attitudes and religious beliefs amongst other things. Examples of ideologies include communism and capitalism. Ideologies guide both what a government thinks that a country should do and the way that they should do it. Political ideologies can influence the way governments view events, and whether governments feel that they should or should not get involved in hosting, staging, running or funding events (Getz, 2012). For some governments, intervention in events is an important strategic objective, whilst other governments may feel that events are the responsibility of the free market, and of individuals. This will be discussed further in the section on how governments get involved in events.

Market failures

Investment in events by governments is often associated with economic returns, and such investment is justified in the expectation of a positive economic outcome, or return on investment. However, there is also an argument that in some cases, if government did not intervene then events would not be able to run (usually for financial reasons). As Getz (2012) points out, the free market does not always provide enough incentive for event organisers to risk their own capital when running an event. Where an event can be shown to provide a public good, then funding by government can be justified in order to underpin the sustainability of the event.

Intangible benefits

As well as the economic benefits of events, particularly in boosting tourism, there are a number of more intangible benefits of hosting events. These are discussed in depth in Chapter 7, but include building national and community pride, increasing levels of social capital, capacity and skill building, promotion of tolerance and diversity, and encouraging participation in leisure, sport and the arts (see e.g. Delamere et al., 2001; Deery and Jago, 2010; Derrett, 2003; Wood, 2006). Events can also be the catalyst for participation and engagement, enhance a city's liveability and encourage ongoing investment in infrastructure (Tourism and Transport Forum, 2014). Such benefits cannot be easily measured, but research has demonstrated that events do have these positive impacts and therefore it is quite justifiable for governments to link their event policy with social and cultural policy, as well as other policy areas such as health and wellbeing and diversity.

Box 3.1 Government major events policy: the case of VMEC

In Victoria, Australia, the state government created a new entity to manage major events. The Victorian Major Events Company (VMEC) was formed in 1991, as part of a Victorian government initiative to attract international cultural and sporting events that require global state-of-the-art facilities and infrastructure (Department of State Development, Business and Innovation, Victorian Government, 2014). VMEC markets Melbourne and Victoria to the owners of events, but does not operate events itself. VMEC was formed following recognition by the state government that events help to raise Victoria's international profile and have a positive financial impact on the state. Victoria has successfully attracted a wide range of major events in areas covering sport, culture and fashion, including the Australian Formula 1 Grand Prix, the Australian Tennis Open Championships, the 2006 Commonwealth Games, the Melbourne Food and Wine Festival, the Melbourne International Jazz Festival and the Melbourne Fashion Festival. An audit of VMEC and the major events in Melbourne and Victoria by the state government demonstrated that major events have undoubtedly delivered economic value to Victoria (Victorian Auditor General, 2007). This value has been in the form of increased visitation to attend the events as well as the opportunities for destination branding which is a powerful and proven tool to create greater awareness and visitation for a destination and hence provide economic benefits to the host city. In 2010, Victoria estimated that its major events calendar contributes around AU$1.4 billion annually to the state's economy (Ernst and Young, 2010). The creation of VMEC allowed government policy (to attract more major events) to become reality with dedicated funding and staffing of VMEC.

Government approaches to involvement in events

There are three broad approaches that governments may take towards events and event policy. They may do nothing, and leave everything to individuals and the free market (the so-called laissez-faire approach), they may take a decision only to regulate certain aspects of events, without any further involvement (the regulatory approach) or they may choose to be involved in a range of aspects of events, including the creation of event policy, and taking decisions as to the level of government support that they may provide to individual events and organisers. This is known as the interventionist approach.

Laissez-faire

The laissez-faire approach proposes that government should not get involved in the private and business decisions of their constituents. It suggests that individuals and organisations should be able to trade and make transactions in an economic environment that is broadly free from government intervention (excepting to protect the rights of the individual). Proponents of this approach may argue that culture, sport and leisure are matters for individual consumption decisions – i.e. it is up to individuals to decide whether they want to be involved in culture, leisure and sport (and associated events). They may also consider that tourism and events are businesses which are best left to the business sector and industry to control and organise (Getz, 2012). Finally, governments may subscribe to a free-market ideology which assumes that the market will make decisions on whether an event should run or not, based on supply and demand.

Regulatory approach

Proponents of the regulatory approach argue that the state should not leave all decisions to the free-market economy, but rather should step in and regulate in order to prevent negative outcomes of the free-market system, including high costs to individuals and bias or discrimination against certain people or groups. Regulations are sometimes used to counteract failures of the market economy, particularly where social equity is threatened.

Interventionist approach

The interventionist approach highlights the importance of events to a number of policy domains (to be discussed in the next section). For example, governments may believe that culture, sport and leisure, and events associated with these, are matters of health and public welfare, and therefore areas that government should be involved in. Governments may also feel that events, and tourism, are social and cultural issues that benefit from government policy and support. It may also be the case that the underlying ideology of the government is based on a belief that governments should intervene and fund as well as regulate various aspects of economic and social life. This is characteristic of the interventionist approach. Governments may intervene in various proactive ways, including direct production of events, where government produce and own events; bidding for major events; establishing the infrastructure (particularly venues such as convention and exhibition centres) and the provision of sponsorship or funding for events (Getz, 2009). Government support may be at a national, state, regional or local level. Where states believe that events represent public goods, then intervention is a common government strategy. Given the economic importance of events, and the close links between events and tourism, many governments are intervening in events policy by creating events-led strategies – a range of policy measures designed to promote events – in order to coordinate their involvement and allocation of resources (Allen et al., 2011). Such strategies may include a portfolio of events (Getz, 2005) and can support existing events as well as attracting and bidding for new events. A good example of a local government events strategy is that of the Sunshine Coast in Queensland, Australia (available online), which documents not only the vision, mission and objectives of the events strategy, but also identifies a range of policies and strategies designed to achieve these objectives (Sunshine Coast Major Events Strategy, 2013).

Box 3.2 Events strategies – the case of the Singapore F1 Grand Prix

In 2005, the government of Singapore set a target to achieve 17 million international tourists, and US$21 billion in income from overseas visitors by 2015 (Henderson et al., 2010). This is known as the Tourism 2015 campaign. At the same time, the government of Singapore set out its aspirations to become the leading hub for leisure, business, education and healthcare tourism by 2015. One of the stated goals of Tourism 2015 is to make Singapore the events and entertainment capital of Asia (Singapore Tourist Board, cited in Henderson et al., 2010). As part of their strategy to achieve this, Singapore applied for, and was awarded approval to host a Formula 1 Grand Prix in 2007. In order to attract such a mega-event, substantial government involvement was required. The costs of staging the event for the first five years was estimated to be over US$100 million, of which the Singapore government contributed 60 per cent (Henderson et al., 2010). The government also invested in alterations to the downtown area of Singapore to allow the race to be run on existing streets in the Marina Bay part of town. Additionally, the race is run at night, requiring extra investment in lighting. In return for their investment, the government expected to see an increase of up to 50,000 extra tourists, as well as increased revenue for those businesses acting as suppliers to the event, including accommodation, catering, security and automotive companies (Chen, 2012). Further, the government recouped some of their initial investment from tax returns and a levy on accommodation prices for the five days of the Grand Prix programme each year (Henderson et al., 2010). As well as the direct economic impacts, the Formula 1 Grand Prix is credited with helping to position Singapore as a 'premier lifestyle destination' (The Straits Times, cited in Henderson et al., 2010), with up to 100 million television viewers around the world seeing striking images of Singapore. Finally, it is hoped that successful staging of the Grand Prix will attract further high profile events to Singapore. This success story is almost entirely attributable to the willingness of the Singapore government to put events at the forefront of their tourism strategy and policy and is a good example of an interventionist approach.

Community involvement in event policy

One of the criticisms levelled at policy in general is a lack of communication with, and input from, the local communities who are most affected by the policies (Hall and Rusher, 2004). Event policy may be local, regional or national, and the communities affected may be villages, towns, regions or a whole country. However, as Whitford (2009) points out, a cohesive event policy that takes into account the views of a range of stakeholders can facilitate local and regional development. There are accepted ways for interested parties to make recommendations and suggestions to those making policy decisions, such as formal submissions to government consultations. However, as events cross over so many different policy areas, it is not always easy for communities to recognise which policies will have a bearing on events in their area. Further, making formal submissions during consultation periods assumes a level of knowledge and ability on the part of the community members which may not in fact be accurate. It should be the responsibility of policymakers to ensure that they have canvassed opinions from a wide range of stakeholders before any decisions are made, but unfortunately, many event policy decisions are still made on an ad hoc basis without sufficient consultation (Whitford, 2009). Until cohesive event strategies are put in place, it is likely that the views of communities will continue to be left out of policy decisions.

Events and government policy domains

Although events are often seen as economic development tools (Getz, 2013), events are linked to a range of different policy domains. These include economic development, cultural policy, social policy and environmental policy.

Economic development

Getz (2012) highlights four different ways in which events contribute to economic development policies. These include tourism 'boosterism'; leveraging events for general economic development; using events to maximise venue efficiency; and using events for place marketing and destination branding. Tourism boosterism suggests that if events are public goods and at the same time attract tourists and media attention and produce positive economic outcomes, then events are worth funding from public money. The argument is that any government investment is money well spent as the economic returns from tourists attending the event will result in profit maximisation. However, it is worth remembering that it can be difficult to gauge the economic impact of an event (see Chapter 5). Leveraging events concerns using the event to foster trade and economic diversification (Getz, 2012) as well as to ensure a positive legacy in terms of both the built environment and urban renewal (see Chapter 4 on events and regeneration). Governments may want to support events as a way to maximise the use of publicly-funded infrastructure, such as convention and exhibition centres and sports facilities. Finally, Getz (2012) discusses the importance of events in place marketing and destination branding, noting that government policy can be put in place to assist events to contribute to image building, branding, destination re-positioning and place marketing. Not only does marketing and branding help to increase visitor numbers (thereby resulting in a positive economic impact), but events can also work with other attractions and developments such as trade missions and city marketing efforts in order to present a coherent destination brand.

Cultural policy

Festivals and arts-related events are often seen as closely linked to cultural policy. However, Getz (2012) argues that all kinds of events should be considered as part of cultural policy, not just those with overt cultural aspects. He points out that business and other types of events can easily have cultural components, such as authentic entertainment and genuine host–guest interactions. According to Quinn (2003), festivals are often important components of urban development and renewal strategies, and can deliver a series of benefits that meet the needs of cultural policies. These are likely to include improving access to cultural events and facilities (such as theatres and art galleries) for local residents as well as improving the liveability of cities and towns. Culture and the arts should be seen as something that enriches society, as long as there is equitable access for all sections of the population (Radbourne, 2002). Events are able to contribute to this policy objective. Getz (2012) also highlights how events can encourage traditional cultures, by providing an opportunity to showcase traditional rituals and celebrations, as well as helping to maintain traditional songs, drama and poetry. Finally, in order to be competitive and sustainable, events should have a cultural aspect that is attractive to visitors and locals alike, in order to help ensure their commercial viability (Getz, 2012).

Social policy

Events have the potential to contribute greatly to social policy, but this is not always recognised. Providing entertainment, culture and the arts remains a non-mandatory part of the remit of local government in many areas of world (Pugh and Wood, 2004). Nonetheless, the public sector remains one of the key providers of festivals and special events. Governments are likely to have policy objectives around social issues such as community development and integration; combatting anti-social behaviour; enhancing health and wellbeing for residents; and developing community resilience to future challenges. In each case, it is possible for events to play a role in achieving these objectives. In the first place, many of the social benefits come directly from the economic benefits – improved job security and boosting the local economy are seen to have social benefits for the local community. In terms of community, events have been shown to be important for building civic and/or community pride, community development, increased community participation and expansion of cultural perspectives (Wood, 2005; Allen et al., 2011). Regarding health and wellbeing, many governments use events as 'social marketing' – campaigns that are undertaken with the aim of changing attitudes and behaviours for the better (such as anti-smoking or anti-drink driving campaigns). Research also suggests that there is a growing interest in using events as a platform for political messages (Sharpe, 2008), and that event organisers, and music festival organisers in particular, feel that they are in a position to advocate for particular environmental and social justice issues (Mair and Laing, 2013). Therefore, there is certainly scope for events to contribute to social policy objectives.

Environmental policy

Many governments have enacted laws or regulations to ensure that various aspects of event organisation and planning take environmental considerations into account. For more detail on sustainable events and the environment, see Chapter 6. However, a policy to foster sustainable events must go beyond simply the practical 'green' aspects of sustainability, such as requiring venues and suppliers to meet environmental regulations or guidelines. Policy for events can consider encouraging events with sustainable or environmental themes. Examples might be eco-fests, or sustainable living festivals, which exhibit new and innovative sustainable options for living, such as technologies and equipment to conserve water or power. Events policy may also be introduced with the aim of encouraging event organisers to include environmental awareness and environmental education into their events, as a way of reaching attendees with social marketing messages.

Sustainable events policy

As has been noted, the primary interest of governments in events and event policy relates to the positive economic outcome of events, in particular their potential to attract tourists to a destination and build a positive destination brand and image. However, Getz (2009) suggests that a more holistic view of events is needed, and that governments should take a triple bottom line approach to event policy. He suggests three phases of a new sustainable events paradigm – conceptualisation, diffusion and institutionalisation – and argues that in most cases, we are still in stage one.

In the conceptualisation stage (stage one), governments recognise the need to evaluate events more broadly than just economically. In addition, the importance and value of events to a range of stakeholders is also recognised. The second stage is diffusion, where the new paradigm or way of viewing events is communicated to the public and politicians, and those in power making decisions about events start to consider this more sustainable approach. Finally, in the institutionalisation stage, sustainability is taken for granted by politicians and the public alike, and its principles are embedded in laws and regulations (Getz, 2009). Both new and established events adopt the principles of responsible and sustainable events.

As Getz (2009) notes, we are not yet in this position generally, although there are several examples of both local and national governments which have begun to take into account sustainability and the triple bottom line in their event policies. For example, Mosman (a local authority in Sydney, Australia) has a sustainable event policy available online (Mosman Council, 2014). This states that their aim is to ensure that sustainability principles are applied to the planning, management and implementation of all events that fall within the scope of the policy – all events taking place with over 50 participants, either organised by Mosman Council, or being staged on land or in buildings owned by the council. Nonetheless, a comprehensive sustainable event policy such as this is the exception rather than the rule at present.

The role of politics within events

As Burbank, Andranovich and Heying (2001: 1) point out 'staging the Olympic Games takes place on the contested territory of politics'. The same could be said for any mega-event, with the rationale for bidding for and staging such events often having more to do with the political ideologies and policies of individual government than with the potential benefits and pitfalls of such events. Governments, which after all are made up of those sharing particular ideologies, use mega-events to pursue what is called 'symbolic politics' – a public display of ideology or intentions (Black, 2007). These may include the opportunity to signal important changes of direction in policy, to reinforce key messages about the host nation, or to re-frame public opinion of the government or nation (Black, 2007). The Olympic Games has over the years been the subject of such symbolic politics nearly every time that they have been held, and at the same time have been the subject of political protest on numerous occasions. Box 3.3 illustrates a range of controversies that have been associated with bidding for and staging the Olympic Games.

Box 3.3 Politics and the Olympics

Toronto Toronto, Canada bid for the Olympic Games in both 1996 and 2008. In both cases, they lost out. One of the factors in their failure to win was the coalition known as Bread Not Circuses (CBC News, 2001). They organised a passionate opposition campaign, demanding that Toronto use the money for housing the homeless and protecting the environment, rather than on bidding for the Games. They may not have been the only reason for Toronto failing to win the bid, but public opposition to the Games acts to discourage the International Olympic Committee (IOC) from awarding the Games to a host nation that may have concerted political opposition.

   Beijing Part of the reason for staging the Olympic Games in Beijing was considered to be the opportunity that it offered to the Chinese government to showcase Chinese development and the importance of China to the global economy (Preuss, 2007). It was also considered that hosting the Olympic Games in China offered a chance for China to promote the benefits of their political system, and potentially divert attention away from negative political issues such as human rights and air pollution (Yardley, 2007). The 2008 Games provoked outrage from human rights groups who said allowing China to host the Games legitimised its repressive regime. Protestors also claimed that China would use the Games as a propaganda tool. However, at the same time it is important to recognise that the presence of the Olympic Games meant that protests and opposition that may otherwise have gone relatively unnoticed, suddenly became international news. Protests about Tibet, for example, received global attention, 'simply because the Olympic Games were in town' (Yardley, 2007).

   Sochi The Sochi Winter Olympics of 2014 were held in Russia. The cost of these Olympics was huge – reported to be US$51 billion – even more than the staging of the Summer Olympics in Beijing and this was one reason for dissent among locals and international onlookers alike (Fedyashin, 2014). There was also much opposition to the Games, both politically and environmentally and a number of protests were held concerning exploitation of workers engaged in Olympic construction; allegations of the illegal dumping of construction waste threatening residents' health and safety; and evictions and displacement of residents to make way for Olympic venues (Mair, 2014b). Protestors against Russia's strict anti-gay laws also used the Olympics as a platform for voicing their objections (Fedyashin, 2014).

Chapter summary

This chapter has considered the relationship between public policy and events, and has identified the policy actors involved. The range of reasons for government involvement in events, including the public good, social equity, ideology and market failure was discussed. The different approaches that governments may take in terms of events – ranging from laissez-faire and the regulatory approach to the interventionist approach – were identified, and the policy domains that are influenced by, and can influence events, which included economic development, cultural, social and environmental policy were explained. Finally, the chapter identified and expanded on the role of politics within events, with particular reference to the Olympic Games.

Learning activities

1   Discuss the extent of government involvement in events in your country, identifying those policy domains where events have particular relevance.
2   Compare and contrast the roles of the different policy domains in terms of the influence they have on event management and planning.
3   Taking a mega-event as an example, consider how national government politics have influenced how the event was staged and how the event was perceived.
4   Identify events where political protests have taken place and discuss ways to deal with these issues.

Case study: Subvention in Malaysia's convention industry

Malaysia is located in South East Asia, and has a population of around 28 million people. In recent years, Malaysia has become a popular tourist destination, particularly its beach resorts, its capital, Kuala Lumpur, Sarawak and Langkawi Island. The Malaysian government has developed a strategy to transform the economy of Malaysia, and to attract more high-yield visitors to the country. As part of that strategy, the Ministry of Tourism has decided to work to attract more conferences and conventions to Malaysia (Malaysia Convention and Exhibition Bureau, 2014). Business events travellers are generally accepted to be a very high-yield visitor (Mair, 2014a), and therefore they are eagerly sought after by many destinations around the world. In recognition of the economic importance of the business events industry, countries across the world are actively seeking to grow their share of the business events market as the benefits of hosting conferences and conventions become clear (Yoo, 2005).

The Asian convention industry has developed rapidly over the past decade and the global share of the convention market held by Asia is gradually growing (Kim et al., 2011). In 2011, Kuala Lumpur was just in the top ten Asian international convention destinations (ICCA, 2012). Malaysia has undertaken a substantial programme of convention infrastructure development, both in Kuala Lumpur and in Sarawak. However, given the level of competition in the industry, the Malaysian government has decided to intervene by providing financial incentives to conventions that take place in Malaysia. As part of the Economic Transformation Programme, the government allocated funds of RM25 million (approximately AU$8 million) each year in 2011 and 2012 to enhance the competitiveness of Malaysia's business tourism industry in the

(Continued)

Case study (continued)

global marketplace (Malaysia Convention and Exhibition Bureau, 2014). According to the Malaysia Convention and Exhibition Bureau (2014), 'to enhance Malaysia's competitiveness, a Subvention Fund has been set aside to encourage companies, especially non-profit organisations, to bid for and host international business events in the country'. Subvention is a financial and/or non-financial incentive designed to attract international business events. The subvention programme focusses on supporting bids for targeted international business events which offer high economic value to the nation.

The level of subvention support is based on an assessment of several criteria:

- The overall economic value of the proposed event
- The number of international participants and their length of stay
- The profile/timing of the event
- The development of an ongoing legacy the event may bring to the community

Malaysia is not the only country to have a subvention fund. The government of Macau has a Convention and Exhibition Stimulation programme to provide assistance and financial support to event organisers – this support assists with the costs of putting together bids, arranging site visits, bringing in keynote speakers and preparing and running event marketing campaigns (Donovan, 2012). However, subventions have been criticised as representing too much government interference in the free market. Some countries (Australia is a notable example), have stated that subventions are not their preferred way of approaching bids, relying rather on trying to make events more attractive for organisers and their delegates, offering value-add rather than cash. Further, for smaller destinations, the budget for large cash subventions is simply not available (Mair, 2014a). However, in a financially unstable climate, money on the table may be the deciding factor for associations and convention planners when it comes to choosing a destination.

Discussion questions

1 Discuss whether you feel that subvention funds are an appropriate way for government to intervene in the free market in order to attract conventions.
2 If you were in charge of event policy for a smaller destination, and didn't have the funds to provide subventions, how else could you try to attract high-yield business events travellers?
3 Discuss alternative ways that governments can support business events without providing financial incentives.

Further reading and online resources

City of Gold Coast Events Strategy. Available online at http://www.goldcoast.qld.gov.au/city-of-gold-coast-events-strategy-23127.html [accessed 20 November, 2014].

Foley, M., McGillivray, D. and McPherson, G. (2012). *Event policy: from theory to strategy*. Abingdon, Oxon: Routledge.

Getz, D. (2009). Policy for sustainable and responsible festivals and events: institutionalization of a new paradigm. *Journal of Policy Research in Tourism, Leisure and Events*, 1 (1), 61–78.

Glasgow Major Events. Available online at http://glasgowmajorevents.com/why-glasgow/events-charter/ [accessed 20 November, 2014].

National Business Events Strategy for Australia 2020. Available online at http://www.businesseventscouncil.org.au/files/BES%20full%20doc%20Nov08.pdf [accessed 20 November, 2014].

References

Allen, J., O'Toole, W., Harris, R. and McDonnell, I. (2011). *Festival and special event management*, NY: John Wiley and Sons.

Black, D. (2007). The symbolic politics of sport mega-events: 2010 in comparative perspective. *Politikon: South African Journal of Political Studies*, 34 (3), 261–76.

Burbank, M., Andranovich, G. and Heying, C. H. (2001). *Olympic dreams: the impact of mega-events on local politics*. Boulder, CO: Lynne Rienner Publishers.

CBC News (2001). Bread Not Circuses voices its concerns to IOC. Online article, available at http://www.cbc.ca/news/canada/bread-not-circuses-voices-concerns-to-ioc-1.295757 [accessed 30 June, 2014].

Chen, S. (2012). Singapore boosts tourism spending with F1 amid slowdown. Bloomberg News online article, available at http://www.bloomberg.com/news/2012-09-18/singapore-boosts-tourism-spending-with-formula-one-amid-slowdown.html [accessed 30 June, 2014].

Deery, M. and Jago, L. (2010). Social impacts of events and the role of anti-social behaviour. *International Journal of Event and Festival Management*, 1 (1), 8–28.

Delamere, T. A., Wankel, L. M. and Hinch, T. D. (2001). Development of a scale to measure resident attitudes toward the social impacts of community festivals. Part I: Item generation and purification of the measure. *Event Management*, 7 (1), 11–24.

Department of State Development, Business and Innovation, Victorian Government (2014). *Entities: Victorian Major Event Corporation*. Available online at http://dsdbi.vic.gov.au/our-department/entities [accessed 27 July, 2014].

Derrett, R. (2003). Festivals and regional destinations: how festivals demonstrate a sense of community and place. *Rural Society*, 13 (1), 35–53.

Donovan, M. (2012). Cruise lines eye MICE market. CEI Asia, Sept.

Dye, T. R. (1992). *Understanding public policy*. Englewood Cliffs, NJ: Prentice Hall.

Ernst & Young (2010). *An eventful year: economic impact of the Victorian major events calendar*. Melbourne: Ernst & Young/Victorian Major Events Company.

Fedyashin, A. (2014). *The real political takeaway from the Olympics: the West needs to get over the cold war. The Guardian*, Tuesday 25 February, available online at http://www.theguardian.com/commentisfree/2014/feb/24/sochi-olympics-west-not-over-cold-war [accessed 30th June 2014].

Foley, M., McGillivray, D. and McPherson, G. (2012). *Event policy: from theory to strategy*. Abingdon, Oxon: Routledge.

Getz, D. (2005). *Event management and event tourism*, Elmsford NY: Cognizant Communication Corporation.

Getz, D. (2009). Policy for sustainable and responsible festivals and events: institution-alization of a new paradigm. *Journal of Policy Research in Tourism, Leisure and Events*, 1 (1), 61–78.

Getz, D. (2012). *Event studies: theory, research and policy for planned events*. Abingdon, Oxon: Routledge.

Getz, D. (2013). *Event tourism: concepts, international case studies and research*. Putnam, NY: Cognizant Communication Corporation.

Hall, M. and Rusher, K. (2004). Politics, public policy and the destination. In Yeoman, I., Robertson, M., Ali-Knight, J., Drummond, S. and McMahon-Beattie, U. (Eds), *Festival and events management*. Oxford: Elsevier Butterworth-Heinemann, pp. 217–31.

Henderson, J. C., Foo, K., Lim, H. and Yip, S. (2010). Sports events and tourism: the Singapore Formula One Grand Prix. *International Journal of Event and Festival Management*, 1 (1), 60–73.

ICCA (2012) *Statistics Report 2002–2011. The International Association Meetings Market*. Abstract for international associations, press, universities, students and consultants, Amsterdam: International Congress and Convention Association.

Kim, S. S., Yoon, S. and Kim, Y. (2011). Competitive positioning among international convention cities in the East Asian Region. *Journal of Convention and Event Tourism*, 12 (2), 86–105.

Mair, J. (2014a). *Conferences and conventions: a research perspective*. Abingdon, Oxon: Routledge.

Mair, J. (2014b). Sochi – a rich green legacy to remember. . . or forget? The Conversation, 9 February. Available online at http://theconversation.com/sochi-2014-a-rich-green-legacy-to-remember-or-forget-22637 [accessed 30 June, 2014].

Mair, J. and Laing, J. H. (2013). Encouraging pro-environmental behaviour: the role of sustainability-focused events. *Journal of Sustainable Tourism*, 21 (8), 1113–28.

Malaysia Convention and Exhibition Bureau. (2014) Subvention Fund. Available online at http://www.myceb.com.my/subvention-programme [accessed 28 July, 2014].

Mosman Council (2014). Sustainable Events. Available online at http://www.mosman.nsw.gov.au/mosman/venues/special-events [accessed 30 July, 2014].

Preuss, H. (2007). Signaling growth: China's major benefit from staging the Olympics in Beijing 2008. *Harvard Asia Pacific Review*, 9 (1), 45–9.

Pugh, C. and Wood, E. H. (2004). The strategic use of events within local government: a study of London Borough Councils. *Event Management*, 9 (1/2), 61–71.

Quinn, B. (2003). Symbols, practices and mythmaking: cultural perspectives on the Wexford Festival Opera. *Tourism Geographies*, 5 (3), 329–49.

Radbourne, J. (2002). Social intervention or market intervention? A problem for governments in promoting the value of the arts. *International Journal of Arts Management*, 5 (1), 50–61.

Sharpe, E. K. (2008). Festivals and social change: intersections of pleasure and politics at a community music festival. *Leisure Sciences*, 30 (3), 217–34.

Solberg, H. A. and Preuss, H. (2007). Major sport events and long-term tourism impacts. *Journal of Sport Management*, 21 (2), 213.

Stokes, R. and Jago, L. (2007). Australia's public sector environment for shaping event tourism strategy. *International Journal of Event Management Research*, 3 (1), 42–53.

Sunshine Coast Major Events Strategy (2013). Sunshine Coast Council: *Sunshine Coast Major Events Strategy 2013–2017*. Available online at http://www.sunshinecoast.qld.gov.au/addfiles/documents/business/major_regional_events_strategy.pdf [accessed 4 September, 2014].

Tourism and Transport Forum (2014). *Backing major events*. Sydney: Tourism and Transport Forum.

Veal, A. J. (2010). *Leisure, sport and tourism, politics, policy and planning*. UK: CABI.

Victorian Auditor General (2007). *State Investment in Major Events*. PP No 14. Melbourne: Victorian Government.

Whitford, M. (2004). Event public policy development in the Northern Sub-regional Organisation of Councils, Queensland, Australia: rhetoric or realisation? *Journal of Convention and Event Tourism*, 6 (3), 81–99.

Whitford, M. (2009). A framework for the development of event public policy: facilitating regional development. *Tourism Management*, 30 (5), 674–82.

Wood, E. H. (2005). Measuring the economic and social impacts of local authority events. *International Journal of Public Sector Management*, 18 (1), 37–53.

Wood, E. H. (2006). Measuring the social impacts of local authority events: a pilot study for a civic pride scale. *International Journal of Nonprofit and Voluntary Sector Marketing*, 11 (3), 165–79.

Yardley, J. (2007). Beijing Olypmics: Let the politics begin. *New York Times*, 13 August. Available online at http://www.nytimes.com/2007/08/13/world/asia/13iht-letter.1.7095421.html?pagewanted=alland_r=0 [accessed 30 June, 2014].

Yoo, J. J.-E. (2005). Development of the convention industry in Korea. *Journal of Convention and Event Tourism*, 6 (4), 81–94.

Chapter 4

Sustainable events and urban regeneration

Learning outcomes

After studying this chapter you should be able to:

- Understand the role of events in urban regeneration
- Compare and contrast event-led and event-themed approaches to urban regeneration
- Appraise the physical, economic and social benefits from regeneration
- Identify the negative consequences of event-led regeneration

Introduction

Regeneration is defined as a comprehensive and integrated vision and action, which leads to the resolution of urban problems, and which seeks to bring about a lasting improvement in the economic, social and environmental conditions of an area that has been subject to change. Using events as a means to improve urban environments is not a new idea and there are examples in Europe dating back to the nineteenth century. For example, the Eiffel Tower in Paris was originally built as the gateway to the 1889 World's Fair and the south bank of the River Thames in London was redeveloped as the show-piece for the 1951 Festival of Britain. However, mega-events are increasingly being used as a means to leverage large scale urban improvements. This is due to a number of factors including the global media attention which a mega-event generates for the host city and an increasing need to brand the host city as a result of the inter-city competition to host events following the 1984 Olympics in Los Angeles (Chalkley and Essex, 1999).

The Olympic Games in particular has been used as a catalyst for large scale urban regeneration since the 1960s and major Olympic Games associated with regeneration include Rome, 1960; Tokyo, 1964; Seoul, 1988; Barcelona, 1992; and Sydney, 2000. Indeed, host cities can use promises of regenerating run-down areas as part of the proposed legacy for the event – Chapters 11 and 12 focus on legacies more broadly. A major event can fast-track urban regeneration, stimulate economic growth, improve transport and cultural facilities and enhance global recognition and prestige for the host destination (Chalkley and Essex, 1999). Typically it is major sporting events, with their requirements for particular sporting venues, international participation and ability to attract substantial sponsorship and media attention, which are the focus of most regeneration projects but other major events such as arts events (see Garcia, 2004), international expos and European capitals of culture can also lead to substantial urban change.

Why do governments use events for regeneration?

Governments can, of course, choose to regenerate any location within their remit if they have the funds, but events are often the direct cause of urban change. This is because of the nature of events and the global media attention that they attract. The event itself provides a reason for intervention – it may be that new facilities are needed and indeed the global bodies that award and oversee major events such as the International Olympic Committee and the Federation of International Football Associations have specific requirements from the host destination, such as an athlete's village in the case of the IOC.

Urban regeneration projects typically take a long time to complete and an event provides a deadline for completion, which usually fast tracks the programme. Indeed a representative from the organising committee for the Delhi 2010 Commonwealth Games commented, in an episode of the Al Jazeera programme *People and Power* (see Further reading and online resources), that the city was able to undertake ten years' worth of regeneration in the space of a couple of years. This is also achievable as events tend to generate new sources of funding not previously available to urban redevelopment (though often taken from other budgets) and are supported by the political will of local politicians, who are keen to see their constituency presented favourably on the international stage.

Urban regeneration as part of the planning for an event can also attract more community support than everyday redevelopments as local residents and businesses may buy in to the need to make improvements for the event.

Event-led and event-themed regeneration

Urban regeneration can be described as both event-led and event-themed, a term coined by Andrew Smith (2012). Event-led regeneration is where the redevelopment is designed simply to meet the needs of the event, without any broader or longer-term impacts. Event-led projects include:

- Investment in new venues
- Re-use of brownfield or industrial land
- Integrating peripheral areas of the city
- Refurbishment of existing facilities

An example of event-led regeneration is provided in Box 4.1.

Box 4.1 Fremantle and the America's Cup

Fremantle near Perth in Western Australia hosted the America's Cup defence in 1983–4 and the preparations for the event involved a total investment in the port city of AU$2.8 billion. Of this, AU$2.3million was provided by competitors with the rest largely provided by the State and Federal Governments. Major works included:

- Construction of the Challenger Harbour
- Refurbishment of the Fishing Boat Harbour and surrounding precinct as the 'Cup City', a waterside leisure precinct for spectators and tourists
- Extension of Perth–Fremantle railway line
- Building of the Esplanade Hotel
- Repair and restoration of historical buildings
- Conversion of existing structures such as warehouses into luxury residential accommodation
- Refurbished infrastructure – water pipes, sewers and cables, roads, cycle ways, parking, sand dunes

Source: Jones, 2007

Event-themed regeneration is about using the event to create longer-term benefits for the host destination by redeveloping the destination physically, economically, socially and culturally rather than simply building a flashy new stadium. Event-themed regeneration is closely linked to creating a positive legacy for the event and successful event legacies are frequently associated with examples of long-term urban renewal such as the redevelopment of Barcelona for the 1992 Olympic Games. See Chapter 12 for further details of the 'Barcelona model'.

The event venues

The scale of the regeneration involved in any event depends partly on the requirements for hosting the event. As noted above, the International Olympic Committee outlines the requirements for a host city in the Olympic Bidding Manual and these include an Olympic Village, which provides accommodation for athletes, officials and the media as well as appropriate standard facilities for each of the sports in the Olympic programme (Pitts and Liao, 2009). The Olympic Games has a 'one city' principle, which means that it must take place in one location, which contrasts with other mega-events, such as the FIFA World Cup and the Rugby World Cup, which use multiple locations. This means that the regeneration associated with hosting the Olympic Games is concentrated in one place. This can lead to the biggest impacts but this geographical clustering of facilities can also cause 'territorial inequity', where the redevelopment benefits only a few of the country's residents, even though they may bear the costs of hosting the event through their taxes.

There are alternative options for spreading the benefits more widely for mono-location events. For example, the 2004 Olympic Games in Athens spread the sporting venues throughout the city. Another option used at the 2012 Olympic Games in London, was to hold most of the events at one site in east London but the canoe and some cycling events took place in locations outside of greater London but still in south east England, while the sailing was held on the south coast at the Weymouth and Portland National Sailing Academy. However, permission to hold events outside the main city is required from the IOC.

New venues are usually the most striking urban development projects associated with events and often serve as flagship components for the event – for example, the media was very excited about the Bird's Nest stadium at the 2008 Beijing Olympic Games. However, with potential requirement for more than 40 venues to host the Olympic Games there is the substantial risk of creating white elephants. White elephant venues are described by Smith as 'under-utilised venues that are expensive to maintain' (2012: 68). Any event that invests heavily in purpose-built new venues for the event, with little thought as to their use afterwards, risks creating white elephants. Smith says there are four main reasons why major events lead to white elephants:

1 Bidding to win – a competitive bidding process encourages cities to include impressive and sometimes extravagant venues
2 Showing off in front of international audiences
3 External pressure from event rights holders about the requirements for staging the event
4 Supply-led development, whereby new venues are developed in the hope that they will generate demand rather than in response to demand

Alternatives to building new venues include using existing venues or refurbishing existing venues; securing a post-event use for the venue in the planning stages of the event; using temporary structures and converting venues to alternative uses after the event. The 2012 Olympic Games in London used structures with temporary components that could be dismantled afterwards to reduce mega-event scale venues to a more usable size for the local community.

Box 4.2 Post-event use of Olympic villages

A major challenge for the organisers of a mega-event is what to do with the venues after the event is over. This is part of the event legacy, which is discussed in more detail in chapters 11 and 12. This should be included in the regeneration plan so that future use is built into the current development. While some venues may need substantial remodelling to prepare them for an alternative, post-event use, the athletes' villages typically lend themselves to be reused as accommodation without much additional work. A review of the Olympic Games since 1936 shows some interesting trends in post-event use. The athletes' village from the 1936 Berlin Games was converted into an army barracks, which is not surprising given that this was just before the Second World War.

From 1952 to 1984, the athletes' villages were all used to provide social housing or student dormitories. Since 1984, athletes' villages have mostly been converted into commercial housing (with the exception of the 1996 Atlanta Games). Why this change? Pitts and Liao (2009) note that up until the 1980s, most Olympic Games were funded publicly which naturally led to the facilities being used for public benefit as social housing post-Games. Since the 1980s, private investment in the Games has substantially increased, leading to concern for post-Games profitability. Olympic Villages have been designed with commercial options in mind with higher quality specifications. While this has brought benefits in terms of the quality of construction and cost efficiency, the focus on building for post-Games use has reduced the emphasis on meeting the needs of the athletes and the post-Games accommodation is frequently unaffordable for local residents.

Source: Pitts and Liao, 2009

Beyond the venues

While the venues typically receive the most attention and are directly related to the event, urban regeneration projects associated with events typically involve much wider redevelopment. This includes primary indirect-related regeneration including transport, such as new public transport facilities or improvements to road systems, communication networks and tourist services such as accommodation. The primary indirect-related regeneration provides support for the event. Additionally, there might be secondary indirect-related regeneration, which can include creating a pleasant environment and improved public domain; branding or rebranding the host destination or improvements to the cultural assets such as museums or other attractions (see Pitts and Liao, 2009: 40). Barcelona's regeneration programme for the 1992 Olympic Games included all of these, with improvements to the transport system, redirecting the train lines to reconnect the port and beaches with the rest of the city, new telecommunications systems, improvements to the streetscapes and museums (Pitts and Liao, 2009).

Outside physical regeneration

As with new venues, physical changes to the host destination as a result of redevelopments associated with the event are the most visible, but physical regeneration is only one aspect of event related regeneration. Major events provide an opportunity to improve the social and economic life of the event location.

Social regeneration

Regeneration, if done sensitively, can be used to improve the social fabric of the host community. The local community – or communities, as destinations usually have a range of different social groupings – can be involved in the event in a variety of ways. These can include consulting with the community during the planning stages of the event, providing opportunities for employment and training in the planning and staging of the event and involving local residents as volunteers in various roles both before and during the event. Upskilling local residents through events-related training and employing them during the event can give them the skills and experience to obtain employment afterwards as well as create an events workforce who can assist with the staging of subsequent events. This approach was adopted by Manchester during the 2002 Commonwealth Games as a means to improve the employment opportunities for local residents from disadvantaged backgrounds (Carlsen and Taylor, 2003).

The event can also be used as a stimulus to try to address broader social problems including crime, obesity and stress. Such programmes are often linked to sporting events, where there can be clear links between the event, promoting sports participation in the region more widely and the potential health benefits associated with increased exercise. Glasgow City Council, for example, produced a Health Impact Assessment in advance of the 2014 Commonwealth Games to provide recommendations for how the health and wellbeing of the region could be improved through hosting the event. Improving the physical environment of the host destination can improve the image of the locality, make it a more pleasant place to live and attract inward migration from skilled people who want to live and work there. However, there is a downside to this – see the section on the dark side of regeneration below. The social benefits of events are discussed in further detail in Chapter 7.

Economic regeneration

Events can also revitalise the local economy of the host destination. Economic regeneration is about creating more business and employment in the locality in the longer term beyond the event. The longer-term economic benefits associated with event-related regeneration are best achieved by augmenting the main event with smaller events and attractions to prolong the impacts, providing training and skills to local people, which will enable them to obtain employment after the event. Hosting subsequent events in the destination can make use of the venues and infrastructure, assist the long-term viability of local businesses by using local suppliers and make use of the newly skilled events workforce. A revitalised image for the host destination can attract tourism and new businesses to the locality. The economic impact of events is examined in Chapter 5.

Sustainable event regeneration

This chapter has outlined two different approaches to regeneration – event-led and event-themed – and also described some of the potential problems associated with urban redevelopment projects linked to major events. What does a successful and sustainable regeneration programme look like? Successful regeneration programmes are typically not focussed on one event but on a series of events, which means that they reuse the venues and infrastructure as well as the expertise and knowledge gained by people living in the host destination. These programmes are usually part of a long-term regeneration agenda, where the initial event provides the investment and impetus for the first steps. Successful examples of such urban renewal programmes include Glasgow and Barcelona, because these cities used the events as part of a longer-term programme, rather than a quick fix solution for the event itself. Singapore offers a further example in Chapter 3.

To be successful and sustainable, urban regeneration associated with one or more major events needs to be planned. Any regeneration should both take into account and be built into the relevant Masterplans for a destination, a Masterplan being a comprehensive document setting out how a locality can be developed in the future. It needs to be part of a longer-term urban renewal programme and associated events policy. All relevant stakeholders should be identified and consulted (Sadd, 2012), including the various local communities, whose homes are about to be irrevocably changed. For example, in the case of Fremantle (Box 4.1), the regeneration associated with the defence of the America's Cup resulted in gentrification of the port city, which priced the original residents out (Jones, 2007). Regeneration projects in the past were typically government-led and funded. Increasingly, these programmes involve partnerships between the public, commercial and sometimes not-for-profit sectors. The increasing involvement of private sector money means that there needs to be a return on investment for these stakeholders, which guides the redevelopment towards post-event commercial uses rather than just public benefit. Smith sets out principles for achieving sustainable regeneration, which are presented in Box 4.3.

Box 4.3 Principles for sustainable event regeneration

1 Embed event strategies within wider urban regeneration.
2 Use the event as a coherent theme and effective stimulus for parallel initiatives and more diverse regeneration projects.
3 Ensure that regeneration planning is fully incorporated into the initial stages of planning for an event.
4 Promote shared ownership and responsibility among all partners of the legacy and events programmes.
5 Design effective organisational and structural arrangements between event regeneration agencies and event management representatives to ensure joint working towards clearly defined and shared goals.
6 Allocate sufficient human and capital resources throughout the lifetime of the event 'to achieve sustained effects'.
7 Design event regeneration projects to prioritise the needs and engagement of the most disadvantaged members of the target community.
8 Try to ensure an even geographical dissemination of positive impacts among targeted areas.

> 9 Ensure that event-themed social and economic regeneration initiatives build
> upon, and connect with, any physical and infrastructural legacy.
> 10 Ensure community representation from the planning stage onwards to pro-
> mote community ownership and engagement.
>
> *Source*: Smith, 2012: 39

Later chapters on the economic, social and environmental impacts of events detail methods of evaluating these impacts. Good practice would indicate that given the enormity of urban regeneration programs, it is essential that they are evaluated and Pitts and Liao (2009) offer criteria for evaluating Olympic regeneration projects. However, there are three factors to consider here:

1 Sustainable development, as Pitts and Liao state, is a 'multi-dimensional, cross-disciplinary process' (2009: 123), therefore evaluation of regeneration projects is extremely complex.
2 Regeneration projects are enormous and take place over a long period of time. Once they are complete, or the event has taken place, evaluation could be too late. The regeneration, good or bad, has already happened.
3 Regeneration projects often change between the bidding, planning and execution stages in response to external factors; in the case of the London 2012 Olympic Games the Global Financial Crisis took place between the award of the Games in 2005 and the event itself in 2012.

To be effective, evaluation of any regeneration project needs to be multidimensional, ongoing and part of the destination's long-term strategy. Ideally preparation of the bid document would include an assessment of whether the destination has the capacity to host the event in the first place, without causing substantial damage to the local area.

The dark side of event-led regeneration

Event-led regeneration usually does not benefit everyone in the destination but it can have a really negative impact on some people. The biggest problem associated with urban redevelopment programmes is displacement of the existing community in order to build venues for the event or event-related infrastructure. As major events are often located in run-down areas, with the aim of the event to improve these localities, it is often the most marginalised communities who are displaced. The Centre for Housing Rights and Evictions (COHRE, undated) has documented these displacements, noting that 1.25 million people in Beijing were displaced due to Olympic urban development.

The problems associated with displacement of a community are manifold. People may be relocated a long way from their workplace or school, which means they may no longer be able to access paid work. In addition, removing people by force from their home can break down community ties, reducing social capital and causing them to lose their identity, which is often linked to their home community, especially if their family has been living in the original location for a long time.

Even if the local community are not forceably relocated, since the aim of the regeneration project is to improve the location, this frequently results in rising house prices and rents, which prices the traditional community out of the area. The process of improving an area so that it rises in value and attracts wealthier new residents at the expense of the traditional community is called gentrification. Sadd (2012) argues that it is important for event-related regeneration to benefit the existing community rather than a new community. However, this can be an unintended outcome of a regeneration project.

A further problem is that planning legislation can be circumvented to speed up urban developments that are needed for the event. This means the proper consultation processes can be absent or cut short and the buildings may not meet certain planning requirements. There can also be wider social and economic impacts resulting from urban regeneration including public debt resulting from the cost of the project since this is usually spread over a much shorter time period than a normal urban renewal programme and the loss of rent and rateable income for local councils due to displacement of businesses.

COHRE has produced guidelines for mega-event organisers (COHRE, 2007) to advise on how best to protect housing rights when hosting a major event such as the Olympic Games. They call on governments to sign up to these guidelines, including:

- Proper assessment, monitoring and evaluation of the impacts of the event on housing.
- The need to develop policies to avoid negative impacts such as gentrification leading to rising house prices following the event.
- To take action to prevent evictions and displacement resulting from the event; to use the event to increase the supply of low-cost, public and social housing and to improve the housing stock of the host destination.
- Enhance the legal and regulatory protection of housing rights.
- Hold violators of housing rights to account.
- Ensure transparency and active public participation in all aspects of hosting the event.

Note that COHRE echo Smith (2012)'s ten principles (Box 4.3) in their call for identification and consultation with all stakeholders as a means to minimise these potential problems.

Chapter summary

This chapter has examined how preparations for mega-events frequently involve major urban redevelopment projects. The redevelopment can be either event-led or event-themed and the two approaches were compared and contrasted, with event-themed bringing longer-term benefits to the destination and local residents. The chapter also appraised the physical, economic and social benefits which are derived from regeneration programmes.

Regeneration projects are not always successful or particularly sustainable. The chapter outlined the risk of creating white elephant venues and also identified the challenges of spreading the regeneration benefits across the destination. Regeneration can also have a dark side, with residents forcibly displaced from their homes, communities and livelihoods, or even unintentionally priced out as an area becomes gentrified and housing more expensive. To maximise the leverage of hosting such a major event and to yield the best results for the community post-event, the chapter reviewed principles for sustainable event regeneration.

Learning activities

1 Using the online resources, review the post-Olympic plans for the London 2012 Olympic Park.
2 Choose a destination that has hosted a mega-event in the past decade and research the event regeneration. Was this event-led or event-themed?
3 Consultation is a major part of sustainable regeneration projects. If your home town was undertaking a major event-themed redevelopment project, which groups should the developers consult with and how?

Case study: The impacts of urban regeneration for the XIX Commonwealth Games, Delhi 2010

The XIX Commonwealth Games in Delhi took place 3–14 October, 2010 and was the largest multi-sport event to be held in Delhi. Staging the event cost US$1.9 billion and is the most expensive Commonwealth Games to date. The planning for the event involved substantial changes to the infrastructure of the city as well as completely refurbishing seven venues and building seven new venues. The preparations for the Games enabled the city to fast track its redevelopment by up to ten years. However, not everyone benefitted from the regeneration projects.

Major projects undertaken as part of the regeneration associated with the XIX Commonwealth Games included:

1 Refurbishing Delhi international airport and building a new terminal – Terminal 3
2 Expanding the Metro train transport system
3 Introducing almost 4,000 new buses, which run on compressed natural gas (CNG), which is more environmentally friendly
4 Improving the tourism infrastructure including:
   o Signage at monuments
   o Improved illumination
   o New laser and sound-and-light shows
   o Easier licensing system for bars and restaurants
   o Promotion of hotels and bed-and-breakfasts
   o Introduction of 'Hop-on, Hop-off' buses

5 Improving air quality by:
   o Setting stringent air quality norms
   o Granting tax exemption to battery-operated vehicles

(Continued)

Case study (continued)

- o Decommissioning two coal-fired power stations and replacing these with CNG plants
- o Establishing 500 Pollution Control Centres to improve monitoring and data collection

6 Other environmental improvements
- o Banning plastic bags in the city
- o Building a new sewage treatment plant
- o Replacing streetlights across Delhi with energy efficient, computer-controlled variants
- o Recycling waste from the Organising Committee of the Commonwealth Games Delhi 2020 Headquarters
- o Minimising the impact of the venues on the environment by introducing compact fluorescent lamp (CFL) and light emitting diode (LED) lighting; rainwater harvesting; reverse osmosis water purification to minimise bottled water consumption; and heat recovery systems to reduce air conditioning load

However, the aftermath of the Games has been marked by allegations of embezzlement of funds and financial irregularities, which have created a damaging perception of the regeneration projects. In addition, the Housing and Land Rights Network (HLRN, 2011) (part of a global non-profit alliance under the umbrella of the Habitat International Coalition) estimate that 200,000 people have been forcibly evicted from their homes as a result of the Commonwealth Games. These are typically the poorest people living in slums, who have limited or no access to legal support. The HLRN have investigated these evictions and found that:

1 At the sites they visited, none of the people had been consulted about the demolition of their homes and no public hearings about the evictions were conducted.
2 In the majority of cases, no notice was given, although in some locations between two and five days' notice was given prior to the forced eviction.
3 People lost or had personal property destroyed or damaged during the forced evictions. They were unable to salvage their possessions and at some sites, people reported losing important documents such as passports and voter identity cards. Families from the banks of River Yamuna (used as the site of the Commonwealth Games Village) lost their plants – their source of livelihood.
4 In the majority of sites, there was no compensation.
5 Many families were left homeless and living in tents, which has increased their risk of disease due to poor sanitation and lack of access to medical facilities.
6 People also reported negative psychological impacts of being forcibly evicted from their homes, including suicidal thoughts and one reported suicide.

7 Approximately 300 children from one site dropped out of school following the eviction and at least three schools were destroyed during the evictions.

The evictions also left people living far from their source of income. Many of the people living in the slums relied on the informal economy of street stalls to make ends meet.

Sources: Organising Committee of the Commonwealth Games 2010 Delhi (2010); Housing and Land Rights Network, 2011.

Discussion questions

1 Who benefited from the urban regeneration associated with the Commonwealth Games in Delhi?
2 Who missed out?
3 Do you think that this is event-led or event-themed regeneration?
4 How could the ten principles of sustainable event regeneration have been implemented in Delhi to create a more inclusive legacy for the Games?

Further reading and online resources

Baim, D. (2009). Olympic-driven urban development. In Poynter, G. and MacRury, I. (Eds), *Olympic cities: 2012 and the remaking of London*. Aldershot: Ashgate.

The London Olympic Park. Available online at http://queenelizabetholympicpark.co.uk/ [accessed 12 November, 2014].

People and Power – slum clearances in Delhi for the 2010 Commonwealth Games. Al Jazeera video. Available online at https://www.youtube.com/watch?v=lNfWF7 YaMio [accessed 12 November, 2014].

The Queen Elizabeth Olympic Park: a visitor's guide. Available online at http://www. theguardian.com/travel/2014/apr/08/queen-elizabeth-olympic-park-london [accessed 12 November, 2014].

References

Carlsen, J. and Taylor, A. (2003). Mega-events and urban renewal: the case of the Manchester 2002 Commonwealth Games, *Event Management*, 8 (1) 15–22.

COHRE (2007). *Multi-stakeholder guidelines on mega-events and the protection and promotion of housing rights.* Geneva: COHRE.

COHRE (undated). 'Mega-events', online article on displacement due to mega-events. Available online at http://www.cohre.org/topics/mega-events [accessed 12 November, 2014].

Chalkley, B. and Essex, S. (1999). Urban development through hosting international events: a history of the Olympic Games. *Planning Perspectives*, 14, 369–94.

Garcia, B. (2004). Urban regeneration, arts programming and major events. *International Journal of Cultural Policy*, 10 (1), 103–18.

Housing and Land Rights Network (2011). *Planned dispossession: forced evictions and the 2010 Commonwealth Games. Fact Finding Mission Report 14.* New Delhi: Housing and Land Rights Network.

Jones, R. (2007). Port, sport and heritage: Fremantle's unholy trinity? In Jones, R. and Shaw, B. (Eds), *Geographies of Australian heritages: loving a sunburnt country?* Aldershot: Ashgate, pp. 169–86.

Organising Committee Commonwealth Games Delhi (2010). *Delhi 2010 Post-Games Report.* Delhi, India: Organising Committee Commonwealth Games Delhi 2010.

Pitts, A. and Liao, H. (2009). *Sustainable Olympic design and urban development.* London: Routledge.

Sadd, D. (2012). What is event-led regeneration? Are we confusing terminology or will London 2012 be the first games to truly benefit the local existing population? *Event Management*, 13, 265–75.

Smith, A. (2012). *Events and urban regeneration.* London: Routledge.

PART II

Impacts of sustainable events

Chapter 5

Economic impacts of events

Learning outcomes

After studying this chapter you should be able to:

- Understand the types of economic impacts of events, both positive and negative
- Understand the range of techniques that have been used in Australia and overseas to assess the economic sustainability of events
- Apply cost–benefit analysis (CBA) to understand potential economic impacts of events and inform government decision-making

Introduction

Australian festivals and events have long been recognised for the economic benefits they generate through the expenditure of visitors, organisers, government agencies and private businesses involved in their staging. Allocation of government funding for events in particular carries with it the requirement to estimate the magnitude of the economic benefits generated and the extent to which events are economically sustainable. There is also a growing imperative to ensure that events, especially recurring events, are socially beneficial and environmentally responsible.

There are other reasons for evaluating events and contributing to their sustainability, such as:

- To determine the success of the event in relation to specific objectives
- To obtain feedback and enable improvement for recurring events
- To report to stakeholders – for example, host organisations, government, sponsors and the media
- To ensure the future funding and recurrence of the event
- To contribute to the understanding of the economic impact of events

Conceptual and technical approaches to economic evaluation of events have emerged during the past 40 years in Australia and around the world, and hundreds of academic articles and many more consultancy reports have been produced in that time (Della Lucia, 2013). Such work has given rise to the development of a range of evaluation techniques for events, some of which lack credibility and rigour and have a tendency to exaggerate economic impacts, which is referred to as boosterism. This creates problems in terms of comparability and consistency of methods, findings and reporting and limits the utility of the evaluation process. In addition, one of the criticisms of economic impact studies is that the full details of how an economic impact has been calculated are not made available, and instead, figures for economic impact are simply publicised without any justification as to how they have been calculated. Box 5.1 illustrates an example of how one event provides economic impact figures without adequate explanations.

Box 5.1 Reported economic impacts of the Indy 500

The Indianapolis 500 Festival takes place in Indianapolis, USA in May each year. As well as the famous motor race, the festival also includes nearly 50 other events during the month of May, such as a street parade, a mini-marathon and a kid's day (500 Festival, 2014). More than 500,000 people attend these events, with a significant number of visitors from outside the local area.

An economic impact study revealed that the 500 Festival events generate a significant tangible economic impact on the city of Indianapolis each year. In 2013, the economic impact was stated to be US$19.7 million in financial impact, including US$5.5 million of direct spending by out-of-area visitors (500 Festival, 2014). In addition to measurements of economic impact in terms of dollars, the 500 Festival in 2013 reported creating an estimated 215 jobs (15 directly by the organisation, 62 from payments to vendors and contractors and 138 as a result of visitor spending). Furthermore, the 500 Festival organisation and events claimed to generate an estimated US$950,000 in additional state and local taxes in 2013 (500 Festival, 2014).

Whilst there is nothing to suggest that these figures are not accurate, there is no way for the general public to verify them, and no further information on how the economic impact was calculated is available in the public domain.

However, a more consistent approach, as recommended by Carlsen and Harris (2013) could overcome the challenges associated with assessment of event economic sustainability.

Positive and negative economic impacts of events

The supporters of events cite a range of positive economic benefits of events, often without acknowledging the negative effects that researchers have identified when conducting post-event analysis. When seeking support for events from government and the tourism industry, the following benefits are often promoted, but the extent of the benefit is also often exaggerated:

- *Employment* – Mega-events are often perceived to 'create' many new jobs due to the investment in venue construction, urban renewal and the event tourism expenditure associated with hosting the event. However, these perceptions are based on economic modelling and employment multipliers that are a function of the additional money coming into the host destination. These jobs are temporary in nature and, in the case of event operations, many are filled by volunteers, not paid full-time equivalent staff. It is more correct to claim that events increase skill and experience levels, which has a beneficial effect on the workforce over time.
- *Income* – Similarly, income in the form of government grants, investment, sponsorship and tourist spending associated with an event is said to be subject to a multiplier effect, whereby the initial injection of funds ripples through the local economy creating additional employment, income and value through the spending of those in receipt of it. However, there is 'leakage' of income from the local economy at all stages of event production in the form of expenditure on imports, taxes, payment for services and prize money for competitors that detracts from the income multiplier effects. In many cases the multiplier effect is less than one, indicating that the local economy is not retaining much of the event income it receives.
- *Inflation* – It is well-recognised that the tourism and retail sectors take advantage of the high demand for transport, accommodation and services associated with an event through increasing prices, in other words, price inflation. This has come to be known as 'gouging' and should be considered as a negative economic impact of events, especially for those that cannot afford to visit or remain in the host destination.

- *Opportunity cost* – Another negative associated with government allocation of public monies to an event is opportunity cost, or the cost of foregoing the alternative uses of those funds such as building hospitals, schools or police stations. It is argued that these have a much longer-term economic benefit to society than the hosting of large, one-off 'parties', but the difficulty in measuring opportunity cost means that it is often disregarded as a negative economic impact of events.
- *Externalities* – Negative 'externalities' such as increased traffic congestion, littering and environmental damage are often associated with events, and very few studies take account of the time lost and cost involved of these impacts. In fact, employment in venue and environmental clean-up are often erroneously counted as a benefit of an event, when it should be counted as a cost.
- *Legacy* – Legacy is a double-edged sword associated with events as the impacts over time can be both positive and negative. If the significant investment of public monies is leveraged correctly the longer-term benefits can include:
  - Enhanced image and branding of the host destination
  - Increased business, trade and investment from outside of the host destination
  - Increased tourism arrivals and expenditure
  - Increased pride amongst the host community
  - Perpetual scholarships and funds to support ongoing community and sporting development

However, there are many factors that cause events to create an economic burden on the host destination that can last for generations. These factors take the form of increased public debt due to cost overruns on construction and operation; ongoing maintenance costs; under-utilised 'white elephant' venues; and lasting negative destination image associated with problems at the event (poor planning, terrorist attacks and even bad weather).

Estimating economic impact of events

There are three main analytical and modelling techniques currently used in economic impact evaluation:

- Cost–benefit analysis
- Input–output models
- Computable general equilibrium models

Each modelling or analytical approach has conceptual and technical strengths and limitations; these are discussed in this chapter, and the recommendations for specific modelling scenarios take them into account. The following pages describe the relative strengths and weaknesses of the three approaches in measuring the positive and negative economic impacts associated with events, as described above.

Generally, the economic effects of events manifest in three ways – directly, indirectly and induced. Direct effects are incurred by those event-related firms who provide goods and services directly to event participants in the form of ticket sales, food and beverages, accommodation, transportation and so on. This has a direct effect on their sales, profits, salaries and wages. Indirect effects arise through business to business transactions and the increased supply of inputs in the form of equipment, fuels and

Table 5.1 Value-added multiplier effects of a AU$10 million event

Scale of economic impact	Value-added multiplier	Total economic impact (AU$m)
Australia	1.67	16.7
Victoria	1.7	17
Queensland	1.33	13.3
Western Australia	1.1 to 1.2	11 to 12
South Australia	0.427 to 0.608	4.27 to 6.08

foodstuffs to these event-related firms. Finally, induced effects are felt in the wider economy when the direct and indirect income effects 'flow-through' the economy in the form of consumer spending and when the initial expenditure of event partici-pants reaches apparently unrelated sectors such as agriculture, communication and personal services.

The sum total of direct, indirect and induced effects of event-related expenditure provides the basis for modelling total impacts, based on the magnitude of the multi-plier effect that the initial event-related expenditure has as it flows through the local economy. However, multiplier effects can be calculated in different and complex ways and the magnitude of the multiplier effect varies significantly from state to state, depending on the structure of the economy, the reliance on imported goods and services and the extent to which event expenditure 'leaks' from their economies. Table 5.1 shows the value-added multipliers used in various states and nationally in Australia and demonstrates that a hypothetical event that generates AU$10 million in direct expenditure would have a significantly different total economic impact, depending on where it was held.

Cost–benefit analysis

Cost–benefit analysis (CBA) is a well-established approach to estimating the net bene-fits of a project when comparisons with alternative projects are required. Governments seek to maximise community and economic benefits when allocating funding and favour the use of CBA to guide their decision-making. In the case of event funding, CBA has been the preferred approach in the Australian Capital Territory since the 2002 Auditor-General's report described advantages of CBA and provided specific guide-lines for the conduct of such analysis (ACT Auditor-General's Office, 2002).

The standard CBA approach is to identify costs and benefits that are directly attribu-table to the project, quantify the costs and benefits, apply a discount rate to future cash flows to calculate net present value, conduct sensitivity tests for uncertainty, and then take account of equity and intangibles. The Auditor-General's report described the approach and its advantages thus:

- It is normal practice for substantial government investment to be subject to CBA.
- CBA provides information to assist evaluation and decision-making.
- CBA considers *on a consistent basis* the costs and benefits of alternatives [emphasis added].
- CBA can assist in the choice between alternative options to achieve a given objective, such as different projects to promote tourism.

- CBA can guide decisions between a range of expenditure proposals directed at a variety of objectives that cannot all proceed due to resource constraints.
- CBA attempts to measure all major costs and benefits associated with a project.
- CBA expresses the costs and benefits in dollar amounts as a convenient measuring tool.
- CBA estimates the difference between the total benefits and total costs as the net benefit of the project. The net benefit can be compared across different projects.
- It is valuable to undertake rigorous and systematic CBA and even if some costs and benefits cannot be assigned a dollar value, it ensures these factors are considered in the decision-making process.
- CBA can help minimise waste and ensure resources are directed to achieving objectives in the most effective way.

In 1997 the New South Wales Treasury listed several additional advantages associated with using CBA:

- CBA provides the framework for consideration of the total costs of providing particular services, and thereby encourages the pursuit of low-cost solutions.
- In emphasising the quantification of benefits, CBA encourages managers of public sector agencies to question and re-examine the strategic objectives of the agency in undertaking the project.
- In quantifying the net contribution of projects in a standard manner, the information base for decisions is improved, thereby assisting in the assessment of relative priorities.

It is also, however, vitally important to recognise the limitations of CBA when applied to events and to take steps to make allowances for them, as follows:

- Evaluate all costs and benefits attributable to an event – tangible and intangible
- Avoid double-counting of benefits – for example, visitor expenditure, which is both revenue for the event and an economic injection for the host destination
- Value all inputs at the prices paid for them, without assuming that these resources had no alternative use
- Apply an appropriate discount rate to future costs and benefits flowing from the event
- Use best estimates of intangible benefits and costs associated with events
- Avoid using CBA for smaller events: the time and cost involved in estimating tangible and intangible costs and benefits make it impractical

The best way of dealing with these limitations is to clearly state all assumptions when conducting CBA and to seek independent expert review of all CBA reports.

Cost–benefit analysis is recommended for use in the pre-event evaluation stage in order to assess the degree to which expected benefits match the funding sought; the results were to be updated after the event. Along similar lines, the now defunct federal Department of Resources, Energy and Tourism commissioned Access Economics to conduct a cost–benefit analysis of the 2022 FIFA World Cup (Access Economics, 2010). This included a sensitivity analysis of three different stadium cost scenarios (full, partial and overlay costs) and a computable general equilibrium model of economic and welfare benefits. Access Economics also provided guidelines for using cost–benefit analysis for pre-event evaluation (see Box 5.2). This analysis examined the economic benefits and costs of Australia potentially hosting the 2022 FIFA World Cup, with a focus on the direct financial aspects of the event to help governments better understand the nature and scale of the impacts

Box 5.2 FIFA World Cup 2022 cost–benefit analysis guidelines

In 2010, as part of a consultancy to produce a cost–benefit analysis of the 2022 FIFA World Cup, Access Economics developed the following guidelines:

- *Cost-benefit analysis should be developed with the Australian Government guidelines in mind* – Cost benefit assessments of major events should closely adhere to the Australian government's guidelines. In many areas, however, these are not definitive, making sound judgements and analytical transparency paramount.
- *Looking at the event from a society-wide point of view* – An important part of structuring a cost–benefit study is to establish an appropriate analytical envelope. The CBA framework subsequently aims to measure welfare impacts within this envelope. In the case of a major sporting event which spans different states, has a national element, and can involve large transfers overseas and Australian government support, a whole-of-economy analytical envelope should be adopted.
- *Careful consideration of displacement effects* – Major events, indeed any activity, use economic resources that could be employed for alternative purposes, with only small scope to use unemployed resources or idle capital. In this regard, event-related activities have a range of displacement effects and come at an opportunity cost. Where government support for an event is intrinsic, the displacement of other economic activities should be factored into the cost–benefit analysis. This should include the impacts of the event on other sports where possible. Where an event is large, such displacement and crowding out can be material from a macroeconomic perspective. These dynamic effects should be captured using appropriate analytical techniques.
- *Recognise the opportunity cost of government expenditures (including in-kind contributions)* – All government spending uses real resources which have competing uses and which must be funded by taxation. Where government facilitates a major event, whether through direct financial support or some other form of backing, there are explicit costs involved. Such costs should be recognised in undertaking a cost–benefit analysis of an event.
- *Be careful about claims that costs can generate benefits* – Many large events involve considerable capital expenditures such as for stadia and other facilities. There are good reasons to be highly sceptical of claims that such spending will provide incremental economy-wide benefits through supporting aggregate

(Continued)

FIFA World Cup 2022 cost–benefit analysis guidelines (continued)

demand and employment. Such claims typically ignore the counterfactual effect that multiplier impacts could also be achieved by alternative uses of the project resources. Failing to recognise the forgone stimulus effect from other potential spending priorities can lead to overstating any expansionary benefit from any particular event or project. It may be the case that little or no additional impact is generated.

- **Careful consideration and treatment of guarantees** – Where major events, such as the Olympic Games or FIFA World Cup, involve a competitive bidding process, countries are often required to provide a range of guarantees to the relevant governing organisation. These guarantees are typically broad, covering various financial and operational matters such as the costs of staging the event and the rights to relevant event revenues. They can effectively lock sponsoring governments into expensive commitments and involve substantial risk. Accordingly, the potential impacts of guarantees should be carefully considered and accounted for within the analysis.
- **Explicit treatment of risks and bidding costs** – Many of the costs and benefits of major events are uncertain and therefore involve an element of risk. Importantly, this should be explicitly accounted for in a cost–benefit analysis, primarily through undertaking a sensitivity analysis of key risk elements.
- **Conservatism** – Uncertainty regarding the benefits and costs of a major event (as discussed above) necessarily involves a high degree of judgement in conducting an event analysis. A common analytical flaw is that inherent optimism bias systemically underestimates costs and overstates benefits. Taking a conservative approach to the analysis, and myriad judgements required along the way, is a good way to build a credible and dispassionate analysis.
- **Transparency** – Cost–benefit analyses of events, and indeed most projects, are heavily reliant on judgement. Because of this, it is crucial that the basis for analytical inputs, decisions and conclusions are properly explained and documented. A key benefit is that it allows for more robust scrutiny of the analysis by other (independent) parties, thereby facilitating more informed debate and continual improvements over time.
- **Post-event assessments** – Agencies should conduct post-event assessments of the benefits and costs from hosting major events in the context of government support. Crucially, this will help build a better data and evidence base to support future event analyses. In particular, it can assist in more fully understanding the nature and magnitude of non-financial impacts from events.
- **Ongoing review** – These principles, and other relevant analytical considerations, should be reviewed periodically. No two events are the same and other issues are sure to arise which will require variations to any general approach. Indeed, the ongoing review of how event analyses are conducted should be a core procedural feature which aims to ensure the assessment of major events is continuously strengthened.

Source: Access Economics (2010)

of Australia hosting the event. Three distinct cost scenarios were examined, based on a different allocation of stadium infrastructure costs. These stadium cost scenarios reflect underlying uncertainty regarding the nature and extent of venue infrastructure commitments currently in the development 'pipeline', and therefore which venue costs can be attributed to the tournament. In moving from scenarios one to three, an increasing level of venue development is not contingent on the tournament, therefore reducing the costs of the event. By far, the major cost factor for the tournament relates to the development of stadium infrastructure (under scenario two, for example, venue related costs comprise around 55 per cent of all costs).

The financial benefits of the tournament arise predominantly through international tourism. Accordingly, the main uncertainties relate to these two dominant cost and benefit drivers. In particular, a key risk of staging the tournament concerns cost overruns for major infrastructure works (irrespective of the different stadium scenarios). For example, a 10 per cent increase in infrastructure costs will lower the net benefit by AU$81 million for scenario two, and under scenarios one and two the net benefits to Australia, after taking into account fully or partially the cost of venue development, were negative.

In summary, CBA offers advantages for governments seeking to maximise the net economic and social benefits of hosting of events, and this approach, along with direct in-scope expenditure (DISE), is currently favoured by some Australian states and territories. There will always be problems associated with calculating intangible benefits and costs, but a clear statement of assumptions and the conduct of an independent expert review will help minimise these. Ultimately, it should be not only the quantum of net benefits or costs that informs decision-making but also the distribution of those benefits or costs in the host community. An event that leaves a legacy of debt for taxpayers while benefiting particular stakeholders does not provide a positive net benefit in the long term.

Input–output models

Event operators obtain various inputs for their project, both from within the host destination and from without. Expenditure on inputs generates an increase in outputs in a range of event-related sectors of the economy, and these initial effects give rise to further industrial support effects as event-related sectors obtain their inputs from other areas of the economy. These flow-on effects and sectoral relationships are modelled by the Australian Bureau of Statistics and economic research centres throughout Australia, and the resultant input–output tables provide an indication of the production-induced multiplier effects. The increased expenditure also generates income for those employed in productive sectors, giving rise to consumption-induced economic effects. Thus, increased economic activity is modelled using input–output tables and sectoral coefficients as multipliers to gauge the final increase in production and consumption resulting from the initial injection of funds associated with an event.

Input–output analysis does, however, involve many unrealistic assumptions and limitations associated with the calculation of inter-sectoral relationships and the structure of regional and state economies. There are also temporal problems with input–output tables, which are often outdated and do not reflect the current structure of economies. Among these restrictive assumptions and problems associated with input–output analysis are the following:

- Excess capacity exists in all sectors, and production can expand to meet demand without having any inflationary price or wage effects.
- Regional and state and territory economies do not provide all required inputs for events, and there can be considerable leakage effects – through imports and federal taxes – that cannot be identified in input–output analysis.
- For non-economists, input–output represents a 'black box' type of analysis, and complex assumptions and calculations are neither transparent nor subject to scrutiny.
- Input–output and associated multiplier effects are always assumed to have a positive impact on economic activity but might not correlate with net economic benefits.
- Use of inappropriate income, output and employment multipliers exaggerates the effects of events.
- Typically, induced production effects from events as measured by value-added multipliers are close to or less than one, so the economic impacts beyond first-round direct in-scope expenditure effects are negligible, especially in import-dependent economies.

For these reasons, input–output analysis is at present used to a limited extent in event impact evaluation: only some Australian states apply value-added multipliers to first-round direct in-scope expenditure estimates to measure the increase in gross state product associated with events. This tends, however, to overstate the economic impact of events, since input–output analysis makes broad assumptions about resource availability and factors of production and does not take into account the opportunity cost of these.

Computable general equilibrium models

It is widely recognised that computable general equilibrium (CGE) models provide better estimates of changes in gross state product because they account for leakages resulting from imports and avoid double-counting in the production process by estimating changes in income for the factors of production in the form of wages, business income, rent and interest. CGE models are, however, a more complex version of input–output models and are therefore subject to the same limitations, albeit with more realistic assumptions about the flow of income generated by an event. Finally, an advantage of CGE over input–output modelling of economic impacts lies in the flexibility to accommodate changes in prices, tax revenue, investment and subsidies associated with major events.

Towards sustainable events economic evaluation

Australian event stakeholders charged with accounting for the economic and related impacts of events take a variety of approaches. There is some divergence in the scale, scope and methods used in event evaluation, but there are also common elements that could provide the basis for national consistency. Additionally, the requirements relating to accounting for the widely recognised non-economic impacts related to events vary significantly among jurisdictions, the following being considered in some, but not all, evaluations of event impacts:

- Community impacts
- Media and marketing impacts
- Tourism destination impacts
- Sponsorship impacts
- Attendee impacts
- Environmental impacts
- Urban renewal and infrastructure development impacts
- Political impacts

The first principle of economic impact evaluation involves the assembly of a statistically reliable and valid data set using clearly defined measures of direct in-scope expenditure (DISE). All jurisdictions use the DISE approach, and some have adapted the ENCORE Festival and Evaluation Kit (Jago and Dwyer, 2006) to accommodate it. A review based on a survey of previous users of the ENCORE tool kit found, however, that consideration should be given to the following modifications in redevelopment:

- Training should be provided to smaller festival and event organisers in order to improve access and uptake.
- An interactive web-based platform should be developed to improve usability and flexibility in the logic, order and wording of survey questions.
- Further developments should include a triple-bottom-line focus to capture the social and environmental, as well as economic, impacts of events (Schlenker et al., 2010).

The review and recommendations provided clear templates and guidelines for assessing economic, community and environmental impacts, and these were tested at the Parkes Elvis Festival of 2010. In addition to the visitor and organiser survey components of the ENCORE tool kit, a host-community social impact survey and an organiser environmental impact checklist were incorporated in the redesign and were found to provide a sound basis for further redevelopment of the tool kit. An earlier study by the Sustainable Tourism Cooperative Research Centre (CRC) in Western Australia found, however, that there was a lack of interest in using environmental checklists to evaluate event impacts (Jones et al., 2008). In any case, a range of tools and guidelines exist for assessing the ecological footprint of events (see Chapter 6), including the Victorian Environment Protection Authority's EPA Event Calculator, and the Australian Centre for Event Management, University of Technology, Sydney's event carbon calculator, both of which are available free (see http://www.epa.vic.gov.au/~/media/Publications/1181.pdf [accessed 14 November, 2014] and https://calculator.noco2.com.au/acem/ [accessed 14 November, 2014]).

Chapter summary

In order to refine their economic impact evaluations based on direct in-scope expenditure, some states (including Victoria and South Australia) use multi-sector modelling methods, such as input–output and/or computable general equilibrium modelling.

A 2009 Victorian Auditor-General's Office report considered direct in-scope expenditure to equate to 'induced tourism' and valued events on the basis of event-specific visitor expenditure in Victoria, which was claimed to be AU$1 billion dollars in 2007, with major events receiving some AU$55 million in government funding annually (Victorian Auditor-General, 2007). The Auditor-General acknowledged the complexity and cost involved in developing improved economic impact evaluations and determined that events receiving less than AU$10 million in funding should be required to conduct a direct in-scope expenditure assessment and then apply a general input–output multiplier (currently 1.86) to estimate 'unconstrained economic benefit'. Events receiving more than AU$10 million were to use an evaluation approach specifically designed for that event. Importantly, the recommendations covered, among other things, improved transparency of assumptions that have a material effect on impact modelling outcomes, greater rigour in the approach, and the use of computable general equilibrium modelling for larger events to assess impacts on gross state product.

This chapter has described the positive and negative economic impacts associated with events that will determine the extent to which events are sustainable in the host destination. The decision as to whether an event should receive, or continue to receive, government and industry funding will largely be determined by the net economic benefits and the extent to which the positives exceed the negatives. A range of techniques for measuring those effects, as well as the relative strengths and limitations of each has been provided in this chapter, with examples. It should equip the reader with the knowledge and skills necessary to interpret and critically examine the estimated economic benefits and costs of hosting events.

Learning activities

Source a report on the economic impact of an event and critically review it, by asking the following questions:

1   Are *all* positive and negative economic impacts associated with the event taken into account correctly?
2   Are the most appropriate techniques used to estimate economic benefits, taking particular note of the use of economic multipliers and underlying model assumptions?
3   Based on the report, what legacies does the event leave for future generations in terms of improved destination image or increased public debt?
4   Do you consider that the event enhanced or inhibited sustainability of the host destination?

Case study: Meta-analysis of 18 major events in New Zealand

The New Zealand government established the Major Events Development Fund (MEDF) in recognition of the longer-term economic benefits, new business opportunities, promotion of sports and arts, strengthening of local and national pride and the development of local infrastructure and amenities associated with major events.

The government required that the economic benefits of the funding provided needed to be documented but recognised that there was no standardised international approach to conducting such an evaluation. In 2007, it recommended that the MEDF should manage the balance of economic, social, cultural, legacy and international exposure and implement a cost–benefit analysis approach for evaluating the performance of events to improve decision-making on the basis of net national (and/or regional) benefits.

Subsequently, a meta-evaluation examined 18 events that received an investment from the MEDF between February 2010 and April 2012, for which either a post-event report and/or an economic impact assessment, was submitted to the Ministry of Business, Innovation and Employment (MBIE).

Investment received by each event ranged from NZ$50,000 (three events) to NZ$2 million (one event) with total investment in the 18 events of **NZ$7,243,750**.

Approach

The objective was to understand the economic benefit the fund has made to the national economy, in terms of a full assessment of tangible, and where possible intangible, benefits and costs. A modified cost–benefit analysis framework has been applied to re-evaluate previously reported post-event impact assessments. The net national focus was an explicit requirement of this evaluation, as distinct from attempting to estimate regional or local benefits and costs.

The approach was based on formal cost–benefit analysis methods, but reflected pragmatic considerations relevant to the scale and scope of most major events, with particular regard to acceptable evaluation rigour in the context of the size of central government investment (see Table 5.2).

Findings

Based on the current revised methodology, it is estimated that the 18 events collectively generated approximately **NZ$32.1 million of net economic benefit** to New Zealand. This is in distinct contrast to the estimated NZ$143.8 million of aggregate national economic benefit originally submitted by event organisers and their contracted consultants. There are many reasons for this, but most differences are because the original approaches:

- counted domestic visitor (and participants, officials, etc.) expenditure as a contribution to national economic welfare, when it actually represents only a transfer of expenditure or savings that would have occurred elsewhere in the New Zealand economy;
- applied generic and/or unjustifiably high multipliers to direct event-induced economic activity (e.g. visitor expenditure), to derive questionable indirect and induced effects;

(Continued)

Case study (continued)

Table 5.2 Methodology for post-event estimation of the national cost and benefits

National costs	Value (NZ$)
Total operating expenditure	$
Redistribution of public funds cost (20% of the total value of central government funding)	$
Total costs	**$**

National benefits	Value (NZ$)
Total operating income	$
Consumer surplus (20% of the total value of estimated domestic ticket sales; 2% of operating expenditure for non-ticketed events)	$
International visitor expenditure contribution to GDP (75% of total international visitor expenditure, where main reason for visit was attending the event)	$
Value of international airfare expenditure that accrues to New Zealand (25% of international airfares)	$
Total benefits	**$**

Net benefits to New Zealand (benefits minus cost)	**$**

- relied on often imprecise or inflated estimates of per day expenditure due to sub-standard or non-existent primary survey collections to collect critical visitor and participant expenditure estimation;
- directly attributed to the event expenditure by either or both domestic or international visitors who were visiting the host region irrespective of the event, i.e. 'coincidental' rather than 'additional' event visitors.

Summary of the study

This case study is evidence that consultants and event managers intentionally and knowingly exaggerate the economic benefits of their events by neglecting to adopt a rigorous and standardised approach to the design, data collection, analysis and reporting of the economic impact. When the scope and scale of the evaluation is set at the national level, which is appropriate given that the level of funding was provided by the national government and the impacts of major events occur nationally, the net economic benefits are considerably lower that the gross economic benefits reported by the organisers and their consultants. In fact, the difference of NZ$111.7 or 77 per cent of the originally reported benefits highlights that government, and therefore community, support for events needs to be based on sound decisions and reliable information regarding their true net benefits as part of the process of transformation towards sustainability.

Discussion questions

1 Why do event organisers and their consultants exaggerate the economic benefits of their events in post-event evaluations?
2 In what ways can evaluation methods be manipulated in order to inflate the findings of economic impact studies?
3 Why is the rigorous and standardised economic evaluation of events a necessary prerequisite in the process of developing sustainable events?

Further reading and online resources

Beach events in Poole have a positive economic impact. Youtube video. Available online at http://www.youtube.com/watch?v=VSsNrcOUH0o [accessed 14 November, 2014].

Hodur, N. and Leistritz, F. (2007). Estimating the economic impact of event tourism. *Journal of Convention and Event Tourism*, 8 (4) 63–79.

Olympic economic benefits in doubt. FT.com video, 26 July, 2011. Available online at http://video.ft.com/1080350867001/Olympic-economic-benefits-in-doubt/World [accessed 14 November, 2014].

References

500 Festival (2014). *Economic impacts*. Available online at http://www.500festival.com/node/553 [accessed 12 September, 2014].

Access Economics (2010). *Cost–benefit analysis of the 2022 FIFA World Cup*. Canberra: Access Economics.

ACT Auditor-General's Office (2002). *Performance audit report: V8 car races in Canberra – costs and benefits*. Canberra: ACT Auditor-General.

Carlsen, J. and Harris, R. (2013). *Developing a consistent approach to analysing the economic impact of festivals and major events*. Australian Centre for Event Management, University of Technology Sydney.

Della Lucia, M. (2013). Economic performance measurement systems for event planning and investment decision making. *Tourism Management*, 34, 91–100.

Jago, L. and Dwyer, L. (2006). *Economic evaluation of special events: a practitioner's guide*. Gold Coast, Queensland: Sustainable Tourism Cooperative Research Centre, Griffith University.

Jones, R., Pilgrim, A., Thompson, G. and MacGregor, C. (2008). *Assessing the environmental impacts of events*. Gold Coast, Australia: Sustainable Tourism CRC.

Schlenker, K., Foley, C. and Getz, D. (2010). *Encore festival and event evaluation kit: review and redevelopment*. Gold Coast, Queensland: Sustainable Tourism Cooperative Research Centre, Griffith University.

Victorian Auditor-General (2007). *State investment in major events*. Melbourne: Auditor-General.

Chapter 6

Environmental impacts of events

Learning outcomes

After studying this chapter you should be able to:

- Define what 'the environment' refers to and what 'impact' means
- Understand how events can impact on the environment
- Identify issues associated with measuring impacts
- Identify general approaches to environmental impact management

Introduction

Environmental impacts of planned events have gained increased attention over the past two decades as part of a greater awareness of a need for sustainable events. One of the first major events to set environmental standards was the 1994 Lillehammer Winter Olympic Games, which was branded as a 'Green Games'. Environmental impact management has since become more prominent in event management, especially with increasing awareness of global environmental issues such as climate change (Getz, 2009; Laing and Frost, 2010). Some researchers and authors such as Robbins, Dickinson and Calver (2007) think that environmental impact assessment and management systems should be a central part of event management.

Planned events are hugely diverse in terms of type, size, duration, location, time of year, theme, focus and so on. This means that the potential environmental impacts of events are equally diverse in terms of scale, type and affect.

However, researchers point to some common aspects of events associated with environmental impacts including:

- Transport and traffic
- Crowds of attendees
- Infrastructure and construction
- Energy use and resource consumption
- Waste production

These can generate a range of negative environmental impacts including:

- Air pollution
- Water pollution
- Litter and waste
- Vegetation trampling
- Congestion and crowding

An event may also have positive impacts. This can result from direct management actions associated with the event or through a demonstration effect that subsequently influences behaviour:

- Urban renewal (see also Chapter 4)
- Nature conservation/rehabilitation
- Demonstration effects – pro-environmental behaviour, environmental awareness

Depending on the characteristics of a planned event, different impacts may occur to different degrees across varying geographical and temporal scales. This chapter discusses these impacts and provides some examples and a case study to help put the ideas into a practical context.

What is 'the environment'?

Before we can discuss environmental impacts, it is important to understand the meaning of this term. In the context of this chapter, 'the environment' refers to the setting in which a planned event occurs. This may be a natural setting or a human made (built) setting. There is a large body of literature that discusses the definition and meaning of what a natural setting is that is beyond the scope of this book. In general, 'nature' refers to the sum total of living (biological) and non-living (physical) elements of an environment. The biological elements include organisms able to metabolise, grow, reproduce and die. The physical elements include soil, air, water, rocks and so on, that enable the survival of living organisms. Interactions within and between these biophysical components comprise what is referred to as ecological processes, or ecosystems. Where humans reside within this framework is a considerable area of debate. Humans, and the environments created by humans, are commonly viewed as being distinct from natural places, that is, nature is commonly seen as the non-human components of an environment (Soper, 1995). Others define nature in terms of the presence and viability of self-sustaining ecological processes (Newsome et al., 2012). From this perspective, some natural areas may cease to be viable in the absence of human intervention (bush reserves in urban areas, for example) while others are a product of human intervention (the Australian landscape and ecology is arguably a result of tens of thousands of years of human influence and intervention). In contrast, the built environment commonly refers to settings dominated by human made structures and landscapes, for example urban areas, towns and cities.

Generally, the environment can be thought of as a spectrum of naturalness. This spectrum ranges from completely natural, where ecological processes retain integrity and are self-sustaining with or without the presence of humans, through to built environments entirely created by humans and where there is little or no evidence of self-sustaining ecological processes (Newsome et al., 2012). Between these two ends of the spectrum are semi-natural areas with varying degrees of built and natural components. A planned event may occur in a range of environments, natural, built or a combination of these.

What does 'environmental impact' mean?

A planned event, no matter how well it is planned and implemented, will have environmental impacts. In this instance, impact is defined as any change to the environment, whether damaging or beneficial, that results from the planned event taking place (Thomas and Murfitt, 2011). As with economic and social impacts, environmental impacts can include positive or negative outcomes in terms of enhancing or degrading the quality of the environment and its functions. A planned event will impact on its immediate surroundings but also may have wider local, regional or even global environmental impacts over different lengths of time depending on the character of the event and how it is managed.

Why should environmental impacts be managed?

Environmental impacts of human activity are a core concept of sustainable development and sustainability. The rise of the modern environmental movement from the mid to late twentieth century was founded on a recognition that human survival, and all life, depends on maintaining viability of the Earth's ecological processes. Subsequent global congresses and international agreements facilitated by the United Nations recognised the link between human activity and its potential for negative impacts that degrade essential ecological processes and threaten humanity. Thus, managing environmental impact is important in terms of a moral and pragmatic obligation to sustain life and human society.

Aside from its role as a life support system, research has demonstrated clear links between environmental quality and human wellbeing. For example, at the local scale, the quality of aesthetics, cleanliness or functionality of an environment has been linked to community and individual wellbeing (Korpela and Kinnunen, 2010; Manning et al., 1999; Roberson and Babic, 2009). Research also indicates that while the general public may not always recognise degradation to ecological systems, issues such as the amount of litter, vegetation damage, erosion and other physical evidence of human impact at a location is very negatively viewed and can impact on satisfaction and experience (Tudor and Williams, 2008; Moore and Polley, 2007). Evidence also suggests that local residents are commonly concerned with issues such as noise and traffic congestion linked to an event. If planned events degrade the quality of an environment, for example through physical damage, litter or other types of pollution, it is likely to reduce community and stakeholder support. As a result, there is arguably a demand for sustainable management practices focussed on minimising negative environmental impacts as a means for ensuring continued stakeholder and community support. Many events and festivals of varying scales are thus adopting such practices (Laing and Mair, 2011).

Geographical and temporal scale

Environmental impacts can occur at different scales depending on the size and location of the event, the distance an audience travels to attend the event, where services and supplies are sourced and how waste is managed among many other factors. In geographical terms these may be thought of as a range from micro to macro scale impacts (Case, 2013). Micro scale impacts refer to impacts confined to the event venue or in the immediate vicinity of the event and could include litter, damaged vegetation, noise and soil erosion. There could also be positive impacts such as nature conservation and habitat renewal and refurbishment of built venues, depending on how the event is managed and implemented. There could also be medium scale impacts on the wider local area in which the event occurs, such as impacts on water quality, noise and light emissions and traffic congestion but also urban renewal and increased environmental awareness in local populations. Impacts at the macro scale could include regional and global effects as a consequence of gas emissions among other potential effects.

In addition to physical scale, impacts may include a temporal aspect, in terms of how long the impacts endure. Some impacts may be short term (or temporary), only occurring while the event is in process or ceasing soon after an event ends. For example, traffic congestion, light and noise may all be short-term environmental impacts of an event. Once the event finishes, the short-term impacts are diminished or cease altogether. Other types of impact may be longer term, enduring well after a planned event takes place. Waste and litter, atmospheric emissions, impacts on water quality and urban renewal could all be longer-term impacts of events, also referred to as the event legacy.

Types of impact

The physical location and timing of a planned event, together with the scale and type of event can determine the nature and extent of environmental impacts it will have. Consequently, a wide range of environmental impacts are possible such that the range of possibilities are too numerous to describe in detail here. Event managers have some control over these impacts because they depend on where and when the event is held and how it is managed. Case (2013) provides a useful summary of different types of event related activities and associated potential environmental impacts on natural area locations (Table 6.1).

There are some general impacts that can occur that may either have a negative or positive effect. Some of these are outlined as examples associated in the following sections of this chapter.

Box 6.1 The Event Impacts Project

The Event Impacts Project (http://www.eventimpacts.com) provides some guidelines on identifying what impacts are important to a particular event in terms of monitoring and management. The website suggests event organisers consider the following points in order to identify key environmental indicators for the event:

1 *What are the most significant impacts of the event?* This depends on event type, location, timing, size and so on.
2 *What are the main causes of these impacts?* Identifying the cause enables identification of what needs to be monitored and managed.
3 *Can the impacts be measured and influenced?* Event organisers have limited resources, for practical purposes, a focus on impacts that can be measured and managed within these limits is reasonable.
4 *What is the likely cost of monitoring and measurement?* Important for event budgeting. Some action may be undertaken in-house while some may be outsourced. Volunteers may also be used.
5 *Will this action affect future event management?* Monitoring and understanding impacts ideally leads to dissemination and learning, ultimately influencing future events management.
6 *What is the extent of impact and monitoring?* At what scale and causal context will impacts be monitored? For instance, focus on local, immediate and direct impacts or consider indirect and wider scale impacts (such as carbon emissions and climate change).
7 *Does monitoring provide clear information that can be acted on?* It is important that stakeholders understand the measures and what they mean to facilitate action.
8 *Are the measures of impact comparable across events?* Comparability means that it is easier to establish benchmarks and understand the relative impact of a particular event compared to other events of the same and different types.

Table 6.1 Example of some potential environmental impacts of different types of planned event held in natural area locations

Event activities	Potential environmental impacts	Event types					
		Concerts	Sporting and community events	Filming	Aquatic ecotourism	Terrestrial ecotourism	Encampments
Installation/use/removal of generators	Damage to in-situ cultural resources	✓	✓	✓			✓
Set up/use/removal of sound/lighting equipment	Damage to in-situ cultural resources	✓	✓	✓			✓
Use of camera equipment	Damage to in-situ cultural resources			✓			✓
Set construction/deconstruction	Damage to in-situ cultural resources			✓			
Campfires	Damage to reconstructed buildings						✓
People attending special event	Damage to reconstructed buildings	✓	✓	✓	✓	✓	✓
Use of special effects and/or black powder	Damage to in-situ cultural resources	✓		✓	✓		✓
	Damage to reconstructed buildings	✓		✓	✓		✓
Equipment/crew transportation (terrestrial)	Trampling/destruction of vegetation	✓	✓	✓	✓	✓	✓
Equipment storage	Trampling of grass	✓	✓	✓	✓		✓
Mooring/parking	Trampling/destruction of vegetation	✓		✓	✓	✓	✓

(Continued)

Table 6.1 (Continued)

Event activities	Potential environmental impacts	Event types					
		Concerts	Sporting and community events	Filming	Aquatic ecotourism	Terrestrial ecotourism	Encampments
Set up/dismantle temporary staging, fencing, tents, etc.	Destruction of grass	✓	✓	✓			✓
Installation/removal of portable washrooms	Trampling of grass	✓	✓	✓			✓
Set up/removal of waste facilities	Trampling of grass	✓	✓	✓			✓
Use of vegetative props	Introduction of invasive species			✓			
Set construction/deconstruction	Destruction of grass			✓			
Campfires	Destruction of vegetation						✓
People attending special events	Trampling of grass	✓	✓	✓	✓		✓
Equipment/crew transportation (terrestrial)	Trampling/destruction of vegetation	✓		✓		✓	
Equipment storage	Trampling of vegetation			✓		✓	
Mooring/parking	Trampling/destruction of vegetation			✓		✓	
Set up/dismantle temporary staging, fencing, tents, etc.	Destruction of vegetation			✓			
Use of vegetative props	Introduction of invasive species			✓			

Source: Case, 2013

Negative impacts

The negative environmental impacts of events include a range of direct and indirect effects resulting from event related activities. The event operation itself can generate negative impacts as can the behaviour of an event audience. Some planned event impacts commonly noted by researchers include:

- Air pollution
- Water pollution
- Litter and waste
- Vegetation trampling
- Congestion and crowding

For any event, the biggest impact is generated by participant and spectator travel to the event.

Air pollution

Air pollution can be thought of in terms of the immediate impact on air quality and also the longer-term effects on climate and health. Air pollution associated with events primarily results from fuel combustion for transport and energy generation to run the event. This occurs both onsite at the event location but also through transport of supplies, equipment and people to and from the event from other regional locations or from around the world. The planned event may also use generators or mains power, both of which can result in increased emissions. Energy consumption can produce various gas emissions including:

- Nitrogen oxides (NOx)
- Carbon monoxide and carbon dioxide (CO and CO_2)
- Sulphur oxides (SOx)
- Methane (CH_4)
- Airborne smoke particles (particulates)

Air pollution includes immediate effects on air quality as well as longer term and macro effects on climate patterns. Local air quality can be reduced by emissions from vehicles and generators present at the event. This includes locally raised levels of particulates and other noxious gases that can have adverse effects on short-term and long-term human health. Aside from emissions from transport and energy generation, there are also reports of temporary and local air quality impacts from event activities themselves. For example, events involving fireworks generate gas and smoke particle emissions. The use of fireworks as part of the Chinese Spring Festival was reported to increase air pollution by about five times more than the non-festival day norm in Beijing, Lanzhuo City and Yuzhong Country (Wang et al., 2007; Shi et al., 2011). Case (2013) observes that events that involve camping and associated camp fires may also result in reduce local air quality. Particulates from burning fuel and materials such as wood can reduce air quality in the immediate vicinity of the event but also disperse into the atmosphere and result in longer-term impacts.

In terms of macro scale impacts, the first four gases in the list are referred to as Greenhouse Gases (GHGs) and are associated with enhanced climate change effects as they accumulate in the Earth's atmosphere. Some of these GHGs have a greater influence than others. For example, methane is known to have a much stronger influence on climate change than carbon dioxide due to its chemical properties and greater ability to trap heat in the atmosphere.

Water pollution

Water pollution may include pollution of water bodies (lakes, dams, oceans), groundwater and waterways from event site runoff or waste water entering these same systems. This may occur at the local site level or more broadly. Significant spills at the event venue that involve oil, fuel, solvents, detergents or other liquid pollutants can enter water bodies, seep into waterways or subsurface (ground) water, impacting on water quality through the introduction of toxins and other substances that potentially damage aquatic ecosystems. Wider impacts might include waste water and sewage generated by event participants that enters mainstream treatment processes and is discharged into waterways and the ocean. Each of these scenarios can result in reduced water quality and negative human health effects as well as degraded ecosystems.

For example, it is inevitable that when there are a number of people at an event for any period of time, they will eventually need to use the toilet, wash their hands or otherwise use water in some capacity that involves consuming water and subsequently generating waste water. Depending on the venue this will result in certain impacts requiring management. A dedicated event venue such as a stadium or convention centre will certainly have facilities that enable waste water to be taken away by an existing sewerage system. However, an outdoor or green field location may be more prone to water pollution given its potentially limited infrastructure to deal with water supply and waste disposal. Event goers at outdoor venues may opt to avoid the overcrowded and perhaps unsanitary toilets provided and urinate in a secluded outdoor location. A large number of people urinating on the ground can result in excess nutrients entering groundwater and waterways. This in turn could result in eutrophication. Eutrophication refers to water with a large concentration of nutrients that promotes the growth of algae and certain types of bacteria. The growth, byproducts and death of excess algae and bacteria in a water body can reduce the light and oxygen levels in the water, killing aquatic plants and animals. Certain types of bacteria that grow in nutrient rich water can also product toxins as a byproduct, such as botulinum. This results in a disease known as botulism that kills animals that ingest the toxin with the water. It can also have health implications for humans using the water. To avoid such impacts, it is important to ensure adequate numbers of toilets are provided for the event and they are maintained in a sanitary state.

Litter and waste

Litter is a common issue for planned events, especially outdoor events that include vendors selling pre-packaged food and other disposable items. In terms of the immediate and micro scale effect, litter is a significant factor influencing public perceptions of environmental quality, especially when it comes to natural area settings. The general public are more likely to notice and negatively react to litter than any form of ecological degradation, especially in natural settings (Tudor and Williams, 2008). An event venue that has obvious quantities of litter lying about can potentially negatively affect the audience experience and satisfaction with the event.

As well as being unsightly, litter may also have ecological impacts if it enters and fouls up waterways, is ingested by animals, injures or entangles animals, or consists of toxic or damaging substances (such as cigarette butts and plastic containers for chemicals and oils). Persistence of non-biodegradable substances, such as plastics, in the general environment in the absence of effective management or clean-up efforts presents a significant longer-term issue.

Longer-term macro impacts of solid waste mainly relate to disposal in landfill sites and other means of disposal. Land fill sites present a finite solution given the limited space available for such practices. Waste that is buried can leach toxins into the ground, persist for long periods of time without decomposing or produce emissions such as methane as organic materials decompose. Use of biodegradable and recyclable containers and packaging can reduce such impacts as can incentives for attendees to collect litter, such as a cash or discounts for return of cans and bottles.

Vegetation trampling

Vegetation trampling presents a micro scale impact in terms of geographical area but the effects may endure for some time after an event takes place. When an event is held in an outdoor location, be it a manicured lawn or a natural setting, the presence of large numbers of people and vehicles can result in trampling, leading to vegetation loss, soil compaction and erosion. This is especially the case where there are little or no paved or hardened surfaces for pedestrians and traffic. Alternatively, events may include spectators or participants accessing sensitive areas such as riverbanks or coastal dune areas that are highly susceptible to trampling related damage (Carlson and Godfrey, 1989; Rust and Illenberger, 1996). Research into environmental impacts associated with trampling demonstrate that the majority of impact occurs very rapidly in the early stages of initial human use whether it is car or pedestrian traffic (Turton, 2005). The impacts of further use then tend to accumulate less rapidly.

Trampling can have multiple consequences depending on the environmental setting. In general, trampling will result in vegetation loss as plants (including lawn) are crushed by repeated foot or vehicle traffic. Trampling can also result in soil compaction that acts to reduce the amount of air and water penetration, subsequently killing existing plants and inhibiting future seed germination and plant regrowth in the trampled area. Plant damage and death leads to soil exposure, or bare areas of ground. In the absence of plants to bind the soil, erosion is more likely, especially in sloping terrain that experiences water runoff or wave action. Erosion removes soil and nutrients, preventing establishment of new plants, exacerbating the damage caused by the initial trampling. Management of trampling is best done through a preventative approach, before event related human activity and impacts occur at the location. This can be approached by providing hardened surfaces such as boardwalks or confining attendees to harden areas (such as paved surfaces) or clearly defined pathways that confine attendees to certain areas and routes.

Congestion and crowding

Planned events are obviously intended to attract an audience, resulting in crowds of people converging on a venue and/or the surrounding environment. This can lead to congestion in terms of large numbers of vehicles and/or people attempting to access a given area using the available transport network (for example roads, footpaths, rail).

Congestion relates to the physical capacity of a venue or event location and the numbers of people or vehicles attempting to access and move through that location or venue at any given time. If an event is attended by a greater number of people than the venue is physically able to cater for within a given time period, congestion occurs and vehicle or attendee flows will be inhibited. Selection of a venue or location with adequate capacity for the estimated attendance, traffic, crowd and event attendee flow management are important means for reducing congestion.

Crowding can be framed as a judgement based on the negative perceptions of numbers of people in a location. However, large crowds of people do not always result in negative feelings associated with crowding. For example, convergence of large numbers of people on the small rural town of Parkes in New South Wales, Australia, for an annual Elvis music festival, was welcomed by most town residents and festival attendees. The positive response was because of the excitement and activity generated by the presence of crowds in an otherwise sleepy country town (Gibson and Connell, 2012). Furthermore, perceptions of crowding may differ between event attendees, local residents and those directly involved in implementing the event (entertainers, suppliers, managers). Some studies have demonstrated the event setting and context, activity, demographics, personal tolerance and motivations could all influence the perception of crowding at an event location (for example, Tarrant et al.,1997; Navarro Jurado et al., 2013). So while congestion is a function of the physical capacity of a venue or setting, the numbers of attendees and the extent to which the flow of people is inhibited, determination of crowding relies on understanding the perceptions of those attending the event or who are otherwise affected by the event.

Positive impacts

With careful and responsible planning and management, events can also have positive impacts on the environment. This can include tangible outcomes such as improved environmental quality or intangible outcomes such as public awareness and influences on environmental attitudes and behaviour. Some commonly observed positive impacts of planned events include:

- Urban renewal
- Nature conservation and rehabilitation
- Demonstration effects – pro-environmental behaviour, environmental awareness

Urban renewal

Urban renewal can have social, economic and environmental aspects that are strongly integrated. In terms of environmental impacts, urban renewal generally refers to improvements to the quality of the built environment. This might include restoration of old buildings, physical improvements to urban layout, removal of dilapidated buildings and construction or enhancement of infrastructure. Some mega-events are associated with urban renewal on a significant scale. Chalkley and Essex (1999) describe a long history of mega-events and resulting impacts on urban areas through event-led urban renewal, especially the Olympic Games, but also other large events such as the 1889 World's Fair and other large scale exhibitions. The Crystal Palace, Eiffel Tower and

Wembley Stadium were all products of 'Great Exhibitions' in the nineteenth and early twentieth centuries resulting in long-term changes to the built environment. On a larger scale, the Olympic Games has been used as a catalyst for broad scale redevelopment, improvement of transport networks, construction of parks and improved residential housing to varying degrees of success or failure throughout the twentieth and twenty-first centuries. However, while urban renewal is often highlighted as a positive impact of larger planned events, it can also have adverse social and economic consequences as outlined in Chapters 4, 7 and 11 of this book. For example urban renewal may result in displacement of disadvantaged communities that can then result in further social and economic disparity in a region.

Nature conservation and rehabilitation

Nature conservation refers to actions focussed on maintaining the endemic plant and animal species and/or essential ecological processes in a given area. Rehabilitation refers to the restoration of nature in an ecologically degraded area. Some events have a focus on rehabilitating or re-creating natural areas such as clean-up days where litter and weeds are removed from natural areas, as well as on local re-planting of native vegetation focussed events. These types of event are intended to make a direct contribution to conservation of nature in a specific location. On a larger scale, events may also incorporate nature conservation and rehabilitation through creation of parks, waterways and other natural or semi-natural areas as well as removal of contaminated soil or water as part of urban renewal. Other types of event, such as garden festivals can act to promote the creation of natural areas in a community while also providing education and raising environmental awareness as well as encouraging environmentally responsible behaviour.

Demonstration effects

Demonstration effects relate to the impact of the event on behaviour and attitudes of attendees and the wider community. Events with a sustainability focus typically incorporate promotion of this approach into the programme. This may include direct education using workshops or presentations as part of the event, or through promoting the sustainable practices of the event to attendees and the wider community as an awareness raising effort. Some events include participant involvement in environmental conservation activities such as habitat renewal through replanting native vegetation or removal of exotic species, water quality monitoring, litter and waste collection among other activities. Direct communication of a sustainability ethos based on activities or educational presentations as well as indirect communication through promoting sustainable event practices is assumed to encourage pro-environmental behaviour and attitudes amongst attendees and the wider community.

The evidence is mixed in this regard. Events with an overt focus on environmental conservation and sustainability may tend to attract people with sympathetic views. It may not be clear whether such events 'cause' people to be more environmentally aware and to act responsibly or are simply 'preaching to the converted'. There is also a recognised gap between stated behavioural intentions and actual behaviour, especially over the longer term. That is, what people say they will do, or report that they do, may not be reflected in their actual behaviour once the event is over and they return to their daily lives.

Measuring environmental impacts

Measurement (monitoring) of an event provides an understanding of the extent to which certain impacts have occurred. Monitoring environmental impacts can be challenging, especially in terms of the extent to which specific impacts are attributable to a particular planned event. It is also difficult to measure the extent to which environmental management measures have reduced impacts that would otherwise occur. Difficulties are based on the complex nature of many events in terms of the variety of activities and people involved in making an event happen. It also relates to the difficulty in determining the boundaries for impact measurement.

For example, at what point are emissions from vehicles attributed to the event? What if a person travels to an event as part of a longer trip? What percentage of the transport emissions during this trip are because of the event occurring? What if a caterer at an event uses mostly local products but also imported packaged food items? What proportion of the emissions generated importing the products should be attributable to the event, given the products might be used elsewhere if the event didn't occur? Setting the boundaries of event impacts is therefore important and is mainly at the discretion of the event manager.

All of these questions present complex issues that could be addressed given adequate time and resources. Not all event organisers have such resources. However, there are general guides on emissions and other impacts that can be used by event managers (Table 6.2). For example, impacts can be expressed in terms of the amount of carbon dioxide (CO_2) per unit of activity linked to the event. This presents a standardised way of measuring impacts that can be compared across activities and between events and also related to a wider scale of impact. It can also be used to estimate what is referred to as a carbon footprint, or the total amount of carbon emitted by an event. Table 6.2 outlines some common CO_2 related measures used and issues associated with these measures. All of these measures require detailed monitoring of impacts before, during and after the event and gathering of data on attendees and event suppliers in terms of transport, and other activities that potentially generate impacts linked to the event. Understanding the impacts of various activities can help with planning the event to minimise these impacts.

When managing impacts such as CO_2 emissions, the lower the quantity of impact the better the outcome, where zero is the ideal. Unfortunately, an event will always have impacts because activities such as transport and energy consumption are absolutely vital for running a planned event; hence offsets can technically be used to reduce the overall impact (net impact) to zero.

Offsetting means that action is taken such that there is no overall impact at the regional or global scale. For example, carbon emissions may be offset by planting trees equivalent to the number of trees required to absorb the estimated carbon emitted by the event. There are numerous offset calculators and programs available to help event managers. Offsetting requires information and understanding of the environmental impacts of an event in order to calculate the amount of offsetting required. The cost of offsetting may be incorporated into the price the audience pays to attend the event.

Table 6.2 Examples of standardised average estimated CO_2 emissions from different event-related sources

Source	Emissions	Unit of measure	Notes
Transport – car	0.22 kg CO_2	Per km travelled	Based on an average car. Varies depending on car type.
Transport – road freight	0.27 kg CO_2	Per km travelled	Based on an average van. Varies depending on type of vehicle and weight of freight.
Transport – aviation	0.16 kg CO_2	Per passenger per km travelled short haul	Highly variable depending on calculation method used, aircraft type, freight loading, seating configuration among other factors.
	0.13 kg CO_2	Per passenger per km travelled medium haul	
	0.11 kg CO_2	Per passenger per km travelled long haul	
Energy – diesel generator	2.63 kg CO_2	Per litre of diesel consumed	Varies depending on type and quality of generator.
Energy – biodiesel generator	0.83 kg CO_2	Per litre of biodiesel consumed	Varies depending on type of generator and quality of biodiesel.
Energy – wind/ solar	0	–	Does not factor in the emissions associated with manufacturing, installation and management of energy generators.
Waste – landfill	0.26 kg CO_2	Per kg of waste in landfill	Varies depending on type of waste and type of landfill site.
Waste – sewage	0.48 kg CO_2	Per cubic metre (1000 litres) created	
Hotel accommodation	34.3 kg CO_2	Per person per night	Includes all energy use, waste, sewage and other activity associated with staying in a hotel. Can vary widely depending on guest and hotel characteristics.

Sources: Collins et al., 2009; Jardine, 2009; Biofuels Association of Australia, 2013

Managing environmental impacts

Monitoring environmental impacts provides information on what has already occurred. Managing event environmental impacts can focus on prevention, or at least minimisation of impacts. Impacts may also be managed by offsetting them, as an indirect mode of management.

Some event impacts may be governed by both legal requirements (regulatory) and self-imposed voluntary systems. Voluntary impact management systems can be aligned with certain standards and then certified, or based on more general guidelines and checklists (Case, 2013).

Depending on the location, type and scale of event, there will be laws and regulations determining how certain aspects of the event are managed to mitigate negative environmental impacts. This can include legislation for environmental issues such as:

- Limiting noise and nuisance
- Air quality thresholds
- Water quality thresholds
- Effective waste management and litter control
- Toxins, chemicals and dangerous goods management
- Nature/cultural heritage conservation

Failure to demonstrate compliance with legal requirements can result in financial penalties or withdrawal of official approval to implement the event.

Chapter summary

This chapter discussed some core issues regarding environmental impacts of planned events, including general types, causes and how they may be managed. The chapter provided a definition of the environment and environmental impact and then discussed the different scales at which these exist. The chapter outlined some common positive and negative impacts that often result from planned events of all types, what causes them and how they can be managed. This was followed by a discussion of impact measurement using the concept of carbon emissions. The chapter also highlighted the importance of integrating environmental impact management with economic and social issues. The chapter finishes with a case study of the Peats Ridge Festival and the various management techniques used to minimise negative and enhance positive environmental impacts.

Learning activities

1   Think about a recent local event in your town or city. List the environmental impacts that were evident. Do you think these impacts were reasonable, or best avoided? Why?
2   Scholars suggest that eventgoers are becoming more aware of, and concerned with, environmental impacts and yet the Peats Ridge Festival reportedly failed due to poor ticket sales while events such as the Formula 1 Grand Prix attract huge crowds. Do you think the environmental impacts of an event are an important factor in the decision to attend? Why?

3 Have you ever attended an event that changed the way you behave in order to reduce your environmental impacts? What are the reasons for this? Discuss with your peers.

4 Using mega-events as an example, discuss whether you think it is possible for such an event to be truly sustainable from an environmental perspective.

Case study: Peats Ridge Festival, Glenworth Valley, Australia

Peats Ridge Festival was an art and music festival founded in 2004 to promote music, art and the idea of sustainability (Peats Ridge Festival, 2009). The festival's primary attraction was a programme of local and international artists and musicians. The programme also included educational workshops for event attendees, covering issues such as corporate social responsibility, composting and grey water treatment systems (Laranjo et al., 2012). The annual festival was located on a farm in the Glenworth Valley, about 60 km north of Sydney, Australia. It was touted as an ideal example of sustainable event management from an environmental and social perspective (Henderson, 2011).

However, it fared less well in terms of economic sustainability. Due to reported poor ticket sales in 2012, there was no festival held in 2013 and the organiser announced cessation of the event a short time later owing to financial difficulties (Taylor, 2013). This case study highlights some of the practices that reflect environmentally sustainable practice but also demonstrates that focussing on one aspect of sustainability while not addressing other components is in fact not sustainable.

Peats Ridge Festival was driven by a series of self-imposed policy documents outlining a range of issues such as procurement, transport, communications and climate change. Event staff and volunteers signed contracts that bound them to progress indicators as a means for encouraging adherence to the sustainability theme of the festival. The festival relied on a large number of volunteers to undertake many of the required tasks such as waste monitoring and collection and traffic direction (Laranjo et al., 2012). Peats Ridge Festival's focus on environmental issues was evident in some of the management initiatives outlined in the following.

Waste Management

Peats Ridge managed waste based on return rates of recyclables including food waste. This was done using a system of three bins for the three different streams of waste:

● Compostable waste such as biodegradable containers and food waste
● Recyclable waste such as cans, glass, cardboard and plastic vessels
● General waste for landfill disposal

(Continued)

Case study (continued)

The three bin layout was monitored by volunteers to assist event participants in correctly sorting their waste. Monitoring was intended to reduce the risk of contamination and helped the festival generate high grade waste streams to facilitate reuse. As part of this effort, some material was sorted and composted onsite for use in farming operations on the rural property. The rest of the compostable waste stream was sent to a local professional composter to be reprocessed into agricultural supplies (Peats Ridge Festival, 2009).

Recyclable material was sorted on site by volunteers. Recovery of material was encouraged using an onsite container deposit levy. A dollar deposit attached to each can or bottle was designed to encourage return of these items for recycling by attendees. This reportedly resulted in reduced numbers of discarded bottles and cans around the festival location (Peats Ridge Festival, 2009).

Energy

Peats Ridge Festival (2009) reported that they used renewable energy to power the entire operation. This included energy sourced via accredited grid supplied solar power and onsite biodiesel generators. The festival organisers also used energy efficient equipment including low power sound and lighting as well as encouraging appropriate behaviour amongst staff, entertainers and volunteers such as switching off electrical equipment when not in use.

Green procurement

In terms of procurement, the festival organisers attempted to source all food locally, to minimise transport distances and reuse decorations and materials to minimise waste. The event organisers claimed that most of the decorations and furniture used onsite were also made from recycled and reused materials. The compostable and recycled materials were intended for reuse or incorporated into the festival's waste recycling and composting streams. Stallholders were also encouraged to use biodegradable packaging in line with event management policy (Peats Ridge Festival, 2009).

Sustainability capacity building

Part of the ethos of the event revolved around sustainability education to build capacity amongst festival goers. The intent was to translate the experience of the festival into the daily lives of participants. This was done in two ways. Firstly, messages conveyed by signs and other means highlighted the festival's sustainable management efforts. This was intended to raise awareness amongst event goers that the event promoted sustainable practice as well as providing indications of how this was done. Secondly, the festival itself included educational workshops focussing on various social and environmental topics such as composting and social responsibility (Peats Ridge Festival, 2009). There appears to be no evaluation of the success of this approach by Peats Ridge Festival.

Transport

The amount of travel time and distance used to transport supplies and equipment to the event was reduced through coordination and streamlining of logistics to minimise emissions. Using local products was also seen to reduce travel distance and the associated emissions from vehicles.

The event location was not entirely convenient for scheduled public transport. If travelling from the cities of Sydney or Newcastle, attendees could catch a train to the town of Gosford but then needed a car or taxi to travel the 19 km from Gosford to the Glenworth Valley. Public transport options were promoted by event managers along with car-pooling. Car-pooling was arranged through an online portal where festival participants could organise themselves to share cars, with the intent of reducing traffic. Buses were provided as were escorted bicycle convoys. A levy on private cars aimed to encourage car-pooling and reduce car numbers (Peats Ridge Festival, 2009). This was also considered a means for reducing emissions from transport. However, there does not appear to be any available evaluation of the effectiveness of this approach.

Conclusion

Peats Ridge Festival was well recognised for its focus on sustainable practices and education. Despite these recognised efforts, there appears to be little available evaluation by managers of the extent to which environmental impacts were reduced. What is worth noting is that as an enterprise, the festival ultimately failed. Festivals are known to be very sensitive to factors such as weather, competition and lack of adequate forward planning (Arthurs, 2013). The failure of the Peats Ridge Festival was reportedly attributed to poorer than expected ticket sales in 2012 but also an error in budgeting where the festival manager did not account for additional employment costs. The employment costs were higher due to the need for employment of a larger workforce rather than the primary reliance on volunteers in previous years. One or both of these issues resulted in a significant financial loss for the festival (Taylor, 2013). It appears that the festival was unable to implement adequate economic measures to prevent its closure. Thus, while the event had a strong sustainability focus on environmental issues, the economic aspect was less than ideal (Arthurs, 2013). This case demonstrates some common environmentally responsible actions but also highlights the need for a holistic approach to sustainable event management.

Discussion questions

1 Given Peats Ridge had a strong focus on sustainability, discuss the merits of the event's location in terms of accessibility. What actions are taken to reduce emissions from transport? Can you think of any other solutions?
2 Peats Ridge Festival had a strong focus on education for sustainability. Do you think a music and arts festival is an effective way of changing behaviour at home? Why?
3 Was Peats Ridge truly a sustainable event given that it appeared to fail economically? What are the key lessons that could be learnt from this example?

Further reading and online resources

Event Impacts (2014). Why measure environmental impact? Online article identifying indicators and measuring impacts, available at: http://www.eventimpacts.com/environmental [accessed 14 November, 2014].

Jones, M. (2010). *Sustainable event management: a practical guide.* London: Earthscan.

Mair, J. and Jago, L. (2009). The development of a conceptual model of greening in the business events sector. *Journal of Sustainable Tourism*, 18 (1) 77–94.

References

Arthurs, A. (2013). Music festivals are in trouble but the shows must go on. *The Conversation,* December 12, available online at http://theconversation.com/music-festivals-are-in-trouble-but-the-shows-must-go-on-21035 [accessed 2 September, 2014].

Biofuels Association of Australia (2013). Biodiesel on emission reductions. Available online at http://www.biofuelsassociation.com.au/biodiesel-on-emission-reductions [accessed 3 September, 2014].

Carlson, L. and Godfrey, P. (1989). Human impact management in a coastal recreation and natural area. *Biological Conservation*, 49, 141–56.

Case, R. (2013). *Events and the environment.* UK: Routledge.

Chalkley, B. and Essex, S. (1999). Sydney 2000: The 'Green Games'? *Geography*, 64 (4), 299–307.

Collins, A., Jones, C. and Munday, M. (2009). Assessing the environmental impact of mega-sporting events: two options? *Tourism Management*, 30, 828–37.

Gibson, C. and Connell, J. (2012). *Music festivals and regional development in Australia.* Farnham, UK: Ashgate Publishing Ltd.

Getz, D. (2009). Policy for sustainable and responsible festivals and events: institutionalization of a new paradigm. *Journal of Policy Research in Tourism, Leisure and Events*, 1 (1), 61–78.

Henderson, S. (2011). The development of competitive advantage through sustainable event management. *Worldwide Hospitality and Tourism Themes*, 3 (3), 245–57.

Jardine, C. (2009). *Calculating the carbon dioxide emissions of flights.* Final report, Environmental Change Institute. UK: Oxford University Centre for the Environment.

Korpela, K. and Kinnunen, U. (2010). How is leisure time interacting with nature related to the need for recovery from work demands? Testing multiple mediators. *Leisure Sciences*, 33 (1), 1–14.

Laing, J. and Frost, W. (2010). How green was my festival? Exploring challenges and opportunities associated with staging green events. *International Journal of Hospitality Management* 29, 261–67.

Laing, J. H. and Mair, J. (2011). Exploring the role of 'greening' in festival planning and management [online]. In: Gross, Michael J. (Ed.). *CAUTHE 2011: National Conference: Tourism: creating a brilliant blend*. Adelaide, South Australia: University of South Australia, 1162–5.

Laranjo, F. F., Wunderlich, J. and Thompson, A. (2012). Maximising the benefits of event volunteering: a case study of the Peats Ridge Sustainable Arts and Music Festival. In Harris, R., Schlenker, K., Foley, C. and Edwards, D. (Eds), *Proceedings of the Australian event symposium 2012*, 21–5. Sydney, Australia: Australian Centre for Event Management, University of Technology, Sydney.

Manning, R., Valliere, W. and Minteer, B. (1999). Values, ethics, and attitudes toward national forest management: an empirical study. *Society and Natural Resources*, 12 (5), 421–36.

Moore, S. and Polley, A. (2007). Defining indicators and standards for tourism impacts in protected areas: Cape Range National Park, Australia. *Environmental Management*, 39 (3), 291–300.

Navarro Jurado, E., Damian, I. M. and Fernández-Morales, A. (2013). Carrying capacity model applied in coastal destinations. *Annals of Tourism Research*, 43, 1–19.

Newsome, D., Moore, S. and Dowling, R. (2012). *Natural area tourism: ecology, impacts and management*. Clevedon: Channel View Publications.

Peats Ridge Festival (2009). *Introduction*. Available online at http://www.peatsridge-festival.com.au/ [accessed 1 May, 2014].

Robbins, D., Dickinson, J. and Calver, S. (2007). Planning transport for special events: a conceptual framework and future agenda for research. *International Journal of Tourism Research*, 9 (5), 303–14.

Roberson, D. and Babic, V. (2009). Remedy for modernity: experiences of walkers and hikers on Medvednica Mountain. *Leisure Studies*, 28 (1), 105–12.

Rust, I. and Illenberger, W. (1996). Coastal dunes: sensitive or not? *Landscape and Urban Planning*, 34 (3/4) 165–9.

Shi, Y., Zhang, N., Gao, J., Li, X. and Cai, Y. (2011). Effect of fireworks display on perchlorate in air aerosols during the Spring Festival. *Atmospheric Environment*, 45 (6), 1323–7.

Soper, K. (1995). *What is nature? Culture, politics and the non-human*. Oxford, UK: Wiley-Blackwell.

Tarrant, M. A., Cordell, H. K. and Kibler, T. L. (1997). Measuring perceived crowding for high-density river recreation: the effects of situational conditions and personal factors. *Leisure Sciences*, 19, 97–112.

Taylor, A. (2013). Performers left unpaid as festival folds. *Sydney Morning Herald*, 24 January.

Thomas, I. and Murfitt, P. (2011). Environmental management systems. In Thomas, I. (Ed.) *Environmental management: processes and practices for Australia*, 2nd edn. Sydney: The Federation Press, pp. 189–232.

Tudor, D. and Williams, A. (2008). Important aspects of beach pollution to managers: Wales and the Bristol Channel, UK. *Journal of Coastal Research*, 735–45.

Turton, S. (2005). Managing environmental impacts of recreation and tourism in rainforests of the wet tropics of Queensland World Heritage Area. *Geographic Research*, 43 (2),140–51.

Wang, Y., Zhuang, G., Xu, C. and An, Z. (2007). The air pollution caused by the burning of fireworks during the lantern festival in Beijing. *Atmospheric Environment*, 41 (2), 417–31.

Chapter 7

Socio-cultural impacts of events

Learning outcomes

After studying this chapter you should be able to:

- Identify the positive and negative socio-cultural impacts of events
- Examine how socio-cultural impacts of events can be measured
- Understand how social capital can be used to understand the relationship between events and the community
- Discuss community perceptions and contested meanings of events

Introduction

What are socio-cultural impacts?

Events of all types have an effect on the people who live in the town or city where the event is taking place. These effects are known as 'impacts' and can be positive or negative, short term or long term and minor or more troublesome. Socio-cultural impacts have been defined as 'any impacts that potentially have an impact on the quality of life for local residents' (Fredline et al., 2003: 26). Positive impacts naturally have some benefit for the residents, whilst negative impacts can cause difficulties for residents. Short-term impacts tend to last only during the event itself, while long-term impacts last well beyond the duration of the event, and can be permanent. Finally, while many socio-cultural impacts are relatively minor (such as congestion in the town caused by extra visitors attending the event) some can be more troublesome for residents (for example, anti-social behaviour by attendees, perhaps due to alcohol or drug abuse).

Many festivals and events rely on positive economic impacts for their continued funding. However, the socio-cultural impacts are very important, given the effects that hosting festivals and events can have on a local community. Deery and Jago (2010) identify three key reasons for studying socio-cultural impacts, noting that if festivals and events are to be sustainable we need to be able to:

- Accurately assess the social benefits and costs
- Assess residents' support, or otherwise
- Provide recommendations for how to enhance the positive socio-cultural impacts of events

Table 7.1 shows a range of positive and negative socio-cultural impacts of events, divided into short-term and long-term impacts. It is clear that the majority of the negative impacts take place during the event itself, while many of the positive impacts last beyond the duration of the event (Deery and Jago, 2010; Gibson et al., 2014). Note also that some of the impacts (in italics) are actually economic impacts which have a positive or negative effect on residents, which highlights the blurred lines between economic and socio-cultural impacts of events.

Another point to note when considering socio-cultural impacts is that for the most part, the negative impacts are relatively tangible – they can be seen, felt or otherwise identified, while many of the positive impacts are intangible. They are harder to understand and measure. For example, during an event, the host community might have to contend with loud noise, congested highways and busy shops. These are tangible issues. On the other hand, a community may enjoy the opportunity to take part in an event and have fun with friends and family, sharing an experience. Or, members of the community may feel that hosting the event makes their town look good, and therefore they enjoy the prestige of the event. Festivals and events can also create 'vibrant communities' (Derrett, 2003: 49). Such feelings and concepts are intangible.

On the contrary, many of the longer-lasting positive socio-cultural impacts are more tangible – capacity and skills building for community members might include training and skills development in administration, logistics and risk management. For example, in research on festivals and events, Mair and Laing (2013) noted that the festival directors in their study were proud to offer the opportunity to 'upskill the

Table 7.1 Positive and negative socio-cultural impacts of events

Positive impacts	Negative impacts
Short term (during the event)	
Increased community participation in the event	Increased noise
A shared experience	Increased traffic
Expansion of cultural perspectives	Overcrowding
Opportunity for entertainment	Anti-social behaviour by attendees (alcohol and/or drug abuse, vandalism, crime, property damage)
Volunteering opportunities	Loss of amenity (perhaps loss of use of the local park or town hall while the event is running)
Prestige for the host community	Social dislocation (residents stay away from their usual cafes/restaurants/bars etc. while the event is running)
Increased visitor numbers	*Inflated prices*
Increased commercial activity (accommodation, retail, hospitality etc)	*Money spent on the event, not on other community needs*
Long term (after the event)	
Building community pride/community cohesion	Development of negative community image
Increasing tolerance of diversity	Community alienation
Revitalisation of traditions	Loss of authenticity of traditions
Capacity and skills building for the local community	Limited employment opportunities post-event
Engaging sections of the community not normally participating in community life/affairs	Reversion to ethnic and cultural divisions post-event
Development of new infrastructure (usually associated with larger events)	*Mounting public debt servicing requirements and ongoing budget deficits*
Improved destination image for potential tourists	*Negative media coverage of problems in the destination creates negative destination image*
Job creation	*Job losses post-event*

Sources: Allen et al., 2011; Delamere, Wankel and Hinch, 2001; Deery and Jago, 2010; Derrett, 2003; Finkel, 2010; Fredline and Faulkner, 2001; Getz, 2013; Johnson et al., 2011; Wood, 2006

community'. The revitalisation of traditions made possible by hosting an event may result in future opportunities for communities to take part in festival and events. However, this needs to be balanced with the risk of losing authentic traditions by turning them into a commercial product. Further, some of the long-term negative impacts are more intangible in nature – examples include community alienation, where members of the community do not like to associate themselves with the event, and choose not to attend, or support it in any way.

Measuring socio-cultural impacts

The most commonly used way to measure the socio-cultural impacts of a festival or event is the resident survey. For the most part, resident surveys appear to show that members of the local community can be split into two main camps – those who love the event and those who hate it (Fredline and Faulkner, 2001; Deery and Jago, 2010).

The surveys are usually made up of scales – a series of questions that respondents give their answers to on a pre-determined scale (an example would be a scale where 1 = very dissatisfied and 5 = very satisfied). One of the first scales to be developed was the Festival Social Impact Attitude Scale (FSIAS), which was proposed in 2001 by Delamere, Wankel and Hinch (2001). This scale included 47 statements for residents to agree or disagree with – a few samples are given below:

- 'The festival provides my community with an opportunity to discover and develop cultural skills and talents.'
- 'The festival contributes to a sense of community well-being.'
- 'Noise levels increase to an unacceptable level during the festival.'
- 'The festival is an intrusion into the lives of community residents.'

This research identified that festivals and events have social benefits and social costs (Delamere et al., 2001). Examples of the social benefits are community benefits (such as a sense of community wellbeing and togetherness) and cultural/educational bene-fits (such as opportunities for residents to learn new things, and opportunities for community groups to work together). Social costs included concerns about quality of life (such as an increase in vandalism, petty crime and overcrowding) and also concerns about the use of community resources (financial and social resources).

Another example of a research instrument designed to understand socio-cultural impacts of events is the Social Impact Perception (SIP) scale, initially developed by Small and Edwards (2003), and further refined by Small (2008). This scale focuses on smaller community events, and includes 41 statements for residents to consider. For each state-ment, residents were asked to identify whether there was an impact, and also how significant the impact was (–5 = *very large negative impact;* 0 = *no impact* and +5 = *very large positive impact*). Figure 7.1 shows how this kind of scale is laid out.

Impact statement	Impact		Level of impact
The footpaths and streets were crowded during the festival	Y N	Don't know	–5 –4 –3 –2 –1 0 +1 +2 +3 +4 +5

Figure 7.1 Social Impact Perception scale (sample question)

Small (2008) found that the impacts on residents could be classified into six main types, some of which are clearly personal to residents, whilst others are more about community and society:

- *Inconvenience* – Increased traffic, noise and crowding
- *Community identity and cohesion* – Increased pride in the town and a positive image of the town
- *Personal frustration* – Too many visitors, disruption to normal routines
- *Entertainment and socialisation opportunities* – Meeting new people, sharing a family experience
- *Community growth and development* – Learning new skills, job opportunities
- *Behaviour consequences* – Increased vandalism and anti-social behaviour

Given the importance of community satisfaction to the continued viability of festivals and events, it is very important to understand how residents of the local community feel about hosting festivals and events. Box 7.1 illustrates a case study example of how local communities feel about hosting a mega-event – in this case, the 2010 FIFA World Cup.

Box 7.1 FIFA World Cup 2010, South Africa

The nineteenth FIFA World Cup was held in June and July, 2010 in nine cities in South Africa. As well as having economic and political aims, the World Cup aimed to improve social conditions for South Africans. South African President, Jacob Zuma, was quoted as saying '...the explosion of national pride is a priceless benefit of the World Cup tournament. It is clear that millions of our people look upon the tournament with hope, pride and a sense of belonging' (Bell, 2010, cited in Heere et al., 2013). According to FIFA, the World Cup is about more than just football – it's about social progress, political unity and cultural understanding (FIFA 2010, cited in Walker et al., 2013).

This mega-event example is particularly salient because of the multi-faceted and diverse nature of South African communities. In hosting the World Cup, the South African government hoped to enhance a sense of community and national identity through sport. Football was chosen as traditionally it has been viewed in South Africa as a 'people's game', attractive to the black population as well as to whites. In this way, the World Cup hoped to 'reignite the spirit of the rainbow nation' (Gibson et al., 2014: 114).

Previous research on the 2002 World Cup held jointly in Japan and Korea suggested that anticipated problems such as crime and traffic congestion were less problematic than expected, and that most residents noted that social benefits were more highly rated after the event (Kim et al., 2006). Ohmann, Jones and Wilkes (2006) also noted that enhanced community and national pride, and an overall sense of friendliness resulted from hosting the World Cup in Germany in 2006.

Gibson et al., (2014) undertook a survey of residents of six cities in South Africa that were hosting soccer matches during the 2010 World Cup. Their results showed that before the event, residents perceived the World Cup as positive, promoting a sense of community and pride, and bringing people together in celebration. After the event, residents were even more positive about the event, leading commentators to suggest that South Africa had made great progress in transforming into the rainbow nation (Ndlovu-Gatsheni, 2011, cited in Gibson et al., 2014). However, research has yet to demonstrate that this so-called 'feel-good' factor will translate into permanent change.

Using perceived quality of life of residents as their measure of socio-cultural impacts, Kaplanidou et al. (2013) identified that residents felt that hosting the World Cup had had a positive impact on their quality of life. Kaplanidou et al. (2013) define quality of life as a multidimensional construct composed of a range of social and cultural factors, such as life satisfaction, satisfaction with community and neighbourhood, satisfaction with family life and happiness.

Finally, Heere et al. (2013) chose to study changes in social and national identity among residents of South Africa as a result of the staging of the World Cup. Governments have tended to assume that hosting a mega-event will positively influence how residents identify with their nation. However, the results of Heere et al.'s (2013) study show that there is little empirical evidence to demonstrate that this is the case. This result must call into question some of the assumptions behind the social benefits that may accrue from hosting mega-events.

This case study serves to highlight the range of ways in which the socio-cultural impacts of one event may be measured, as well as the difficulties in assessing whether the hoped-for benefits to communities and societies will accrue, or last.

Social capital

As a way to try to understand how events can affect people in the locations where they are hosted, scholars have looked to a number of different social theories as ways to explain the connections between events and communities. The theories include social exchange theory (see Deery and Jago, 2010) and stakeholder theory (see Hede, 2007). Whilst none of the theories explains everything, each has its own strengths. Perhaps one of the best ways to understand social impacts is to use social capital.

The term 'social capital' is somewhat contested, as many authors use it in different ways (Arcodia and Whitford, 2006). However, it focusses on the various features of social organisation, such as networks, norms and trust that facilitate human interaction and cooperation (Putnam, 1993). This means things like membership of local associations and clubs, having good relationships with neighbours and community members, and being active or at least interested in local government and politics. As Arcodia and Whitford (2006) argue, festivals and events can impact on a community and its social life in positive or negative ways. Some of the positive impacts of events that translate into the development of social capital include developing community resources (building skills among the event organisers and their local contacts); efficient use of community resources (finding locals to work with the event organisers rather than bringing in supplies or resources from outside the local area); the development of community partnerships (such as with volunteers, and with providers of local facilities, such as the local government); and by simply bringing the community together to have fun and enjoy themselves (Arcodia and Whitford, 2006).

Box 7.2 Using social capital to assess socio-cultural impacts of events

Using three different types of music festivals (folk music, opera and indie-pop), Wilks (2011) examined the role of social capital in the event experience. She used both a survey and in-depth interviews to ascertain whether attending such events makes people feel that they are closer to their community. She studied two different types of social capital in this research – 'bridging social capital' and 'bonding social capital'. Bridging social capital is where people make new connections – friendships, networks or relationships. Bonding social capital refers to strengthening existing ties with friends and those already in our social groups. At the festivals that she studied, it seemed that most people travelled and attended with friends, spent most of their time with their existing friendship group, and did not really meet many new people. Therefore, these festivals are important sites of bonding social capital. Despite meeting new people during the festivals, respondents in this research reported that these were only temporary friendships, rather than the beginning of any lasting relationships. So, there was little evidence of the development of long term bridging capital.

Some respondents interviewed by Wilks (2011) even suggested that they purposely avoided trying to make new friends during the festivals, choosing to spend the time enjoying the music rather than socialising. If festivals and events are being held with the purpose of bringing people together, perhaps to increase tolerance and understanding of diversity in a community, then this research suggests that this is unlikely to be successful. However, if the aim of the festival or event is simply to strengthen existing community relationships and give locals and residents an opportunity to relax in each others' company, then it is likely that strong bonding social capital will be the result.

Community perceptions of events

The underlying assumption behind many festivals and events is that they act as nation or community building activities. This type of impact is much harder to pin down than tangible things like job creation or congestion during an event. There are many ways to define 'nation' and 'community' and so it is important to understand who is being referred to. For the most part, it is the geographical community which resides in the place where the event is being held, either the country, or the town or village. It is important to remember that this should include a range of stakeholders – not just residents, but as Hede (2007) points out, business, community groups, sponsors and media. However, occasionally, the community refers to a community of interest – a group of people brought together by their shared interest. This might be the case for an opera festival for example, where the 'community' may refer to the group of opera lovers who have come together to experience the event.

There are a number of things that can be studied in connection with festivals and communities – how the event contributes to community sense of place (Derrett, 2003), national or community identity (Mair and Duffy, 2014), civic pride (Wood, 2006) and more broadly sense of community itself (Van Winkle et al., 2013). Each will be examined in turn, although it should be remembered that they all share key characteristics relating to place and membership of a group.

Sense of community

Derrett (2003: 51) defines sense of community as 'an almost invisible yet critical part of a healthy community. It includes notions of community image, community spirit, community pride, community relationships and community networks (Derrett, 2003). She concludes that what festivals display clearly identifies distinctive features of a community and can therefore be said to represent a clear sense of the place. A sense of community stems from historical and current forces which have shaped the image and identity of a place. She also suggests that one of the main outcomes of a strong sense of community is community wellbeing, as demonstrated by conviviality, equity and vitality. The community festivals that she studied included a Beef Week in Casino (a food and wine festival), the Byron Bay New Year's Eve festival, the Grafton Jacaranda Festival and the Nimbin MardiGrass festival. All festivals were in New South Wales, Australia. These types of community festival often have long-standing ties with the place where they are held, reflecting history and identity over a long period of time. This kind of festival offers opportunities for communities to get together and reinforce their visions and notions of what their community represents to them.

Identity

National or community identity is similar to the idea of 'place identity', and refers to the meaning and significance that a country or place has for an individual, or a group. Festivals and events can be ways to strengthen place or identity, by showcasing traditions, culture and history in such a way as to engender pride and a feeling of belonging among residents (De Bres and Davis, 2001). Festivals and events can also be opportunities for residents to express their affinity and identification with their nation or their community and with its values and way of life (Van Winkle et al., 2013).

Community identity is more likely to be associated with a long-running community event or festival, rather than any new events that have been introduced, or any festivals or events that only take place in a given location once before moving on (Mair and Duffy, 2014). In a study of a small community festival in Pakenham, Australia, Mair and Duffy (2014) note that one of the key aims of the festival has always been to bring people together and provide community recreation in a celebration of the town's farming heritage. However, over time the community of Pakenham has changed from a rural county town to a suburb of south-east Melbourne and in that time, the make-up of Pakenham has changed. Therefore, the history and traditions celebrated at the festival no longer reflect the identity of the community. In this case, the festival does not strengthen community identity for the majority of the new residents of the town.

National identity is often associated with mega-events such as the Olympics or Commonwealth Games, which are seen to be ways to bring a nation together to celebrate the event (Heere et al., 2013). For example, the London Olympics were seen as an important celebration of all things British, whilst being inclusive of the multicultural nature of the United Kingdom. Other types of events which are closely related to national identity are commemorative events and anniversaries. In this case, the event brings together a country or nation to remember a past sacrifice, tragedy or other important part of the national history (Frost and Laing, 2011). One example of this type of event is Anzac Day, celebrated in Australia and New Zealand, which commemorates the fallen of World War I, as well as being an opportunity to remember and pay respect to all members of the armed forces killed during battles and wars. Anzac Day is marked in almost all Australian and New Zealand towns and cities with dawn services and marches, and brings people together in a day of national commemoration.

Civic pride

For Wood (2006), civic pride represents those aspects of social benefits which can be defined in terms of the residents' attitudes to their local area. She points out that even if some festivals and events do not bring about substantial economic benefit, they are still valuable additions to a community and region, through the provision of social value. Civic pride is about the shared image of a city, town or region that is held by the residents, and where the shared image is positive, residents can be said to have high levels of civic pride. Wood's (2006) research aimed to examine whether festivals and events can increase levels of civic pride. She surveyed nearly 500 local residents in Blackburn, north-west England in order to test whether their image of the town had improved following the staging of two different events. Her findings suggest that there is a relationship between changes in levels of civic pride and the hosting of local events, and therefore, that events and festivals can assist in boosting levels of civic pride.

Sense of community

Festivals and events are considered part of the social life of a community and therefore may contribute to sense of community (Van Winkle et al., 2013). Arising from the field of community studies, the idea of sense of community relates to many aspects of community life. It includes membership – feeling involved and belonging; influence – feeling that one has some influence over how a community acts; integration – feeling that one has status and shares values with the community; and shared emotional connections – some understanding and experience of the community, its history and its stories (McMillan and Chavis, 1986). Research by Van Winkle et al. (2013) in Texas suggests that attending local festivals may contribute to creating shared emotional connections, one of the aspects of sense of community noted above. It certainly appears plausible that festivals can help to form, or strengthen, a sense of community. However, this concept has not been studied in enough depth yet to explain exactly how this happens.

What do events mean to communities?

Despite the discussion above about how festivals and events can contribute to communities, whether that is through strengthening identity, pride or sense of community, it is worth noting that many communities are not homogenous. Rather, they are made up of groups of individuals with different values, cultures, traditions and beliefs. In this context, it is worth asking the question – who is the community? Events can mean different things to different people. There are also multiple stakeholders involved in events, and so each may have their own view of what an event means to them. Identity and sense of community are contested terms, and for any given community, there are likely to be those who identify with a festival or event, and those who do not. There may even be some who vigorously oppose an event or festival taking place in their town. An example of an event with highly contested meanings is Australia Day. Celebrated annually in January, in recognition both of the discovery and colonisation of Australia, and of the Federation of the States into the country we know today, Australia Day is a public holiday which is associated with summer pastimes – beaches, barbeques and picnics. However, for many indigenous people in Australia, the day is known as 'Invasion Day' and is marked by protests about the inequities suffered by the indigenous people today and in the past. Clearly, these two meanings are difficult to reconcile.

In addition, events, and their meanings, can change over time. For example, the Notting Hill Carnival in London was originally created as a small grassroots festival to celebrate the West Indian community. It is now an international street music festival attracting up to a million people (Frost and Laing, 2011). The Sydney Gay and Lesbian Mardi Gras was originally a protest against unfair treatment of gay and lesbian people, but is now primarily a carnival and spectacle, about enjoyment and having fun.

In order to ensure the sustainability of an event, organisers must confront the difficulties associated with contested and changing meanings. Frost and Laing (2011) identify three options for event organisers under such circumstances:

1 *Reaction* – No planning for any unforseen difficulties, simply reacting to events as they occur. This is not advised, as a poorly chosen response may further inflame a difficult situation.
2 *Limitation* – This is a form of risk management, where organisers consider potential difficulties that may arise and put in place measures to counter them. This may involve excluding certain stakeholders, or potentially working closely with the media to ensure a positive message.
3 *Inclusion* – This is the preferred strategy, and involves negotiating and collaborating with a range of stakeholders who bring multiple meanings to the event. In this way, difficulties are identified and solutions sought by negotiation, long before they are able to negatively affect the event.

Box 7.3 illustrates how an event in a small town can mean different things to different stakeholders and residents.

Box 7.3 Contested meanings at the Parkes Elvis Festival

Parkes is a rural town of around 12,000 inhabitants, approximately 350 kilometres from Sydney in New South Wales, Australia. On the second weekend in January, the Parkes Elvis Festival is held, coinciding with Elvis Presley's birthday. The Parkes Elvis Festival represents a community-led approach to event development where a group of passionate Elvis fans living in the town decided in 1993 to

(Continued)

Contested meanings at the Parkes Elvis Festival (continued)

create a festival to celebrate the legacy of Elvis Presley, and the event has been running each year since then. Despite the clear economic success of this event, the local community is somewhat divided over the event. For some, Elvis is a means for the town to generate income and national notoriety, while others prefer less 'kitsch' tourism attractions such as a nearby (and nationally famous) radio telescope (Brennan-Horley et al., 2007). Nonetheless, the Elvis Festival has succeeded despite opposition from some local residents who feel that the image and status of the town is being put at risk by such a close association with one event, and one which relies on an invented tradition at that.

Chapter summary

This chapter has examined some of the most important socio-cultural impacts of events, and has identified both positive and negative impacts. The chapter considered how socio-cultural impacts can be measured and demonstrated the difficulties associated with events. The chapter then moved on to consider how we might understand the relationship between events and the community, and proposed social capital as being one theory that would be helpful in achieving this. Finally, the chapter considered the meanings and perceptions of events to communities, and highlighted the issues that can arise when there are multiple, or conflicting meanings associated with events.

Learning activities

1   Choose an event that you are familiar with. Consider how well it maximises any positive socio-cultural impacts and minimises any negative socio-cultural impacts.
2   Taking an event that you are familiar with, discuss how we might understand the relationship between events and communities.
3   Using an example of an event that you are familiar with, examine the different perspectives of the event that various members of the community may have, and discuss how the organisers of the event could take these differing perspectives into account when delivering a socio-culturally sustainable event.

Case study: Community relevance at Bluesfest Blues and Roots Festival, Byron Bay

Bluesfest is a blues music festival that takes place annually in Byron Bay, in New South Wales, Australia. They have a very comprehensive sustainability policy, which includes a commitment to building institutional capacity, presenting a culturally relevant festival, organising a zero-waste festival and implementing a range of carbon neutral initiatives. Of particular importance is their Strategic Goal 3: A Festival that Respects, Transforms and Grows Local Community. The key features of this goal are noted below:

- By committing to a permanent site the Bluesfest management realises the opportunity of building in attributes such as belonging, being locally relevant and contributing to local economic stability. A value added statement will be published following the 2009 event and for each year thereafter. The statement will highlight new local suppliers and report on why non-Northern Rivers suppliers were used over local suppliers. The statement will be prepared in consultation with local industry groups (including Northern Rivers Tourism Inc).
- We will develop an employment policy that includes an obligation to proactively employ Aboriginal people to the extent where Aboriginality is a requirement for effective service in some aspects of the event. An annual statement will be published detailing the extent of local hiring following the 2009 event and beyond.
- The festival will continue to facilitate the special needs of people with disabilities and their carers. This includes provision of access for children with disabilities. A management plan will be developed for improved access for people with disabilities and the frail aged.
- Bluesfest has a proud record of giving back in terms of donations and other forms of support for a wide range of Northern Rivers based NGOs. The Bluesfest management will re-evaluate its corporate social responsibility (CSR) policies and practices leading up to the 2009 event with the view to improving the positive impacts related to this giving. An annual Statement will be published detailing the corporate social responsibility spend and resultant positive impacts to our society.
- Bluesfest management will engage with artists and involve them more in Bluesfest sustainability initiatives. Artists' travel related emissions will be offset. A review of transportation offset options will form part of the carbon footprint analysis currently underway. The Bluesfest management will communicate these efforts prior to each year's event, so that artists can promote these efforts during their shows.
- The Bluesfest management will build on past efforts where volunteer 'green police' roam the site removing waste for recycling and engaging with our audience around environmental issues. It will also improve 'green' ticket options that offset transport related emissions available to our audience.
- The Bluesfest management will introduce a sustainable procurement policy for suppliers, and will introduce annual 'Responsible Trader Awards' to recognise traders who stand out in terms of lowering their ecological footprints.
- Each year's festival will be used to raise awareness of social/environmental causes and to showcase sustainability solutions. In particular the Bluesfest management will initiate and develop environmental sustainability showcase area/s. Demonstration installations will deal with waste, water conservation,

(Continued)

Case study (continued)

energy conservation and renewable energy and sustainable land management. A number of selected projects/initiatives will be piloted in 2009.

The Bluesfest management have built in these sustainability aspects as core attributes of the Bluesfest brand, thus including sustainability and in particular community relevance as underlying principles of the event (Bluesfest website, 2013).

Discussion questions

1 Why would Bluesfest incorporate community relevance as a core attribute of their brand?
2 How could Bluesfest increase their 'positive' activities of donations and other forms of support?
3 How could Bluesfest improve access to the event for people with disabilities?
4 Why would Bluesfest work closely with local industry groups? How would this improve community relevance of the event?

Further reading and online resources

Love your tent: A Greener Festival Film, the campaign to encourage people to take their tents home from festivals. Available online at http://loveyourtent.com/sub-section.php?s=7andss=13 [accessed 15 November, 2014].
Putnam, R. D. (2000). *Bowling alone: the collapse and revival of American community*. New York: Simon and Schuster.
Quinn, B. (2003). Symbols, practices and mythmaking: cultural perspectives on the Wexford Festival Opera. *Tourism Geographies*, 5 (3), 329–49.

References

Allen, J., O'Toole, W., Harris, R. and McDonnell, I. (2011). *Festival and special event management*, Queensland: John Wiley and Sons.
Arcodia, C. and Whitford, M. (2006). Festival attendance and the development of social capital. *Journal of Convention and Event Tourism*, 8 (2), 1–18.
Bluesfest (2013). Festival website available at http://www.bluesfest.com.au [accessed 18 November, 2014].
Brennan-Horley, C., Connell, J., and Gibson, C. (2007). The Parkes Elvis Revival Festival: economic development and contested place identities in rural Australia. *Geographical Research*, 45 (1), 71–84.
De Bres, K. and Davis, J. (2001). Celebrating group and place identity: a case study of a new regional festival. *Tourism Geographies*, 3 (3), 326–37.

Deery, M. and Jago, L. (2010). Social impacts of events and the role of anti-social behaviour. *International Journal of Event and Festival Management*, 1 (1), 8–28.

Delamere, T. A., Wankel, L. M. and Hinch, T. D. (2001). Development of a scale to measure resident attitudes toward the social impacts of community festivals, Part I: Item generation and purification of the measure. *Event Management*, 7 (1), 11–24.

Derrett, R. (2003). Festivals and regional destinations: how festivals demonstrate a sense of community and place. *Rural Society*, 13 (1), 35–53.

Finkel, R. (2010). 'Dancing around the ring of fire': social capital, tourism resistance and gender dichotomies at Up Helly Aa in Lerwick, Shetland. *Event Management*, 14 (4), 275–85.

Fredline, L., Jago, L. and Deery, M. (2003). The development of a generic scale to measure the social impacts of events. *Event Management*, 8 (1), 23–37.

Fredline, E. and Faulkner, B. (2001). Variations in residents reactions to major motorsport events: why residents perceive the impacts of events differently. *Event Management*, 7 (2), 115–25.

Frost, W. and Laing, J. H. (2011). *Strategic management of festivals and events*. Melbourne, Australia: Cengage.

Getz, D. (2013). *Event tourism: concepts, international case studies, and research*. Putnam Valley, NY: Cognizant Communication Corporation.

Gibson, H. J., Walker, M., Thapa, B., Kaplanidou, K., Geldenhuys, S. and Coetzee, W. (2014). Psychic income and social capital among host nation residents: a pre–post analysis of the 2010 FIFA World Cup in South Africa. *Tourism Management*, 44, 113–22.

Hede, A.-M. (2007). Managing special events in the new era of the triple bottom line. *Event Management*, 11 (1/2), 13–22.

Heere, B., Walker, M., Gibson, H., Thapa, B., Geldenhuys, S. and Coetzee, W. (2013). The power of sport to unite a nation: the social value of the 2010 FIFA World Cup in South Africa. *European Sport Management Quarterly*, 13 (4), 450–71.

Johnson, V., Currie, G. and Stanley, J. (2011). Exploring transport to arts and cultural activities as a facilitator of social inclusion. *Transport Policy*, 18, 68–75.

Kaplanidou, K. K., Karadakis, K., Gibson, H., Thapa, B., Walker, M., Geldenhuys, S. and Coetzee, W. (2013). Quality of life, event impacts, and mega-event support among South African residents before and after the 2010 FIFA World Cup. *Journal of Travel Research*, 52 (5), 631–645.

Kim, H. J., Gursoy, D. and Lee, S. B. (2006). The impact of the 2002 World Cup on South Korea: comparisons of pre- and post-games. *Tourism Management*, 27 (1), 86–96.

McMillan, D. W. and Chavis, D. M. (1986). Sense of community: a definition and theory. *Journal of Community Psychology*, 14 (1), 6–23.

Mair, J. and Duffy, M. (2014) Festivals and sense of community in places of transition: an Australian case study. In Clarke, A. and Jepson, A. (Eds) *Exploring community festivals and events*. Abingdon, Oxon: Routledge.

Mair, J. and Laing, J. H. (2013). Encouraging pro-environmental behaviour: the role of sustainability-focused events. *Journal of Sustainable Tourism*, 21 (8), 1113–28.

Ohmann, S., Jones, I. and Wilkes, K. (2006). The perceived social impacts of the 2006 Football World Cup on Munich residents. *Journal of Sport and Tourism*, 11 (2), 129–52.

Putnam, R. D. (1993). The prosperous community: social capital and public life. *The American Prospect*, 13, 35–42.

Small, K. (2008). Social dimensions of community festivals: an application of factor analysis in the development of the Social Impact Perception (SIP) scale. *Event Management*, 11 (1/2), 1–2.

Small, K. and Edwards, D. (2003). Evaluating the socio-cultural impacts of a festival on a host community: a case study of the Australian Festival of the Book. In Griffin, T. and Harris, R. (Eds). *Proceedings of the 9th Annual Conference of the Asia Pacific Tourism Association*, Sydney: School of Leisure, Sport and Tourism, University of Technology, Sydney, pp. 580–93.

Van Winkle, C. M., Woosnam, K. M. and Mohammed, A. M. (2013). Sense of community and festival attendance. *Event Management*, 17 (2), 155–63.

Walker, M., Kaplanidou, K., Gibson, H., Thapa, B., Geldenhuys, S. and Coetzee, W. (2013). 'Win in Africa, with Africa': social responsibility, event image, and destination benefits. The case of the 2010 FIFA World Cup in South Africa. *Tourism Management*, 34, 80–90.

Wilks, L. (2011). Bridging and bonding: social capital at music festivals. *Journal of Policy Research in Tourism, Leisure and Events*, 3 (3), 281–97.

Wood, E. H. (2006). Measuring the social impacts of local authority events: a pilot study for a civic pride scale. *International Journal of Nonprofit and Voluntary Sector Marketing*, 11 (3), 165–79.

Chapter 8

Delivering the sustainable event

Learning outcomes

After studying this chapter you should be able to:

- Identify practical ways in which event organisers can deliver a financially and economically sustainable event
- Examine practical considerations for event managers to deliver a socio-culturally sustainable event
- Discuss the practical tools and methods for event managers to deliver an environmentally sustainable event
- Understand how event managers can use a systems approach to delivering sustainable events

Introduction

Having considered many of the economic, socio-cultural and environmental impacts of events, it is time to examine how event planners and organisers can take this knowledge and apply it to producing sustainable events. Initially, the individual aspects of sustainability will be examined (economic, socio-cultural and environmental) and then the chapter will consider how to bring each of these aspects together in a systematic way to deliver a sustainable event. In all cases, the primary aim of the event organiser should be to minimise any negative impacts and maximise any positive impacts. However, event organisers can and should go much further than that. By planning and organising their events with sustainability in mind, organisers can not only mitigate any negative impacts, but can actively create positive outcomes for all stakeholders, including visitors, residents, local business and the environment amongst others.

Delivering economic sustainability

One of the simplest measures of economic sustainability for an event is arguably whether it kept to its budget. The most straightforward way to assess this is consider whether income (from ticket sales, sponsorship, merchandising, government grants, etc.) exceeded expenditure (on organising, planning, marketing and running the event). Of course, not all events are run for a profit, but even where the event is strictly not-for-profit, the event should ideally break even rather than lose money. However, there are far more complexities involved than this simple approach (see Chapter 5 on economic impacts of events). Further, for an event to be economically sustainable, it should also contribute to local economies in a sustainable way. Therefore, it is reasonable to suggest that the benefits of the event should be spread as widely as possible in a local area (O'Sullivan and Jackson, 2002). They cite examples of community members living on marginal incomes who can raise what are for them substantial sums of money by selling produce at events, and even those who can afford to pay for college education for their children as a result of selling car parking during a major event. Event visitors bring economic benefits simply by attending events, eating in local cafes and restaurants, staying in local accommodation and making purchases in local retail outlets. O'Sullivan and Jackson (2002) even suggest that events may be one of the most sustainable forms of tourism development.

In their work on regional festivals in Australia, Gibson and Stewart (2009) note that over 75 per cent of these return only a very small operating profit (less than AU$10,000), break even or even operate at a small loss. Therefore, festivals that return a profit (less than 25 per cent) are in the minority. However, as Gibson and Stewart (2009) point out, this does not mean that the festivals cannot generate economic benefits for local communities. They stress that a common characteristic of festivals is that organisers may make little or no direct profit, but instead, the events 'catalyse meaningful monetary benefits for their surrounding communities as a flow on effect' (Gibson and Stewart, 2009: 16). The most likely businesses to benefit directly from an event or festival are those functionally connected to the event – cafes and restaurants, sound and lighting equipment hire, waste management, accommodation providers, printers, advertising agencies, legal services and catering companies (Gibson and Stewart, 2009). However, indirect benefits then flow on to the suppliers and employees of those companies and organisations which benefit directly, and thus the economic impact of the event percolates through the local economy. However, Gibson and Stewart (2009) point out that some aspects of festival and event organisation are likely to rely on suppliers and providers external to the local area (for example, performers or participants). Money earned by those external providers is unlikely to benefit the local economy.

Allen et al. (2011) suggest that there are four areas where events can assist in the sustainable economic development of their host locations:

- Business opportunities
  - How well does the event showcase the expertise and potential of the host location to investors?
  - Does the event make the most of new business opportunities that may arise as a result of hosting the event?
- Leveraging the business outcomes of an event
  - Are strategies in place to make sure that the benefits of the event flow on to the local business community?
  - Are local businesses leveraging the event?
- Employment creation
  - For major and mega-events, are they working to create employment opportunities during the planning, construction and staging of the event?
  - What measures are in place to ensure the longevity of these positions?
- Keeping business local
  - For smaller regional or community events, is the event using local and regional suppliers and produce wherever possible?

Box 8.1 Infrastructure gains from events

Tamworth is a small town in rural New South Wales, Australia. Each year, it hosts the Tamworth Country Music Festival. The event attracts approximately 50,000 attendees over two weeks and is one of the iconic events in the country music calendar. According to the NSW Business Chamber (n.d.), the event contributes around AU$20 million to the local economy each year. As the event has grown, and achieved hallmark status, investment in local infrastructure and facilities to service the event and of course the local population has increased. Tamworth has received investment in new hotels, a museum, a tourist information centre, and a large entertainment centre (Gibson and Stewart, 2009). The funding has come from a mixture of local and state government finances. These new facilities, as well as improvements in local recreation and amenities (parks and gardens and the urban landscape) have provided sustaining benefits for local residents, yet have come about almost entirely as a result of the economic gains generated by hosting a successful festival. Now, the local authorities are looking at further investment in event infrastructure. The NSW Business Chamber (n.d.) believes that Tamworth's existing reputation for festivals and events means that it should be able to compete for other types of events. If the funding could be secured, a

(Continued)

Infrastructure gains from events (continued)

major sports arena in Tamworth would play multiple roles in ensuring the sustainability of the local economy. It would provide leisure, recreation and sporting opportunities for locals, it would allow the town to bid for competitive sporting events, and it would provide a new major venue for the country music festival.

Table 8.1 Examples of how events can support sustainable economies

Sustainable economic development		Examples
Business opportunities	Showcasing the location	Inviting important trading partners to the event to enjoy corporate hospitality
	Making the most of new business opportunities	Tracking new business opportunities so that in future the event can demonstrate its contribution to the local economy
Leveraging business outcomes	Is the event working with local businesses to do this?	Joint marketing or promotions activities
	Are local businesses doing this?	Local restaurants could extend their opening hours to cater for event attendees, or theme their offerings around the event
Employment creation	Creating employment opportunities during all stages of the event	Construction jobs, administration jobs, service jobs such as hospitality and tourism related positions and security jobs
	Longevity of employment opportunities	Examples include recurring major events which support year round permanent employment opportunities for locals
Keeping business local	Buying local	Purchasing locally-grown and produced food and drink, using local suppliers such as technicians, printers and local media for advertising
	Working with local people and community groups to improve their capacity and skills	Training courses in first aid or food hygiene via accredited institutions, or equally may include upskilling local people in administration skills, which improves their job prospects and has a knock-on effect on the local economy

Source: Adapted from Allen et al., 2011

Delivering socio-cultural sustainability

As we saw in Chapter 7, socio-cultural impacts have been defined as 'any impacts that potentially have an impact on the quality of life for local residents' (Fredline et al., 2003: 26). This includes problems such as noise, congestion and pollution, which are clearly negative impacts, but also a range of more positive outcomes, including opportunities for social inclusion, community participation in a shared experience, building community pride, improving the destination image of the host location (Carlsen and Williams, 1999), providing opportunities for volunteering and building the skills and capacity of the local community (Allen et al., 2011; Delamere et al., 2001; Derrett, 2003; Finkel, 2010; Fredline and Faulkner, 2001; Getz, 2013; and Wood, 2006).

One of the key things that event organisers have to take into account when ensuring the socio-cultural sustainability of their events is to consider the issues of access and inclusion. Research to date suggests that social inclusion might be a potential outcome of a festival, in the sense of 'engaging sections of the community not commonly participating in community and political activities' (Johnson et al., 2011: 69), or breaking down barriers and building strong communities (Derrett, 2003; Finkel, 2010).

Further, in order to achieve a socio-culturally sustainable event, organisers must work hard to avoided exclusion. Research suggests that festivals might act as a tool for social exclusion of some groups within the community, perhaps because of the context of the event, or perhaps because of intentional or unintentional marginalisation of some parts of the community. Quinn (2003) notes that some festivals, such as opera or ballet festivals, are established for elite audience groups. Also, some international festivals are criticised for their elitist programmes and high costs, which act as barriers to inclusivity. Therefore, some parts of the community may feel excluded from these events. Lockstone-Binney et al. (2010) note the potential under-representation of socially disadvantaged groups as volunteers, which suggests that the benefits of volunteering in terms of building skills and interacting with a variety of people are not equally accessible to all sections of the community. These negative outcomes of exclusivity can usually be addressed in terms of working towards the positive outcomes of inclusion.

According to Johnson, Currie and Stanley (2011), there are four areas in which event organisers can improve the socio-cultural inclusion outcomes of their events – *consumption*, *production*, *engagement* and *social interaction*. To this may also be added education, as events offer excellent opportunities to educate all those involved in the event – organising, volunteering, performing or attending.

Consumption is about being able to 'consume', or access events. Options for improving access that have been used by various events include:

- Free entry or a nominal entry fee for locals
- Free tickets to paid events for those from financially disadvantaged communities
- Using community spaces (such as town halls or council buildings) that are not usually accessible to the general public
- Using technology (such as websites and social media) to allow access to some event content even when people are not able to attend in person

Impacts of sustainable events

Production refers to how an event is planned, organised and staged. Some suggestions for how event organisers can improve the sustainable production of their events include:

- The use of local suppliers, for catering, staging, security etc.
- Having a large local volunteer contingent in the event
- The generation of public–private partnerships with community-based organisations
- Working with local authorities to regenerate deprived areas
- Showcasing local talent by commissioning local artists, or discovering and presenting new local musicians
- Championing ethnic diversity by working with migrant and refugee groups

Engagement refers to political or active engagement with community life. Not all events may be in a position to work to engage their attendees, but those who wish to may:

- Advocate for social justice or social change
- Invite activist organisations (such as Greenpeace or Amnesty International, or smaller local activist groups) to be part of their event
- Use the event as an opportunity to publicise or lobby for action on a particular cause

Social interaction concerns the opportunities that events provide to bring people together, and help to build community cohesion and community tolerance. Some events work hard to create an interactive atmosphere by:

- Using easily accessible sites that encourage participation
- Creating a relaxed atmosphere
- Providing opportunities for people to gather within the event (cafes or picnic areas)

Education in this context refers to the possibility for event organisers to use their event as a way to educate, or build skills and capacity among attendees and local residents. Such possibilities may include:

- Educational workshops as part of the event (e.g. on aspects of pro-environmental behaviour)
- Outreach programmes to help build community skills (e.g. taking arts productions into schools)
- Building skills among local people by employing them in event organisation
- Using volunteering opportunities as a way to teach local people new skills that will help them in their careers

Box 8.2 Coachella

The Coachella Valley Music and Arts Festival takes place every year in Indio, California. It has been running since 1999 and includes a range of music genres as well as art installations and sculptures. In 2014, the festival attracted 579,000 attendees (Coachella, 2014). Coachella has a strong focus on sustainability and community involvement and a portion of all ticket receipts collected at the festival are used to benefit local charities. In addition, the art festival that takes place alongside the music event attracts both international and local artists, thus engaging the community in the event. In 2014, one of the art installations was called Paraiso, and was an interpretation of the California desert by local youth artists based in the Coachella Valley (Coachella, 2014). This is an example of how events can engage and showcase local talent. The festival also encourages attendees to participate by getting them involved with the Coachella Valley art scene, where attendees can create craft items during the festival. Another example of community involvement was the invitation in 2004 for the local high school marching band to take part in the festival opening (Huang, 2014). Further, Coachella festival tickets include a US$5 contribution to the local authority (Huang, 2014). Locals speak of their pride in their community when the festival comes to town, and the presence of the festival is also seen as something that gives local children something to aspire to – a career in music, art or indeed event organisation (Huang, 2014).

Delivering environmental sustainability

Managing event impacts on the environment may be governed by both legal requirements (regulatory) and self-imposed voluntary systems. Voluntary impact management systems can be aligned with certain standards and then certified, or based on more general guidelines and checklists (Case, 2013).

Depending on the location, type and scale of event, there will be laws and regulations determining how certain aspects of the event are managed to mitigate negative environmental impacts. This can include legislation for environmental issues such as:

- Limiting noise and nuisance
- Air quality thresholds
- Water quality thresholds
- Effective waste management and litter control
- Toxins, chemicals and dangerous goods management
- Nature/cultural heritage conservation

Failure to demonstrate compliance with legal requirements can result in financial penalties or withdrawal of official approval to implement the event.

Environmental management systems

Environmental management systems (EMS) are voluntary, internal, formalised procedures that can help ensure compliance with legal requirements and minimise or negate environmental impacts (Thomas and Murfitt, 2011). The design of effective environmental management systems requires expertise in identifying environmental risks, implementation of best practice and preparation for mitigation measures if impacts occur (Ponsford, 2011). Many larger planned events may hire consultants or environmental management teams for this purpose.

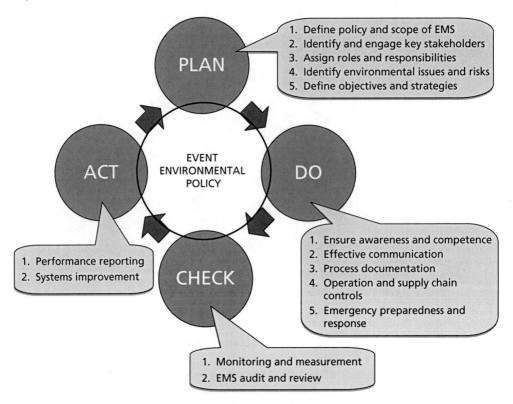

Figure 8.1 A generalised events environmental management system framework (adapted from ISO 20121)

The International Standards Organisation (ISO) and British Standards Institute (BSI) provide tools and guidelines (referred to as ISO 20121 and BS 8901) defining a management systems standard specifically for sustainable events, including environmental management systems. The standards are not environmental checklists but rather, they are complex documents that describe the elements of a management system required for implementing a sustainable event. These types of standard focus on the elements of the event management system, and not the event itself or the impacts of the event. The assumption is that if the management system complies with these standards, event impacts will be effectively managed (ISO, 2012). Figure 8.1 outlines a general framework for a planned event environmental management system based on the ISO 20121 and BS 8901 framework.

Environmental guides and checklists

Developing and implementing an event EMS, or achieving ISO or BSI certification can be complex, costly and time consuming. Many events and festivals may not have the resources to adopt these types of practices, particularly smaller and community based events or one off events. However, there are many resources based on the complex ISO/BS framework that event organisers can access as a voluntary approach to environmental management including:

- Environmental or green event checklists
- Green event guides
- Sustainable event guides
- Green wedding planning ('natural weddings')
- Green meetings
- Guides for sustainable event practices

These resources provide guidance and general tips on how to manage the various environmental (and other) impacts of events. This typically includes appropriate venue or event location selection, strategies for minimising energy consumption, waste, supply transport distances and congestion. They also provide strategies for recycling and composting as well as sustainability education. Effective implementation of these strategies may involve recruitment of volunteers for monitoring and action, staff awareness and compliance, education of event attendees about responsible behaviour, agreements with stakeholders such as government and event sponsors to manage impacts such as waste disposal, recycling, transport and energy consumption.

Carbon offsetting

Once an event has measured its carbon footprint (see Chapter 6), the key ways to manage excess carbon emissions are reduce, re-use, recycle, and then as a last resort, offset whatever is left over (Jones, 2010). Once the organisers have reduced their energy and water use, re-used whatever materials they are able to, and recycled as much as possible, carbon offsetting becomes a suitable way to deal with remaining emissions. There are a number of forms of offsets that can be purchased, including Emission Unit Allowances, Emission Reduction Units, Certified Emission Reductions and Verified Emission Reductions (Gössling et al., 2009). Most offsets sold in the voluntary market are Verified Emission Reductions (Gössling et al., 2009). Verified Emission Reductions are those where emission reductions are validated and verified by independent third parties, but with varying standards. There is a great diversity in types of projects that generate verified emission reductions, but examples include reforestation projects, fossil fuel reduction projects and energy efficiency projects (Mair, 2011). Event organisers can purchase carbon offsets and claim that the event is carbon neutral, however, it is worth remembering that the biggest contributor to emissions in the events context is attendees' travel to and from the event. Some events include a voluntary offset as part of a ticket package, which means that the attendee's travel is offset by the event organiser (see Box 8.3).

Box 8.3 The 'green' ticket at Splendour in the Grass

Splendour in the Grass is a music festival that takes place in Byron Bay, in the north of New South Wales, Australia. The organisers recognise the importance of introducing ways to minimise its negative impacts on the environment, and have introduced a range of measures aimed at doing this. These include waste

(Continued)

The 'green' ticket at Splendour in the Grass (continued)

management improvements, new recycling initiatives and the provision of buses from both Melbourne and Sydney for attendees (Connell and Gibson, 2012). As part of their commitment to producing and staging a carbon neutral event, Splendour in the Grass offsets all internal emissions by purchasing renewable wind farm carbon credits, and also offers attendees the opportunity to purchase a 'green' ticket. This ticket is offered in association with Climate Friendly, a 'profit for purpose' organisation that provides carbon offsetting solutions to businesses and households internationally. This ticket allows patrons to offset their attendance and travel to and from the event in one payment (with the proviso that attendees are not travelling further than a total of 450 kilometres).

The emissions offset by this ticket are calculated based on average carbon emissions by attendees. The proceeds from the green ticket are then spent on renewable energy, more specifically wind power generation, and on forest protection projects. The cost of the green ticket in 2014 was only AU$3 on top of the ticket price (Splendour in the Grass, 2014). According to Soulshine, the website for independent music in Australia, Splendour in the Grass sold 12,415 green or carbon offset tickets between 2008 and 2010. The results of this initiative demonstrate how much of an impact this makes. Over 1,939 tons of greenhouse gas emissions were offset through investment in renewable clean wind farm energy, with a total investment of AU$65,123 in these projects. This equates to taking 538 family sedan cars off the road for a year, or powering 242 average homes for a year (Soulshine News, 2010).

Delivering a holistically sustainable event

Applying holistic thinking to planned events means understanding the connection between the elements that make the event happen and how this relates to the broader context in which the event is taking place. It also needs an understanding of the interdependencies, interactions and feedback loops between the various aspects of the event and a recognition that these may change over time.

Often the economic benefits of an event are considered to be of primary importance by event organisers – if the event cannot sustain itself financially, then it is unlikely to run again. However, many of the economic benefits of an event flow on to the local community, in terms of increased job opportunities, an injection of tourist cash into the local economy and a contribution to the long-term sustainable development of the host location. At the same time, many of these seemingly economic impacts are also of significant benefit to local people in a more intangible way – improved job opportunities can bring improvements in quality of life for residents. Increased money in the local economy may be spent on services and facilities that are of benefit to locals in terms of their health and wellbeing (new parks or recreation facilities, for example). A more sustainable local economic base can also underpin improvements in the environment, for example, in terms of urban renewal. Such long-term improvements in the local environment can also bring about an increase in community pride, which has an impact on quality of life for residents. Community pride can be the catalyst for local people to become more aware of local and global environmental issues, and to take action to improve protection of their local environment.

Events can provide opportunities for local people to gain skills and experience, either as paid staff or volunteers, and larger events can work with accredited institutions to provide nationally recognised qualifications in first aid, occupational health and safety and administration. Not only does this provide a benefit to the local community in general, in terms of improved access to training and education but also offers individuals the chance to improve their long-term job prospects and increase their earnings potential. Even if those involved in the event don't undertake any specific training or gain any qualifications, volunteering is recognised as an important component of building social capital in a community.

Events can also provide a way for culturally and ethnically diverse communities to showcase and revitalise their traditions, and encourage tolerance of the diversity that exists within most communities. This increased tolerance may have a knock-on effect on community pride, and may even contribute towards a reduction in anti-social behaviour. Reductions in anti-social problems like vandalism also have a positive effect on the local environment, particularly in urban areas or town centres, and on quality of life for local residents.

Finally, events often attract tourists, who bring with them a positive direct and indirect economic impact in terms of their spend during the event. If they enjoy their visit then they are more likely to return again in future, and also spread positive word of mouth about the destination. Events can also showcase a destination, work towards improving destination image, and can contribute towards a destination brand. This contributes towards the local economy both now and into the future, and helps with the sustainable development of communities.

Systems thinking

Systems thinking originated in the area of ecological science based on the observation that natural ecological processes consisted of interactions between various elements (biological and physical) that were interdependent. That is, the different elements have various relationships with each other that influenced how each element functions and how the system as a whole functions. It also recognised that systems are dynamic rather than remaining the same over time. That is, relationships and the status of various elements in a system can change in the short and longer term. Systems thinking is thus founded on understanding relationships between the parts of a system and how they influence each other and the whole system over time. As we have seen in previous chapters, there are many different elements and functions involved in organising an event and the overall success and sustainability is a function of these elements and the degree to which they integrate and interact before, during and after the event. Hence systems thinking is a prerequisite in the process of transformation towards the staging of sustainable planned events.

The whole is greater than the sum of the parts

One way of thinking about systems is to think about your body. It is made up of millions of individual cells that each has a certain function. These cells interact and influence each other but individually are limited in what they can do. They combine to form organs (such as skin, heart, stomach, bones, muscle, brain and so on) that in turn combine to form what could be termed 'sub-systems' such as the cardiovascular system, musculoskeletal system, nervous system and digestive system. Each of these sub-systems has a particular function, based on relationships between its parts that is more complex than that of the individual cells and organs. In turn, these sub-systems interact and combine to form your body. When these various elements and their relationships are combined, it enables your body to perform complex tasks that the individual elements could not do alone. As a system, your body is greater than the sum of the individual parts because it is not just the combined functions of each element that matters, but the relationships between them over time that create the system. Events also have multiple sub-systems in simultaneous operation – management, marketing, finance, staffing, venue, performers/competitors, security, logistics and so on – and these must combine and interact in order to deliver the whole sustainable event.

Key attributes of systems thinking

Understanding the relationships between the elements of a system is essential to systems thinking. A systems approach recognises that changes to one part of a system can influence other parts of the system that in turn can result in varying degrees of overall change. This is based on direct and indirect causal relationships and feedback loops.

Direct relationships are those where a change in one element of the system directly affects the state of another element. For example, a shortfall in funding will directly affect the quality of performers or competitors that can be attracted to the event.

Indirect relationships are those were change in one element may influence another through one or more intervening elements. Following on from the previous example, lesser known performers or competitors will limit the marketing messages and prestige of the event, which will in turn impact on ticket sales and financial revenue. Counter-intuitively, this is referred to in systems thinking as a positive or reinforcing feedback loop, where an initial change (shortfall in funding) is further exacerbated by a shortfall in ticket sales, producing an even more exaggerated financial result.

Feedback loops refer to the circumstance where a change in an element results in changes to the system, which in turn can 'feed back' to the source of influence as either a positive or negative effect. The feedback can either balance, offset or reinforce the effects resulting from the original change and subsequent influences on the system. For example, the funding shortfall that leads to limited ticket sales and reinforces poor financial results may be offset by a change in venue and associated reduction in venue costs, thus offsetting the funding shortfall and helping to balance the event budget. Again, counter-intuitively this is referred to as a negative feedback loop, as it moves the system in the opposite direction to the initial change. All functioning systems will have an equal number of offsetting and reinforcing feedback loops, so that the whole system moves dynamically towards a balanced state, referred to as homeostasis.

In understanding the relationships, feedback and dynamics of a system, managers can identify key leverage points to effectively influence that system, introduce balancing feedback loops and achieve sustainable outcomes. Thus, system thinking requires certain attributes (see Table 8.2).

Table 8.2 Attributes of systems thinking

Attribute	What it means
Big picture thinking	Ability to see the dynamics of a whole system and the relationships between its parts
Recognising things change over time	Recognising that systems are dynamic and the components and relationships can change over time
Understanding interdependencies	Understanding that cause and effect are circular rather than linear in nature and can include positive and negative feedback loops in the system
Leverage points	Understanding the key points and relationships in the system where management action can generate change and desired results
Considering short- and long-term consequences	Weighing up the consequences of a decision or action in terms of short-term effects and the possible longer-term consequences
Adaptive management	Managing a dynamic system often needs a 'best guess' action that requires monitoring and adjustment to eventually obtain the desired result
Delayed effects	Management actions in a complex system may take time to manifest as outcomes. Delayed effects need to be factored into systems management

Source: Adapted from Waters Foundation, 2014

Resilience

The concept of resilience was introduced by Holling (1973) as an alternative way of explaining the complex behaviour of natural systems. This approach recognises that nature is dynamic and exists in a state of constant variation. For example, animal and vegetation population characteristics, temperature and rainfall vary over time and influence each other based on these variations. This idea challenges the traditional notions of nature based on stability and the achievement of pristine states of equilibrium. However, the constantly changing variables within a natural system remain within upper and lower limits over time. This is referred to as the range of natural variability. It is the range of natural variability that defines the character of the system (the system state) and not any specific point of balance or equilibrium.

Resilience has been broadly categorised into two forms, engineering resilience and ecological resilience (Gunderson, 2000). Engineering resilience (see Figure 8.2) is the ability to recover from a shock and return to a predefined state after the impact occurs. Ecological resilience (see Figure 8.3) refers to the ability of a dynamic system to absorb disturbances and remain within a given range of variation that maintains a given system's state over time. Resilience, therefore, is the ability of a system to absorb sudden as well as gradual changes without shifting into an alternate system state (Gunderson, 2000).

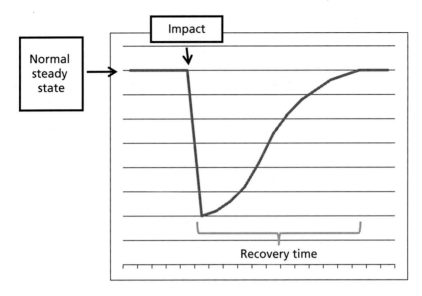

Figure 8.2 Engineering resilience

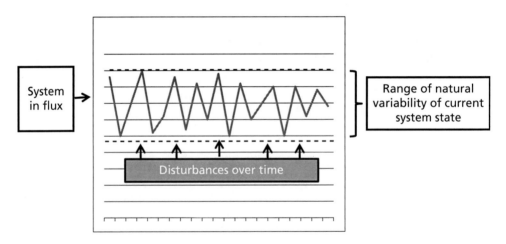

Figure 8.3 Ecological resilience

The idea of dynamic systems and resilience has since spread from ecology across other fields of research and is accepted as a valid framework for understanding social and ecological processes and the broader systems in which they operate (Cochrane, 2010). As it has spread across numerous disciplines, multiple definitions of resilience have been generated. However, most definitions reflect Holling's (1973) original conceptualisation of variability over time as the natural state of being.

Chapter summary

This chapter demonstrates that delivering the sustainable event requires event organisers to consider the practical ways in which they can work towards creating economically and financially sustainable events. They are also required to examine some of the practical considerations for event managers in terms of developing a socio-culturally sustainable event as well as recognise some of the key operational and managerial strategies that they can use to stage an environmentally sustainable event. In summary, this chapter underlined the need for event organisers and planners to take a systematic approach to delivering a sustainable event by considering all aspects of sustainability – economic, social and environmental – in an integrated way.

Learning activities

1   Use an event that you are familiar with as an example. Discuss how the concepts of economic and socio-cultural sustainability are linked.
2   Consider the issues of accessibility and inclusion for events, and identify a range of strategies that event managers can use in order to improve both accessibility and inclusion in events for local residents.
3   Discuss the appropriateness of developing an environmental management system (EMS) for all events.
4   Taking a holistic sustainability approach, critique an event that you are familiar with and suggest ways in which it could improve its overall levels of sustainability.

Case study: London 2012 Olympic Games – delivering a sustainable event

In 2012, the Olympic Games were held in London, UK. As part of their bidding process, the organisers promised the most sustainable and inclusive Games ever. The International Olympic Committee considers that there are three pillars to the Olympic movement – sport, culture and the environment. The London Organising Committee for the Olympic Games (LOCOG) worked hard to include both the socio-cultural and environmental dimensions of the Olympics in their planning and management of the event, as well as delivering an economically successful Games.

The London Olympic Games set out to leave a positive economic legacy for the United Kingdom. A report by Lloyds Banking Group and Oxford Economics into the economic impact of the Games suggested that the total economic impact was significant (Lloyds Banking and Oxford Economics, 2012).

1   **Contribution to UK GDP**. This report estimates that the 2012 Games will support a GBP16.5 billion contribution to the UK's GDP, spread over 12 years. Of this, 82 per cent is expected to result from the pre-Games and legacy construction activity, 12 per cent from tourism and 6 per cent from the infrastructure required to stage the Games. Games-related construction activity therefore makes a very significant contribution, with an estimated spend of

(Continued)

Case study (continued)

GBP11.9 billion. This construction activity is expected to support 267,000 employment years in the UK between 2005 and 2017.

2 **Contribution to tourism.** The Games are also expected to attraction many tourists, with a net increase in visitors of 10.8 million between 2005 and 2017, which is anticipated to generate over GBP2 billion in tourist spend, and support over 61,000 additional years of employment.

3 **Contribution to the labour force.** There is also expected to be an important labour force legacy – the training undertaken by those employed directly and indirectly by the Games is estimated to be worth over GBP500 million in future income over the working lives of those employed. There were also over 3,000 formerly jobless people employed by the Games, and this work experience is expected to earn these people on average an extra GBP40,000 over their working lives.

4 **Contribution to physical legacy.** The provision of 3,850 new affordable homes as a physical legacy of the Games is likely to deliver benefits in relation to better health, fewer lost working days, lower National Health Service costs, and reduced costs of crime.

In addition, the Olympic Games also developed an Employment and Skills Strategy, with commitments in three main areas (LOCOG, 2012a):

1 **Creating employment opportunities.** LOCOG directly employed 8,000 workers in the run-up to, and during the Games (Games-time workforce), as well as indirectly providing work for another 100,000 employed by contractors. Twenty-three per cent of their Games-time workforce lived in the six London boroughs local to the Games, and 39 per cent of their directly employed Games-time workforce was previously unemployed.

2 **Experience and skills development.** LOCOG claims that they provided tens of thousands of opportunities for individuals to gain new skills and experience while working for the Games (LOCOG, 2012a).

3 **Developing young people.** This was primarily addressed though a range of programmes set up by LOCOG, including the Get Ahead apprenticeship schemes, a range of internships and work experience placements, and the Young Games Makers volunteer workforce.

Finally, and by no means least important, LOCOG set out eight key attributes of sustainable event delivery, and following the Games, they measured their achievements in all eight attributes in a post-Games sustainability report entitled 'Legacy for Change' (LOCOG, 2012b).

1 **Provide an accessible and inclusive setting for all.** The venues and services were designed to be accessible as possible, with food services catering for diverse dietary, ethnic, cultural and practical needs, affordable entry options were provided, and a warm welcome was provided by the Games Makers (volunteers).

2 **Provide a safe and secure atmosphere.** There were no major safety or security incidents during the Games. Attendees were screened before entry, and the security and emergency services all worked to a highly detailed plan.

3 **Have minimal negative impacts on the environment.** LOCOG worked hard to avoid waste, make carbon savings, source environmentally friendly products and protect natural and cultural heritage.

4 **Encourage healthy living.** Sporting clubs in the UK have reported a surge in participation in a variety of sports following the Games. Also, during the Games itself, there was a sharp increase in the number of Londoners using public transport, or walking or cycling to work. Finally, the creation of new parklands in east London provided open space for recreation and leisure for local people.

5 **Promote responsible sourcing.** The Games required more than GBP1 billion worth of goods and services. Sustainability was an important part of the procurement and supply chain for the Games, and therefore the Games organisers were in a position to demand high levels of sustainability from their suppliers.

6 **Deliver excellent customer service.** Feedback from athletes and spectators at the Games was generally positive, with particular praise given to the quality of service, the venues, transport and security and the friendliness of the Games Makers.

7 **Encourage more sustainable behaviour.** The Games showcased best practice in waste management and recycling, and introduced a number of initiatives in their Inspire programme to encourage people to get involved in local sustainability efforts.

8 **Leave a positive legacy.** LOCOG notes that legacy is a long-term perspective, but points to a number of their initiatives that have been picked up and used by other large corporations (such as their carbon footprint methodology, and their waste and resources action plan) and the Games were also instrumental in the development of the new international standard for sustainable events, ISO20121.

Discussion questions

1 Given the tendency to boost or inflate impacts studies, how much confidence do you place in these results? Discuss how the organisers can improve the reliability of their impact studies.

2 Discuss the components of the LOCOG sustainability strategy. Are there any important components missing? How could it be improved?

Further reading and online resources

British Standard BS 8901 Sustainability in Event Management. Available online at http://sustainable-event-alliance.org/how-to-guides/projects/bs-8901/ [accessed 27 November, 2014].

Sustainable Event Alliance. Available online at http://sustainable-event-alliance.org/ [accessed 27 November, 2014].

Goldblatt, S., & Goldblatt, J. (2011). *The complete guide to greener meetings and events*. Hoboken, NJ: John Wiley and Sons.

References

Allen, J., O'Toole, W., Harris, R. and McDonnell, I. (2011). *Festival and special event management*. Queensland: John Wiley and Sons.

Carlsen, J. and Williams, A. P. (1999). Events tourism and destination image in Western Australia. In Andersson, T., Persson, C., Sahlberg, B. and Strom, L. (Eds), *The impact of mega events*. European Tourism Research Institute, Sweden.

Case, R. (2013). *Events and the environment*. UK: Routledge.

Coachella (2014). Welcome to Coachella 2014. Available online at www.coachella.com [accessed 23 July, 2014].

Cochrane, J. (2010). The sphere of tourism resilience. *Tourism Recreation Research*, 35 (2), 173–85.

Connell, J. and Gibson, C. (2012). *Music festivals and regional development in Australia*. Farnham, UK: Ashgate Publishing.

Delamere, T. A., Wankel, L. M. and Hinch, T. D. (2001). Development of a scale to measure resident attitudes toward the social impacts of community festivals, Part I: Item generation and purification of the measure. *Event Management*, 7 (1), 11–24.

Derrett, R. (2003). Festivals and regional destinations: how festivals demonstrate a sense of community and place. *Rural Society.* 13 (1), 35–53.

Finkel, R. (2010). 'Dancing around the ring of fire': social capital, tourism resistance and gender dichotomies at Up Helly Aa in Lerwick, Shetland. *Event Management*, 14 (4), 275–85.

Fredline, E. and Faulkner, B. (2001). Variations in residents reactions to major motorsport events: why residents perceive the impacts of events differently. *Event Management*, 7 (2), 115–25.

Fredline, L., Jago, L. and Deery, M. (2003). The development of a generic scale to measure the social impacts of events. *Event Management*, 8 (1), 23–37.

Getz, D. (2013). *Event tourism: concepts, international case studies, and research*. New York: Cognizant Communication Corporation.

Gibson, C. and Stewart, A. (2009). *Reinventing rural places: the extent and impact of festivals in rural and regional Australia*. Wollongong, NSW: University of Wollongong.

Gössling, S., Haglund, L., Kallgren, H., Revahl, M. and Hultman, J. (2009). Swedish air travellers and voluntary carbon offsets: towards the co-creation of environmental value? *Current Issues in Tourism*, 12, 1–19.

Gunderson, L. H. (2000). Ecological resilience: in theory and application. *Annual Review of Ecology and Systematics*, 31, 425–39.

Holling, C. S. (1973). Resilience and stability of ecological systems. *Annual Review of Ecology and Systematics*, 4, 1–23.

Huang, J. (2014). Coachella 2014: locals left out when the world comes to party. Online article, 89.3KPCC Radio news page 18 April. Available at www.scpr.org/programs/take-two/2014/04/18/37025/coachella-2014-locals-left-out-when-world-comes-to/ [accessed 23 July, 2014].

ISO (2012). *Sustainable events with ISO 20121*. Geneva, Switzerland: International Standards Organisation. Available online at http://www.iso20121.org [accessed 15 November, 2014].

Johnson, V., Currie, G. and Stanley, J. (2011). Exploring transport to arts and cultural activities as a facilitator of social inclusion. *Transport Policy*, 18, 68–75.

Jones, M. (2010). *Sustainable event management: a practical guide*. London: Earthscan.

Lloyds Banking and Oxford Economics (2012). *The economic impact of the London 2012 Olympic and Paralympic Games*. Oxford: Oxford Economics.

Lockstone-Binney, L., Holmes, K., Smith, K. and Baum, T. (2010). Volunteers and volunteering in leisure: social science perspectives. *Leisure Studies*, 29 (4), 435–55.

LOCOG (2012a). Employment and Skills Strategy. Available online at http://learninglegacy. independent.gov.uk/documents/pdfs/equality-inclusion-employment-and-skills/ cp-locog-employment-and-skills-strategy.pdf [accessed 25 November, 2014].

LOCOG (2012b). London 2012 Post-Games sustainability report: a legacy of change. Available online at http://learninglegacy.independent.gov.uk/documents/pdfs/ sustainability/5-london-2012-post-games-sustainability-report-interactive-12-12-12. pdf [accessed 25 November, 2014].

Mair, J. (2011). Exploring air travellers' voluntary carbon-offsetting behaviour. *Journal of Sustainable Tourism*, 19 (2), 215–30.

New South Wales Business Chamber (n.d.). Ten big ideas to grow Tamworth. Available online at www.nswbusinesschamber.com.au/NSWBC/media/Misc/Lobbying/ 10BigIdeas/10_big_ideas_Tamworth.pdf [accessed 29 July, 2014].

O'Sullivan, D. and Jackson, M. J. (2002) Festival tourism: a contribution to sustainable local economic development. *Journal of Sustainable Tourism*, 10 (4), 325–42.

Ponsford, I. (2011). Actualising environmental sustainability at Vancouver 2010 venues. *International Journal of Event and Festival Management*, 2 (2), 184–96.

Quinn, B. (2003). Symbols, practices and mythmaking: cultural perspectives on the Wexford Festival Opera. *Tourism Geographies*, 5 (3), 329–49.

Soulshine News (2010). Carbon offset plans for Splendour in the Grass. Available online at http://www.soulshine.com.au/article/2010/04/21/672-carbon-offset-plans-for-splendour-in-the-grass.html [accessed 23 July, 2014].

Splendour in the Grass (2014). Ticket info. Available online at www.splendourinthegrass. com/ticket-information.html [accessed 23 July, 2014].

Thomas, I. and Murfitt, P. (2011). Environmental Management Systems. In Thomas, I. (Ed.), *Environmental management: processes and practices for Australia*, 2nd edn, Sydney: The Federation Press, pp. 189–232.

Waters Foundation (2014). Systems thinking: habits of a system thinker. Available online at http://watersfoundation.org/systems-thinking/habits-of-a-systems-thinker [accessed 23 July 2014].

Wood, E. H. (2006). Measuring the social impacts of local authority events: a pilot study for a civic pride scale. *International Journal of Nonprofit and Voluntary Sector Marketing*, 11 (3), 165–79.

PART III

Logistics of sustainable events

Employment, volunteering and sustainable events

Learning outcomes

After studying this chapter you should be able to:

- Understand the employment and volunteering issues in relation to sustainable events
- Identify ways of sustainably staffing an event
- Recognise the different ways of managing event volunteers
- Identify how to recruit, motivate and manage volunteers
- Analyse how mega-events try to create employment and employability legacies

Introduction

Event management as a field of work has experienced enormous growth over the past decade (Mair, 2009). This is the result of both demand and supply issues. The events sector is growing fast and in more specialist directions. For example, in the early 2000s, the UK's Cultural and Creative Sector Skills Council predicted a need for 30,000 new recruits for the live entertainment events industry over the next decade (DCMS, 2002). Other areas such as the exhibitions and conventions sector have also experienced expansion as destinations seek to market themselves to the lucrative business events industry (McCabe, 2008).

Events management has emerged as a specialised area of work with new jobs appearing such as wedding planner or an events coordinator in a school. This has been matched by the increasing number of event management programmes available at universities and further education colleges and sustained demand for these programmes from students. The idea of event management as a distinct profession is still being debated (Arcodia, 2009), but this is clearly a growth industry with many opportunities at all levels. This chapter explores event staffing models, the role of volunteers and the ways in which events can be used to upskill the local community leading to an employment legacy for the event.

Issues in sustainable event staffing

Increased employment in a destination is frequently cited as an economic benefit of hosting events (see Chapter 5). While events often do create jobs, these may not be ongoing, skilled or highly paid as most paid work in events is casual and episodic. As noted above, events and festivals are extremely varied and require staff with a range of skills including event management, design, staging, catering, marketing and public relations and people management (Arcodia, 2009). An event's staffing needs can also change between the planning and operations phases.

Events and festivals can be organised by professional (commercial) event organisers, local or national governments and not-for-profit organisations. To be financially viable, event management companies will run a series of events throughout the year. Governments often have in-house event teams, who run regular, annual events in a destination, sometimes sub-contracting to professional event organisers. Typically regular events have a core of ongoing events management and specialist staff who will work throughout the year to organise and stage the event or series of events. This core is supplemented with a much larger group of casual staff and/or volunteers who can be brought in for the event itself. These organisations can be described as pulsating organisations, in that they grow and decrease in size depending on the needs of the event (Hanlon and Jago, 2009). The event organisers can recruit the casual staff directly or sub-contract the recruitment to an event staffing company, who provide staff for a range of different events in a destination. These companies can typically provide bar staff, stewards, entertainers, stage crew, promotions and security staff and will usually have a specialism such as outdoor music festivals or sporting events.

For one-off events, particularly roaming mega-events which change location each time, an entire event management organisation is created to run the event. The build up to a mega-event like the Olympic Games takes a number of years, with the local organising committee usually being established after the city has been awarded the event and dissolved after the event is held and the organising committee has submitted their report to the International Olympic Committee. The Organising Committee of the Sochi Olympic and Paralympic Games was established in 2007, three months after the 2014 Winter Olympic Games was awarded to Sochi in the Russian Federation and began to dissolve itself in August 2014 (Shirinian, 2014). These mega-event organising committees are massive operations. The Beijing Organising Committee of the Olympic Games was expected to have 4,000 staff across 30 departments by 2008 (Theodoraki, 2007).

Box 9.1 Staffing at the Vancouver Winter Olympics

The Vancouver Organising Committee for the 2010 Olympic and Paralympic Winter Games (VANOC) was established on 30 September, 2003, four months after the event had been awarded to Vancouver. A not-for-profit organisation, VANOC had responsibility for planning, organising, financing and staging the 2010 Winter Olympics. The organisation grew from an initial 100 employees to 2,500 by the staging of the event, with 500 of these recruited just for the actual year of the Games.

Managing such a large, complex and short term organisation is a challenge and posts to the online job reviews site Glassdoor (2014) reveal particular problems with the organisation. These include the need to hire people who are both good in planning and operational roles, the long hours involved and the lack of any subsequent employment plan once the event was over. In spite of the negative comments, all posters commented that working at VANOC was a once in a lifetime opportunity and that they were able to work with amazing people.

Staffing at events can therefore be in-house, outsourced to a professional staffing agency or specialist suppliers, seasonal, casual, temporary or volunteer. Sustainability concerns for event staffing are focussed on ensuring the viability of the event and creating employment and training benefits for local residents.

Mega-events involve enormous numbers of people for a short period of time, as the example of VANOC illustrates. There is a risk that in the race to get the destination ready for the event, sustainable employment practices are not always followed. Greece, for example, resorted to employing three shifts of workers a day to ensure the venues were completed on time for the 2004 Athens Olympic Games, which added to the cost overrun of the event (see Chapter 11). Another mega-event has attracted global media attention for the wrong reasons. The 2022 FIFA World Cup was awarded to Qatar. Qatar is an extremely wealthy country and most of the workers employed to complete the construction of the new stadia for the event are migrant workers operating in conditions which have been described as 'modern day slavery' (Booth, 2014).

Workers are toiling in hot desert conditions, allegedly working 30 days a month for as little as five pounds (GBP) per day. The workers are from developing countries including India, Sri Lanka and Nepal who journalists have described as living in dirty, crowded and dangerous conditions. In Brazil, the 2014 host of the tournament, eight construction workers died while working on the new stadia, which is a higher casualty rate than other recent tournaments, which typically have only 1–2 fatalities. While Qatar reports that no workers have died in the preparation works for the 2022 event, this may simply be because work has not yet begun on the new stadia.

Qatar has a poor record of safety for migrant construction workers and 184 Nepali workers have been reported killed in the past year, with India stating that 450 of their emigrant workers have died in 2012 and 2013. According to the *Guardian* newspaper, Qatar has reported that 882 migrant workers from India and Nepal died in the country in 2012 and 2013 and Nepalese Human Rights campaigners claim that almost every day a Nepali worker dies (see Pattisson, 2014). This has generated negative publicity for the host destination and also the client organisation, FIFA, which has recently introduced environmental and social chapters into its bidding process for countries wanting to hold the tournament. In response, Qatar has announced it will amend its labour laws and FIFA has announced that it will be closely monitoring any claims of mistreatment of the workers.

Challenges for community events

Community events often have no paid staff at all and rely on local people to give their time voluntarily to organise and run the event. This approach raises questions about the long term sustainability of the event if the main event organisers are unable or unwilling to continue in their role. This happened with Snowfest, a community event organised in the early 2000s in New South Wales (Davies, 2011). The event ran for three years but in 2004 the two leaders who had driven the event were unable to continue for various reasons and the event closed. An additional reason given at the time was also that the event grew too large for the local community to manage (ABC News, 2004).

The example of Snowfest raises two sustainability challenges for community events. Firstly, there is rarely a succession plan in place to run the event if the original leaders are unable to continue in their role. Secondly, the size of the event needs to be managed. If an event grows too big, it can become too difficult to organise and outgrows its community. In terms of succession planning, successful community events can be taken over either by government or a professional event manager. The challenge here is to ensure that the event is transferred before the community event organisers burn out and also to ensure that the event does not substantially change in meaning and lose its connection to the local community.

Volunteers and sustainable events

Events and festivals are heavily dependent on volunteer labour. Mega-events such as the Olympic Games involve enormous numbers of volunteers, with the London 2012 Olympics recruiting upwards of 70,000 individuals from 240,000 applicants for their various volunteer programmes (Smith et al., 2014). Smaller events may involve fewer volunteers in number but they would still not be able to go ahead without their volunteer support. Many community events are entirely volunteer-run, which raises specific challenges addressed above.

Where do these volunteers come from? Why are they giving up their free time to support the event and how should volunteers be managed? Studies show that volunteers are attracted to specific events. For example, they may want to volunteer at a golf tournament because they are keen golfers. They may also be attracted to volunteer at an event because it is prestigious in the case of a one-off mega-event, because it gives them access to the performers, so that they can attend the event for free or because they are looking for experience to further a career in event management. Various researchers have sought to develop scales for examining the motivation of event volunteers. The most widely used is the Special Event Volunteer Motivation Scale (SEVMS), which was developed by a group of Canadian researchers (Farrell et al., 1998). They identified four groups of motives for event volunteers. The first two are:

- Purposive (contribution to the community and event, linked to altruism)
- Solidary motives (social interaction and personal development)

Two additional motives were identified, which are specific to the event context:

- External traditions (external obligations linked to extrinsic motivations)
- Commitments (fulfilling obligations to the event or community)

These last two were later combined as material motives by the SEVMS team (Johnston et al., 1999/2000). As can be seen, event volunteer motivation is complex and ideally event managers should seek to identify each volunteer's individual motives and assign them a role which will meet this. However, when a volunteer manager is recruiting 70,000 volunteers, this is just not feasible.

Volunteer labour is not free. Event volunteers need to be recruited, trained, supervised and rewarded properly, for example by ensuring that their out of pocket expenses such as travel are reimbursed. This is important as otherwise the event is at risk of exploiting the volunteers' goodwill. At a community event, where everyone is a volunteer, the volunteer programme may be much more informal with no expenses available. However, at any event which is organised by paid staff, the volunteer programme needs to be properly managed. The risk of exploitation is greatest at a commercial event, where the volunteers are contributing to the event organisers' profit margin. An example of where volunteers may be involved in a commercial event is a music festival, where people can volunteer as stewards in return for free entry to the event.

Management of event volunteer programmes

There are several ways in which event volunteers can be organised. Most event management texts, which provide advice on how to manage volunteers, advocate the programme management approach. This is the most widely used approach for event volunteer programmes and involves treating the volunteers largely as unpaid staff, replicating typical human resource management processes (Holmes and Smith, 2009). The volunteer programme is normally managed in-house by either a paid or voluntary coordinator.

1 First of all the event organisers need to identify how many volunteers they need and what skills will be required.

2 Next, they should develop a role description for each of the different roles needed for the event.
3 The next stage is recruitment and selection. This should be as simple as possible but ideally will involve meeting each volunteer (individually or as a group) and identifying their suitability for the different roles.

Good volunteer management tries to match the volunteer's interests and skills with the appropriate role. The volunteers will need training prior to and supervision during the event. They should also be provided with refreshments, breaks and travel expenses depending on the event's resources. The event organisers could offer additional rewards such as a uniform (this could just be a t-shirt with a logo) and recognition in the form of a special and public thank you at the end of the event and/or a thank you party.

However, there are alternative ways of managing event volunteer programs. These include:

Outsourcing

While events can outsource their paid staff requirements, many events also outsource their volunteer needs. Event organisers recruit local sport, community or special interest groups who then recruit volunteers from among their members. The volunteers can be directly managed by the event organisers or their group can be given responsibility for a specific task, which they manage among themselves. Typically, the group will be given a donation by the event organisers. The advantages for the event organisers is that they save time and funds on recruiting and managing the volunteers. The disadvantage is the loss of direct control, which is less of a risk with unskilled, simple tasks. For example, at the Busselton Ironman contest in Western Australia, the car parking was organised by the local Lions Club, a not-for-profit community group.

Box 9.2 Establishing a volunteer programme for the Commonwealth Heads of Government Meeting, Perth 2011

In October 2011, Perth, Western Australia, hosted the Commonwealth Heads of Government Meeting (CHOGM), a biennial gathering of heads of government from all Commonwealth nations. The state peak body for volunteering, Volunteering WA, was charged with recruiting, training and managing the 500 volunteers needed for the event in partnership with the Australian Government's Department of Prime Minister and Cabinet CHOGM 2011 Taskforce. Volunteering WA advises volunteer organisations on good practice in volunteer management so it was essential that their own programme was exemplary.

The CHOGM 2011 Volunteer Program was launched in April 2011 to generate publicity for the programme and assist with recruitment. Volunteers were needed for a range of roles including drivers, transport officers and venue officers. Applications opened in May and 1,152 applications were lodged online. Over a period of five weeks, the team spent 300 hours interviewing 538 potential volunteers.

A team of ten volunteer interns were also recruited to assist with the management of the programme, many being recruited from a university event management programme.

The nature of the event meant that all volunteers needed to undergo rigorous security checks by both Federal and State Government agencies. The volunteers also received specialised training which included 'volunteers rights and responsibilities, uniforms, transport, basic logistics, venues, protocols, OHS, cultural awareness, incident management, personal grooming, volunteer insurance, out of pocket expenses, security, media and communications, customer service and delegate relations' (Volunteering WA, 2012).

Membership management

The membership management approach focusses on meeting the volunteers' expectations and matching tasks to these (Meijs and Karr, 2004). It is an alternative method for developing a volunteer programme, which takes a bottom up approach to designing and assigning volunteer roles. It is most appropriate for an all-volunteer community event and is generally more work-intensive for the volunteers.

Bring your own

Some events require participants to provide a volunteer to help stage and clear up after the event. This is common in equestrian events. The participant can choose to do the volunteering themselves or nominate a family member or support team. Newer, amateur participants are most likely to nominate themselves, whereas more established competitors will be able to nominate a member of their support team.

Creating a pool of event volunteers

Destinations which host a lot of events can establish a pool of trained and experienced event volunteers. This is similar to commercial companies that supply event staff but is not run for profit. This is a relatively unique concept, which has formed part of the volunteer legacies of mega-events. London Borough of Newham established a pool of event volunteers to support the London Olympic bid in 2004 (Nichols, 2009). The aim was to create a volunteering legacy for the borough, which would continue after the Games. Newham Volunteers recruited and trained volunteers, who then selected which local events they want to volunteer for. The programme gave the volunteers complete flexibility and they could volunteer as often or as little as they chose.

Newham Volunteers provided induction and training for new volunteers as well as optional career development advice. Newham Volunteers worked with event managers to manage their expectations of the volunteers and to encourage good practice in volunteer management. Newham Volunteers continues to operate following the Olympic Games (http://www.activenewham.org.uk/volunteering) and is not solely focussed on events. Volunteers can be placed with any community organisation.

The employment and employability legacies

Creating a legacy, which outlasts the immediate event is important for mega-events. Indeed, it is a requirement of bid documents that candidate cities or countries outline their proposed legacy for the event (see Chapters 11 and 12). While events can create direct employment before and during the event, creating both an employability and a volunteering legacy are frequently cited as potential benefits from hosting the event.

An employability legacy involves using the event as an opportunity to train the workforce within the destination so that they can gain employment both during the event and afterwards. This can link to a broader events strategy where the destination markets itself after the major event as having increased capacity to host subsequent events in terms of facilities, infrastructure and workforce. Queensland's legacy plan for the 2018 Commonwealth Games, which will take place on the Gold Coast in Australia, includes the statement:

'People from the Gold Coast and throughout Queensland will have a chance to learn new skills and gain valuable practical experience by supporting GC2018 and related activities through our pre-volunteering program' (State of Queensland, 2013: 14). The document also states that the training will upskill and grow the workforce, which will be needed due to increased demand for tourism businesses resulting from the event.

Box 9.2 and the case study below provide evidence of how events can lead to a volunteer legacy. However, what about paid jobs? As we noted above, events typically provide short term employment but mega-event organisers make big claims about the employment potential of the event. What happens in reality? The 2012 London Olympics took place in a deprived area of London's East End, which experienced myriad social problems including high unemployment, particularly for young people. Typically, the people most likely to be employed on Olympic projects are those who are already skilled and in work (Minnaert, 2014). However, the UK Government promised that the Games would create 20,000 jobs for local residents. Yet, local people were only able to access 9,700 of these jobs (Ali, 2013).

Minnaert (2014) provides a cautionary analysis of the 2012 London Olympic Games employment legacy plans, noting that the direct jobs created by the event were small in number in construction and very short term in other sectors. Two legacy employability projects have failed to deliver results including the 2012 Employment Legacy project and the Host Borough Skills and Employment project, which were both set up to leverage off the event and create longer term employment across London and specifically in six of the London boroughs closest to the Olympic site (Donovan, 2013). Together both projects cost GBP19.5 million. Part of the problem has been that the projects were too late in being established. For example, the 2012 Employment Legacy project sought to create employment during and after the Games but by the time it was launched in 2011, many contractors had already appointed their staff. Contrast this with Newham Volunteers, which began operations in 2004.

Further problems identified with the 2012 Employment Legacy scheme include the challenge of reaching the target group – unemployment and low-skilled workers from diverse ethnic backgrounds – and also a payment by results model. The model pays the contractor a bonus for keeping staff in employment for 12 months. The tough economic conditions make this model extremely difficult and the 12 month figure has been revised to 6 months.

How can a mega-event be leveraged to create sustainable employment opportunities post-event? To a certain extent this will depend on the local economy of the event location. Event employment legacies often involve building a capacity for hosting future events. This approach has been successful in Glasgow, which has hosted various major events but it is not always realistic. A successful employment legacy is frequently related to the regeneration associated with a mega-event. For example, Barcelona's regeneration for the 1992 Olympic Games involved building additional rail services. London's regeneration included building a new shopping centre, which has created more employment in nearby boroughs. It is also clear that the employment legacy needs to be part of the overall event planning, rather than leaving it to the last minute.

Box 9.3 Glasgow 2014's employability legacy

Glasgow's employability legacy from the 2014 Commonwealth Games is only just beginning. An analysis of Glasgow's legacy notes that there are a number of programmes designed to increase employment during and after the event. Before and during the Games, the organising committee has employed 1,100 staff. Construction and refurbishment of the venues and athlete's village has created approximately 1,000 jobs per annum in the six years leading up to the event. As venues are constructed they provide employment for their operation and lead to job creation in other sectors such as food and beverage and security.

Employability projects for the future include:

- Legacy 2014 Young Person's Fund, launched in 2012 by the Scottish Government, which aims to provide employment for 1,500 young people at events which Scotland will host in the future.
- Skills Development Scotland is providing incentives to employers to offer apprenticeships to 16–19 year olds in sports and events-related areas.
- Glasgow City Council has included a clause in Games-related contracts, requiring that the contractor employs at least 10 per cent of their staff locally.

It will be interesting to revisit these programmes in the future to evaluate their short term and longer term outcomes.

Source: Scottish Government Social Research, 2012

Chapter summary

This chapter has examined staffing issues within events and how these related to sustainability. Three themes emerged in this chapter. The first theme is about how staffing models can be developed which ensure that events are economically viable. This means that events need to be able to draw on large numbers of temporary and casual workers or volunteers to be able to stage the event. This is typically achieved either by using an event staffing agency or volunteers. The primary concern within this theme is the viability of the event and little consideration is given to what happens to the paid workers after the event.

Volunteer management is itself a sub-theme and there are a range of issues which event organisers need to manage. The key concern is to avoid exploiting volunteers. Volunteers need to be properly trained, managed and rewarded. Volunteers are not free labour and just because they are not being paid, does not mean that a volunteer programme should not be properly resourced or rewarded in non-pecuniary ways.

The second theme focusses on how events – particularly mega-events – can have questionable staffing practices in the urgency to deliver the event on time and within the budget. Two examples were discussed – one which added to the event's cost and one which clearly exploited the workers. The third theme examines how mega-events link staffing to longer-term legacy benefits for the resident population. This last theme uses examples to illustrate how efforts to create more sustainable approaches to event staffing are challenging and queries whether legacy plans are unrealistic given the economic and time pressures to deliver the event. This is explored further in Chapters 11 and 12.

Learning activities

1   What would be the most appropriate staffing model for:
    o   A two-day annual gourmet food and wine festival?
    o   An annual industry conference organised by a professional conference organiser and held in a dedicated convention centre?
    o   An annual community arts festival held in public parks and buildings?
2   Draw up a plan for recruiting volunteers to assist at a university open day event.
3   Compare and contrast the employability legacy plans for the London 2012 Olympic Games and the Glasgow 2014 Commonwealth Games.

Case study: Manchester Event Volunteers

Manchester hosted the XVII Commonwealth Games in 2002 and a major part of the event was to secure a positive and longer-lasting economic and social legacy for the city, with the event venues located in East Manchester, a deprived part of the city. The legacy programme involved a number of event-themed projects including the Manchester Pre-Volunteer programme (PVP). While mega-events have involved increasing numbers of volunteers, these are typically recruited and trained specifically for the event itself. The Manchester PVP sought to target individuals from disadvantaged groups who would be unlikely to either apply or be selected in the competitive recruitment associated with a mega-event volunteer programme. The PVP provided these individuals with accredited training and volunteer experience which would prepare them to volunteer at the Commonwealth Games.

Participants were recruited through a series of group and then one-to-one meetings in locations around the Greater Manchester area. The project targeted people from disadvantaged areas as well as the long-term unemployed, people with disabilities and people from minority ethnic backgrounds. A team from colleges across the region designed an Event Volunteering study programme, which was delivered in two courses of 30 hours each. As well as preparing the volunteers for the event, the two courses were designed to promote further training opportunities to participants.

A total of 2,134 individuals completed one or both of the courses. Participants who completed both training programmes could apply to volunteer at the Commonwealth Games and 700 PVP graduates did so. A PVP project team provided ongoing support to these volunteers throughout the event. Benefits from the programme included 160 PVP graduates reporting that they found paid employment as a result of the programme. Graduates also reported increased confidence and raised aspirations. The PVP held a graduation ceremony for participants to celebrate their achievements.

The longer term legacy of the PVP is Manchester Event Volunteers (MEV). It is open to all volunteers, not just those from disadvantaged groups, and provides an ongoing broker service for event managers and a means for individuals to become involved in their community. The majority of MEV volunteers are aged over 60 years old and retired. However, MEV continues to offer participants advice on job opportunities, preparing CVs and for job interviews, and offers support during periods of unemployment.

Manchester Event Volunteers faces a number of challenges. It is under pressure from funding cuts to Manchester City Council and has had its staff reduced from three to one person. There is no formal link between the city council's in-house events unit, which runs a number of events around the city each year and MEV. The nature of MEV's funding and remit means that it is limited in recruiting volunteers from within the Greater Manchester boundary. The success of the PVP was attributed to early planning and encouragement of training outside of a formal education setting. The volunteer team was also quick to take advantage of the brief period (estimated at five weeks) of euphoria following the event.

Source: Nichols and Ralston, 2011

Discussion questions

1 Why is it more difficult to attract people from disadvantaged backgrounds to volunteer?
2 Look at the Facebook page for Manchester Event Volunteers – what volunteer legacy has the 2002 Commonwealth Games PVP programme created for Manchester?
3 What are the challenges for maintaining a program such as MEV in the long term?

Further reading and online resources

Baum, T., Deery, M., Hanlon, C., Lockstone, L. and Smith, K. (2009). *People and work in events and conventions: a research perspective.* Wallingford: CABI.
Manchester Event Volunteers. http://www.facebook.com/mevofficial [accessed 23 February, 2014].

References

ABC News (2004). Hopes melt away for Snowfest. Available online at http://www.abc.net.au/news/2004-07-05/hopes-melt-away-for-snowfest/2003920 [accessed 15 November, 2014].

Ali, R. (2013). London Olympics has failed to bring jobs to London's East End. *The Guardian*, 28 January, available online at http://www.theguardian.com/commentisfree/2013/jan/27/olympic-legacy-failed-jobs-london [accessed 27 November, 2014].

Arcodia, C. (2009). Event management employment in Australia: a nationwide investigation of labour trends in Australian event management. In Baum, T., Deery, M., Hanlon, C., Lockstone, L. and Smith, K. (Eds), *People and work in events and conventions: a research perspective*. Wallingford: CABI, pp. 17–25.

Booth, R. (2014). FIFA: we will monitor Qatar's treatment of migrant World Cup workers closely. *The Guardian*, 30 July. Available online at http://www.theguardian.com/global-development/2014/jul/30/fifa-monitor-qatar-treatment-migrant-world-cup-workers-closely [accessed 20 November, 2014].

Davies, A. (2011). Local leadership and rural renewal through festival fun: the case of Snowfest. In Gibson, C. and Connell, J. (Eds) *Festival places: revitalising rural Australia*, Bristol: Channel View Publications, pp. 61–73.

DCMS (2002). *Creative industries factfile*. London: Department of Culture, Media and Sport.

Donovan, T. (2013). Mayor missed long-term Olympic jobs targets, says report. *The Guardian*, 19 July. Available online at http://www.bbc.com/news/uk-england-london-23371731 [accessed 19 November, 2014].

Farrell, J., Johnston, M. and Twynam, D. (1998). Volunteer motivation, satisfaction and management at an elite sporting competition. *Journal of Sport Management*, 12, 288–300.

Glassdoor (2014). Online job reviews site. Available at http://www.glassdoor.com.au/Reviews/vancouver-winter-olympics-reviews-SRCH_KE0,25.htm [accessed 27 November, 2014].

Hanlon, C. and Jago, L. (2009). Managing pulsating major sporting event organizations. In Baum, T., Deery, M., Hanlon, C., Lockstone, L. and Smith, K. (Eds), *People and work in events and conventions: a research perspective*. Wallingford: CABI, pp. 93–107.

Holmes, K. and Smith, K. (Eds) (2009). *Managing volunteers in tourism: attractions, destinations, and events*. Oxford: Routledge.

Johnston, M., Twynam, D., and Farrell, J. (1999/2000). Motivation and satisfaction of event volunteers for a major youth organisation. *Leisure/Loisir*, 24 (1/2), 161–77.

McCabe, V. (2008). Strategies for career planning and development in the convention and exhibition industry in Australia. *International Journal of Hospitality Management*, 27 (2), 222–31.

Mair, J. (2009). The events industry: the employment context. In Baum, T., Deery, M., Hanlon, C., Lockstone, L. and Smith, K. (Eds), *People and work in events and conventions: a research perspective*. Wallingford: CABI, pp. 3–16.

Meijs, L. and Karr, L. (2004). Managing volunteers in different settings: membership and program management. In Stebbins, R. and Graham, M. (Eds), *Volunteering as leisure/leisure as volunteering: an international assessment*. Wallingford: CABI, pp. 177–93.

Minnaert, L. (2014). Making the Olympics work: interpreting diversity and inclusivity in employment and skills development pre-London 2012. *Contemporary Social Science*, 9 (2), 196–209.

Nichols, G. (2009). Newham Volunteers, United Kingdom: developing a pool of event volunteers as part of a mega event legacy. In Holmes, K. and Smith, K. (Eds), *Managing volunteers in tourism: attractions, destinations, and events*. Oxford: Routledge, pp. 225–35.

Nichols, G. and Ralston, R. (2011). Manchester Event Volunteers: a legacy and a role model. Available at http://www.shef.ac.uk/polopoly_fs/1.227269!/file/MEV_2012_with_cover.pdf [accessed 20 November, 2014].

Pattisson, P. (2014). Qatar should not hold World Cup, say relatives of missing human rights workers. *The Guardian*, 5 September. Available online at http://www.theguardian.com/world/2014/sep/05/qatar-world-cup-yuvraj-ghimire-questions-human-rights-krishna-upadhyaya [accessed 15 November, 2014].

Scottish Government Social Research (2012). *An evaluation of the 2014 Commonwealth Games Legacy for Scotland.* Edinburgh: The Scottish Government. Available online at http://www.scotland.gov.uk/Resource/0040/00408160.pdf [accessed 20 November, 2014].

Shirinian, Z. (2014). Sochi 2014 Organising Committee being dissolved. *Inside the Games*, 12 August. Available online at http://www.insidethegames.biz/olympics/winter-olympics/2014/1021835-sochi-2014-organising-committee-being-dissolved [accessed 19 November, 2014].

Smith, K., Baum, T., Holmes, K. and Lockstone-Binney, L. (2014). Introduction to event volunteering. In Smith, K., Lockstone-Binney, L., Holmes, K. and Baum, T. (Eds), *Event volunteering: international perspectives on the event volunteering experience.* London: Routledge, pp. 1–15.

State of Queensland (2013). *Embracing our Games legacy*. Brisbane: State of Queensland. Available online at http://www.dtesb.qld.gov.au/__data/assets/pdf_file/0003/117606/gccg-legacy-strategy.pdf [accessed 19 November, 2014].

Theodoraki, E. (2007). *Olympic event organisation*. London: Routledge.

Volunteering WA (2012). *Volunteering WA 2011 annual report*. Perth: Volunteering WA.

Chapter 10

Risk and crisis management for sustainable events

Learning outcomes

After studying this chapter you should be able to:

- Understand the risk management process
- Identify a range of potential risks faced by event organisers
- Explain how risk is related to sustainability
- Discuss crisis and disaster management for events

Introduction

Whilst it may seem that events are about fun and enjoyment, it is important to remember that many things can go wrong at events (Silvers, 2007). Events are particularly vulnerable to a range of risks. According to Allen et al. (2011), a unique venue, large crowds, new inexperienced staff and volunteers, movement of equipment and general excitement are all a recipe for potential hazards. Event planners have a legal, professional and ethical duty to ensure the safety of the people who attend their events (Hilliard et al., 2011). Risk management is a key part of event planning and an integral part of the larger picture of event strategic management. For an event to continue sustainably, risks must be managed and addressed. Risks can be considered to be any future incident that will negatively impact the event (Allen et al., 2011). Silvers (2007) identifies both what is at risk (people, property, finances, systems, environment and image) as well as some of the risks that events bring (bodily injury, property loss or damage, reduced revenue, reduced capacity or capability, resource availability, increased demand, and possible loss of goodwill or reputation).

Definitions of risk, crisis and disaster management

According to Shone and Parry (2010: 171), 'risk management can be regarded as the mechanism by which we attempt to be aware of those things that can go wrong at an event or venue, and for which we should make plans, or take steps to prevent or mitigate these risks'.

There is an international standard on risk management – ISO 31000. This outlines the steps that event organisers should be taking in order to manage and minimise risk. 'Risk management should be embedded in all the organisation's practices and processes in a way that is relevant, effective and efficient. The risk management process should become part of, and not separate from, those organisational processes' (AS/NZS ISO 31000 2009: 20).

The terms 'crisis' and 'disaster' are often used interchangeably in the media and indeed in some academic circles. However, a distinction has been made (Faulkner, 2001: 136) with 'disaster' referring to 'a situation where an enterprise or a destination is confronted with sudden unpredictable catastrophic changes over which it has little control'. The definition of 'crisis' is on the other hand is 'a situation where the root cause of an event is, to some extent, self-inflicted through such problems as inept management structures and practices or a failure to adapt to change' (Faulkner, 2001). In this chapter, the term risk management will be used to cover all types of risk, crisis and disaster.

All the various parts of an event's organisation are subject to a range of risks, and it is important to consider each area when assessing and managing risks. Berlonghi (1990) suggests that there are six key sub-sectors of event organisation that carry specific risks and that should be included in risk assessment. These are shown in Table 10.1.

Types of risk

The types of risks that event planners have to plan for include economic risks, performance risks, psychological risks, legal risks and physical risks (Shone and Parry, 2010).

Table 10.1 Areas of event risk

Event organisation sub-sector	Issues to consider
Administration	Contracts must be in place and carefully checked. Permits and licences must be obtained
Marketing and public relations	The marketing and promotions department must consider the risks associated with the event and make sure that these are not ignored
Health and safety	Food hygiene Sanitation Water provision
Crowd management	Managing crowd flow Managing noise control
Security	Managing safety of all attendees, suppliers, organisers, volunteers and any other people at the event site Managing security of valuable equipment and facilities Liaising with police, fire, ambulance and other agencies and organisations
Transport	Deliveries of equipment and supplies Parking and shuttle bus services Public transport safety Managing car and pedestrian traffic on site

Sources: Adapted from Berlonghi,1990 and Allen et al., 2011

These include risks to the organisers, to the participants, to the venue or destination and risks to the continued sustainability of the event. A further category, disaster, can also be added.

- *Economic risks* – These include such issues as financial losses, lack of sponsorship, lack of other financial support and failure to pay suppliers or performers.
- *Performance risks* – These would relate to problems with the performance of the event such as performers failing to turn up, competitors failing to turn up, inclement weather preventing the event from running and technological failure.
- *Psychological risks* – These risks have more to do with the location or venue of the event having a poor reputation or image, which may dissuade people from attending.
- *Legal risks* – This covers issues such as licensing laws for the sale of alcohol, food handling regulations, entertainment and performance licences, insurance and contractual arrangements with suppliers.
- *Physical risks* – These risks involve danger to the public, attendees, organisers or participants, crowd management, alcohol sales management, health and safety issues, hygiene and sanitation, crime, drug and alcohol abuse, anti-social behaviour and security problems.

● *Risk of disaster* – These risks are those which are unusual, unlikely and unforseen. These could include terrorism and unpredictable natural disasters such as earthquakes, extreme weather and flooding.

Box 10.1 Economic risks: the collapse of Peats Ridge Festival

Peats Ridge Music Festival was created with the aim of showcasing best practice for environmental sustainability by a large festival. It took place annually from 2004 to 2013 in the Glenworth Valley north of Sydney, Australia. However, by 2013 it was clear that the festival was no longer financially viable (Taylor, 2013). The reasons for this collapse remain uncertain, although it appears that the festival simply did not generate enough income to cover its costs in 2012 (Music Feed, 2013). The collapse of the festival led to hundreds of performers and production crew being unpaid. The debts of the festival were rumoured to be over AU$1 million (GBP 580,000), with one particular band, the John Butler Trio, owed AU$95,000 (GBP 56,000) (Music Feed, 2013). The auditors were called in and attempts made to pay all creditors (Taylor, 2013). However, there are still some question marks over the collapse of the festival, and the Festival Director has even been accused of embezzling funds, although there has been no proof of this (Music Feed, 2013). This case highlights the financial difficulties associated with running a large festival, and shows how a previously successful event can fail after only one year of less than sufficient revenue.

Risks and event sustainability

The easiest way to understand the links between risks and event sustainability is to consider the ultimate issue of whether an event can sustain, or continue following a major crisis or emergency. For some events, continuing is simply not possible, either for financial reasons (costs of cancellations, extra security, etc.), or because it would be inappropriate to continue (particularly if there have been serious injuries or death). For example, as Rojek (2013) notes, security issues have become more and more prominent since the 2001 terrorist attacks of 9/11, and the costs of the security operations, particularly those for major and mega-events may prove prohibitive to the sustainability of the event. The security bill for the Beijing Olympics was estimated to be US$6.5 billion, and at the London Olympics, security costs were estimated to be GBP563 million (Rojek, 2013). Indeed, the security costs for protecting the athletes at the London Olympics have been estimated at GBP59,000 per competitor (Rojek, 2013).

Other times, it is because the reputation of the event has been tarnished, and attendee perceptions altered. This may result in a drop in the number of tickets sold as well as a reduction in the number of sponsors willing to be associated with the event. These are the results of an event failing to prepare adequately for physical, financial or psychological risks. For other events, perhaps where there has been a breach of legal responsibilities, this too can result in the collapse of the event, a result of a failure to plan for legal risks.

Box 10.2 Death and injury at festivals and events

Sadly, almost every year there are fatalities at events. Some of the best known sporting examples include the Heysel Stadium disaster in 1985 in Belgium and the Hillsborough Disaster in 1989 in the UK. However, disasters have occurred at other event types too, with the Love Parade festival in Germany one of the worst cases.

The Heysel Stadium disaster occurred just before the start of the Juventus versus Liverpool European Cup final. Thirty-nine fans were killed and over 600 injured. The cause appeared to be a group of Liverpool football fans who breached a fence that was separating them from the Juventus fans. The Juventus fans were pushed back into a wall which eventually collapsed. After the disaster, all English football clubs were barred from European football competitions for three years, and 14 Liverpool supporters were found guilty of manslaughter and sentenced to time in prison.

During the Football Association Cup semi-final match between Liverpool and Nottingham Forest, held at the Hillsborough Stadium in Sheffield, 96 people were crushed to death and 766 injured. The cause was dangerous overcrowding outside the ground before kick-off, coupled with the collapse of a crush barrier which resulted in fans falling on top of each other. Initially, the organisers were blamed, however, the Taylor Report, the official inquiry into the incident in 1990, concluded that the police, and their failure to control the fans, was the key cause of the disaster.

The Love Parade festival was a popular festival that took place each year in Duisberg, Germany. As it was a free entry festival, numbers were difficult to judge, but it is estimated that between 250,000 and 1 million people attended the event in 2010, the year of the disaster. The capacity of the venue was only 250,000 people. Only one entrance and exit point (a tunnel) was provided to the attendees, and police closed off one end of the tunnel and asked those in the tunnel to turn back. However, this message did not get through to those at the beginning of the tunnel. As a result, 21 people died and more than 500 were injured. The cause of the disaster and exactly who should bear the responsibility for it have not yet been ascertained.

There are of course other links between risk and sustainability, and one example is the risk associated with a changing climate. The impacts of climate change are likely to intensify in the coming decades, including the potential for more frequent and more severe weather events (Stocker et al., 2013). The travel and tourism industry, and by extension, the events industry is particularly vulnerable to changes in climate and impacts such as increased global temperatures, sea-level rise and increasingly intense and frequent storm events, as these are likely to cause significant bio-physical and socio-economic impacts (DeLacy, 2007).

Table 10.2 Events and festivals cancelled due to severe weather

Weather	Event/Festival	Year	Country
Flooding/heavy rain	Sunrise Celebration	2008	UK
	Phnom Penh Water Festival	2011	Cambodia
	Olympic Torch relay	2012	UK
	Sled Island Music Festival	2013	Canada
	Australian Festival of Chamber Music	2014	Australia
Storms/high winds	AFOS Festival of Speed	2010	Asia
	Pukkelpop Festival	2011	Belgium
	Colour Run 5k Road Race	2012	Australia
	Hudson Project Festival	2014	USA
	Boardmasters Festival	2014	UK
Bushfire	Yarra Valley Grape Grazing	2009	Australia
	Cool Summer Festival	2013	Australia

Sources: Morris, 2007; BBC, 2008; Johnson, 2009; AFOS, 2010; Batty, 2011; BBC, 2012; Color Run, 2012; Sled Island Festival, 2013; Snow Reservation Centre, 2013; AFCM, 2014; Agence Presse Kampuchea, 2014; Hudson Project, 2014; Mair, in press; Metro, 2014

In terms of taking action, event organisers and event stakeholders may choose one of three options, similar to those outlined by Dubois and Ceron (2006) for tourism stakeholders. These are characterised as follows (adapted from Mair, 2011):

1 *Wait and see* – since the impacts of climate change are not yet certain, there has been a tendency amongst tourism stakeholders to adopt a waiting game. Event organisers may choose to do the same, although this may simply be postponing the inevitable.
2 *Trust technology and science to cope* – ski resorts are increasingly making artificial snow, beaches threatened with coastal erosion can be maintained with artificial sand. Event organisers may trust to the various technical adaptation options open to them (roofs on venues, new constructions etc.).
3 *Adopt a precautionary approach* – integrate vulnerability assessments into event planning and revise risk management plans to include potential climate change impacts.

However, as yet little research attention has been focussed on the potential issues for events that may result from our changing climate (Mair, 2011). Some limited research suggests that there will be different impacts from climate change on different types of events, and concludes that smaller, community events and larger hallmark events are likely to be most seriously affected by climate change, as they are types of events which rely on specific locations and venues (Mair, 2011). Larger major, and mega-events on the other hand have more ability to move venues, or to implement expensive technical solutions to climate-related issues, such as flood prevention at venues, artificial snow-making at winter sporting events, or moving away from beachside destinations where sea-level rise or storm surges are potential problems.

Risk management process

Given that we are able to identify a wide range of possible risks, some more likely to occur then others, and the range of potential consequences that may result, it is important to put in place a rigorous process to manage these risks should they occur, and to minimise any harm that may be caused to the event, its organisers, its attendees and the general public. There are many reasons for introducing a risk management policy or strategy:

● Organisers have a duty of care to provide safe environment for staff, volunteers, participants and spectators
● Risk management can protect the event owner and partners from legal action, civil claims and law suits
● Risk management is often required to comply with legal and insurance requirements
● Risk management helps to protect the reputation of the event

According to Allen et al. (2011), the process for risk management involves five stages. These are:

1　Establish the context
2　Identify the risks
3　Analyse and evaluate the risks
4　Assess options
5　Implement options

1 Establish the context

In order to establish the risk management context, the organisers need to do a scan of their external and internal environments and assess a range of factors. These include the type of event (music festival, sporting event, religious ceremony etc.), the stakeholders (funding bodies, sponsors, suppliers, local government, media etc.) and the general risk environment (any incidents that have occurred in the past, any specific warnings from police or security).

2 Identify the risks

Once the context for the event has been established, the next stage is to identify possible risks that the event may be subject to. For the largest events, a professional event risk analyst may be engaged. However, for most events, identifying risks involves meetings and discussions during which brainstorming sessions take place and a wide range of possible risks is identified. It is important to identify risks specifically – as Allen et al. (2011) point out – 'weather' is not specific enough for the risk management process. Rather, the risk may relate to extreme heat, high winds or heavy rain.

3 Analyse and evaluate the risks

Clearly, some risks are more likely than others. At the same time, some risks are more serious than others. In order to analyse and evaluate risks, it is common practice for event organisers to plot or map their identified risks on a graph, chart or matrix (Shone

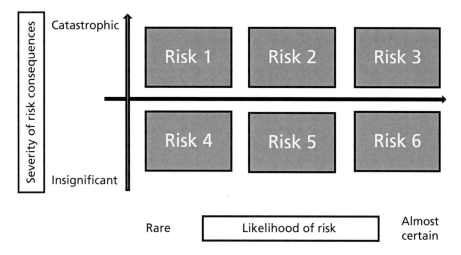

Figure 10.1 Risk matrix for events

and Parry, 2010). There are many risk graphs that can be used, but often they include the likelihood of a risk occurring (from extremely unlikely to extremely likely), and the severity of consequence should the risk occur (from minor to catastrophic) (Figure 10.1).

For example, inclement weather in the shape of some rain showers may be a highly likely risk, but one which would only have minor consequences. However, high winds, heavy rain or flooding may result in damage to equipment or may be dangerous to patrons and therefore would be considered as having severe consequences (Carlsen et al., 2010).

4 Assess options

Assessing the risks in this way will give event planners and organisers a good idea of which risks need most management, and indeed, which risks are too great for the event to bear. It allows event organisers to understand the support that they may need from other services (for example, the emergency services), and which risks they will be able to manage themselves. It also provides the opportunity for organisers to assess which options they have for mitigating risks. For example, heavy rain is problematic for an outdoor event, therefore the risk management plan allows the event organiser to allow for this possibility in advance, and decide in advance what action should be taken if heavy rain is forecast. Further, the risk management plan will assign responsibility for a range of potential occurrences to different staff members or stakeholder groups. Financial risks would be the responsibility of the financial manager. Mitigating risks that may harm the reputation of the event may be the responsibility of the marketing manager, or external advertising or public relations company.

Getz (2013) identifies five strategic options for dealing with risks. These are avoidance, reduction, diffusion, reallocation and insurance. Avoidance as a strategy refers to making changes in the way that the event is planned, managed or staged in order to avoid a particular risk. An example might be moving a festival away from a particular time of the year if inclement weather is likely. Reduction refers to minimising either the likelihood of a risk, or the consequences of it occurring, through better management, training or operations. For example, while misuse of alcohol and drugs may happen during an event, better security procedures and better trained security staff will help to reduce this risk. Diffusion means spreading the risk around many stakeholders, such as ensuring that all contractors and suppliers provide their own insurance cover. Reallocation refers to the process of moving responsibility for a particular risk away from the event organisers, perhaps to a municipal authority, or another regulatory body. Finally, insurance is necessary in all cases, but a good risk management strategy will help to keep the costs of insurance premiums to a minimum.

5 Implement options

Once the risk management plan has been finalised, and all staff and volunteers made aware of it (so that they know their responsibilities in the event of any incidents), the final step is to implement any relevant options at the first sign of a potential risk or hazard. Having a risk management plan in place means that actions taken have been chosen in a considered way as being the best option available under a given set of circumstances. This will help to prevent ad hoc or unplanned reactions to situations as they arise.

Crisis and disaster management for events

Despite the best efforts of event organisers and planners, sometimes things do go wrong. There have been many incidents of accidents, injuries and fatalities at events over the years, and in many cases it seems that there is little that organisers could have done to prevent the risk or to minimise its effects. One of the severest risks (in terms of consequences) is the potential for acts of terrorism. Whilst organisers can take account of the political environment at the time of the event and can plan for stringent security measures, there are some risks that really cannot be managed in advance. When a terrorist attack takes place, the responsibility of the organisers and all the other agencies that they have been liaising with (emergency services, local and state authorities and other stakeholders) is to manage the emergency in accordance with their risk management plan, and this is exactly why risk management plans have to be robust, clear and well-organised.

Box 10.3 Risk of disaster: the Boston Marathon bombing

On 15 April, 2013, two home-made bombs exploded during the Boston Marathon. Three people were killed, including an eight-year-old boy and over 250 were injured (McPhee, 2014). The bombs exploded near the finish line. The bombers were later identified as being two Chechen brothers who were motivated by their extremist Islamic beliefs and who were protesting against US foreign policy. One of the brothers was killed by police when resisting arrest. The trial of the other brother commenced in 2015.

The risk of terrorism at major events has been with us for a long time. In 1972, at the Munich Olympics, Israeli athletes and officials were killed by terrorists (Taylor and Toohey, 2005). The extended media coverage of this tragedy demonstrated to terrorists how they could focus the world's attention. Of course, since then security at events has been tightened, but sport events remain a potential terrorist target (Taylor and Toohey, 2005). Following the September 11 attack in New York, many large events introduced more sophisticated security measures (Allen et al., 2011). Nonetheless, even stringent security measures are not always enough to prevent this kind of attack, particularly in a public place such as the city streets on which a marathon is run.

Chapter summary

This chapter began by emphasising the importance of risk management and introducing the risk management process. It identified a range of potential risks that may be faced by event organisers and discussed the relationship between risk and sustainability. Finally, the chapter examined how event managers and organisers can deal with crisis and disaster management through risk management planning processes.

Learning activities

Using an event that you are familiar with as an example, undertake a risk assessment, create a risk matrix, and identify options for dealing with these risks should they occur.

1   Assess the risk context of the event (consider the type of event, the stakeholders involved and the general risk environment)
2   Brainstorm a range of possible risks that that event may have to face
3   Allocate each of the identified risks to a risk matrix in terms of likelihood of occurrence, and severity of consequence
4   Assess the possible options for reducing or removing the risk

Case study: Risk management at Edinburgh's Hogmanay

Scotland is internationally recognised as the home of Hogmanay (a Scottish word for New Year's Eve). Every year, the city of Edinburgh in Scotland celebrates New Year's Eve with a huge street party named Edinburgh's Hogmanay. This is one of the largest New Year's Eve parties in the world, and has had up to 400,000 attendees in the past, although numbers have been reduced considerably in recent years in order to improve crowd safety at the event. The event was initially unticketed, however, some years back a ticketing system was introduced to limit attendee numbers. Revellers now have to buy a street party pass wristband and must have a street party pass to enter the huge Princes St Edinburgh New Year's Eve party. Princes Street (one of the main streets in Edinburgh city centre) is blocked off at

(Continued)

Case study (continued)

dusk on 31 December in an effort to control numbers. Only those with official passes (wristbands) are allowed entry. Approximately 80,000 people now attend each year (Group 4 Security, 2014). In addition, the street party and associated events are not recommended for those under 16 years of age and anyone under 16 years must be accompanied by an adult over 21 years of age (Edinburgh's Hogmanay, 2014). Despite such large numbers attending, the event is famous for its relaxed party atmosphere, and there are comparatively few issues of disorder.

The event has expanded over the years and now includes a street carnival which runs from 27 December and a huge torchlight procession through the city with massed pipers, a bonfire and fireworks display on 30 December. The main part of the event is held on 31 December and includes a concert, the street party in Princes Street, a ceilidh (Scottish dance) and a fireworks display. A substantial proportion of the visitors each year are not local and so the event facilitates their enjoyment of the New Year in the city centre.

However, New Year in Scotland is mid-winter and there is always a risk of poor weather. Naturally the organisers are aware of this possibility and make every effort to ensure that their plans allow for wintry weather. They also remind visitors to wrap up warmly and to check the weather forecasts before leaving home to attend the event. However, on several occasions over the past decade, the event has had to be cancelled completely. In 2003/2004, the entire event was cancelled due to gale force winds which made both the concert, and particularly the fireworks display, too dangerous to hold. The high winds ripped the awnings and the roof from the stage, and the rain damaged the electrics around the stage area. In addition, the police decided that the high winds would make it too dangerous to set off the fireworks. Thousands of ticket holders were disappointed. The 2006/2007 event was also called off because of poor weather, although a small firework display did proceed.

Naturally there were some losses to local businesses in the short term, however, the greater concern has been for the long term reputation of the event and its ability to continue to attract tourist interest and revenue to the city in the winter holiday season. Headlines such as 'Street party blown away' and 'Weather spoils the party' (BBC, 2007) show the risk to the reputation of the event. In addition, it is likely to become more problematic in the future. Edinburgh City Council has identified climate change, and its attendant risks of disruption and/or cancellation of winter festival and Hogmanay celebrations as a significant risk to tourism and economic development (Edinburgh City Council, 2014).

Discussion questions

1 What practical steps can the city of Edinburgh take to make its Hogmanay events more resistant to inclement weather?
2 How can the city of Edinburgh protect the reputation of its Hogmanay events?
3 Identify and discuss avoidance, reduction, diffusion, reallocation and insurance options for the city of Edinburgh Hogmanay events.

Further reading and online resources

Allen, J., O'Toole, W., Harris, R. and McDonnell, I. (2011). *Festival and special event management*, Milton, QLD: John Wiley and Sons, (Chapter 18, Risk Management).

The original Derby: Shrovetide football in Ashbourne. Video available online at http://www.guardian.co.uk/travel/video/2010/feb/18/uk-peakdistrict-ashbourne-derby-football-shrovetide [accessed 19 November, 2014].

References

AFCM (2014). Australian Festival of Chamber Music Sounds like Paradise concert cancelled. Available online at http://www.afcm.com.au/ [accessed 14 August, 2014].

AFOS (2010). Combined races to mark season finale for GT3 Asia and GT4 Asia Cup. Available online at http://www.afos.com/index.php?option=com_contentandview=articleandid=632:combined-races-to-mark-season-finale-for-gt3-asia-and-gt4-asia-cupandcatid=38:afos-newsandItemid=242 [accessed 20 November, 2014].

Agence Presse Kampuchea (2014). Cambodia to resume Water Festival celebration this year. Available online at http://www.akp.gov.kh/?p=50321 [accessed 25 November, 2014].

Allen, J., O'Toole, W., Harris, R. and McDonnell, I. (2011). *Festival and special event management*. Milton, QLD: John Wiley and Sons.

AS/NZS ISO31000 (2009). *Risk management principles and guidelines*. Sydney, Australia: SAI Global.

Batty, D. (2011). Storm at Belgium's Pukkelpop music festival kills five after stage collapses. *The Guardian*, 19 August. Available online at http://www.guardian.co.uk/world/2011/aug/18/pukkelpop-belgium-festival-killer-storm [accessed 20 November, 2014].

BBC News (2007). Weather spoils Hogmanay parties, 1 January. Available online at http://news.bbc.co.uk/go/pr/fr/-/2/hi/uk_news/scotland/6221557.stm [accessed 24 July, 2014].

BBC News (2008). Festival goers' anger at Sunrise cancellation. Available online at http://www.bbc.co.uk/somerset/content/articles/2008/05/30/sunrisecancelation_feature.shtml [accessed 20 November, 2014].

BBC News (2012). Olympic torch: rain changes torch plans but ballroom finale brightens day, 22 June. Available online at http://www.bbc.co.uk/news/uk-18541486 [accessed 20 November, 2014].

Berlonghi, A. (1990). *The special event risk management manual*. Mansfield, Ohio: Bookmasters.

Carlsen, J., Andersson, T., Ali-Knight, J., Jaeger, K. and Taylor, R. (2010). Festival management innovation and failure. *International Journal of Event and Festival Management*, 1 (2), 120–31.

Color Run (2012). News. Available online at http://thecolorrun.com/australia/gold-coast/ [accessed 20 November, 2014].

DeLacy, T. (2007). *Tourism and climate change: a background paper*. Victoria University, Melbourne: The Centre for Tourism and Services Research.

Dubois, G. and Ceron, J. P. (2006). Tourism and climate change: proposals for a research agenda. *Journal of Sustainable Tourism*, 14 (4), 399–415.

Edinburgh City Council (2014). *Resilient Edinburgh: climate change adaptation framework for Edinburgh 2014–2020.* Edinburgh: Edinburgh City Council. Available online at http://www.edinburgh.gov.uk/info/20029/consultations_and_participation/1063/climate_change_adaptation [accessed 24 July, 2014].

Edinburgh's Hogmanay (2014). Edinburgh's Hogmanay Street Party: buy tickets. Available online at http://www.edinburghshogmanay.com/buy-tickets [accessed 28 July, 2014].

Faulkner, B. (2001). Towards a framework for tourism disaster management. *Tourism Management*, 22 (2), 135–47.

Getz, D. (2013). *Event tourism: concepts, international case studies and research.* Abingdon, Oxon: Routledge.

Group 4 Security (2014). Security at Edinburgh's Hogmanay. Available online at http://www.g4s.uk.com/en-GB/Media%20Centre/Case%20Studies/Event%20security%20solutions/Events%20-%20Hogmanay%202011/ [accessed 24 July, 2014].

Hilliard, T. W., Scott-Halsell, S. and Palakurthi, R. (2011). Core crisis preparedness measures implemented by meeting planners. *Journal of Hospitality Marketing and Management.* 20 (6), 638–60.

Hudson Project (2014). Hudson Project Festival cancelled. Available online at http://sensiblereason.com/hudson-project-festival-canceled/ [accessed 14 August, 2014].

Johnson, M. (2009). Grape grazing festival cancelled after bushfires. *The Age* (online edition), 10 February. Available online at http://www.theage.com.au/national/grape-grazing-festival-cancelled-after-bushfires-20090210-82wk.html [accessed 25 November, 2014].

Mair, J. (2011). Events and climate change: an Australian perspective. *International Journal of Event and Festival Management*, 2 (3), 245–53.

Mair, J. (in press). Events and climate change: an Asia-Pacific perspective. In Ruhanen, L. (Ed). *Tourism's response to climate change: an examination of tourism related initiatives in Asia and the Pacific.* Madrid, Spain: United Nations World Tourism Organization (UNWTO).

McPhee, M. (2014). Trial date set for accused Boston marathon bomber. ABC News, 12 February. Available online at http://abcnews.go.com/Blotter/trial-date-set-accused-boston-marathon-bomber/story?id=22478389 [accessed 21 May, 2014].

Metro (2014). Bastille gutted as Boardmaster's Festival cancelled. Available online at http://metro.co.uk/2014/08/10/bastille-gutted-as-boardmasters-festival-cancelled-due-to-hurricane-bertha-4827650/ [accessed 14 August, 2014].

Morris, S. (2007). Edinburgh's Hogmanay party falls foul of atrocious weather as 2007 enters with a blast. *The Guardian*, 1 January. Available online at http://www.guardian.co.uk/uk/2007/jan/01/topstories3.mainsection [accessed 20 November, 2014].

Music Feed (2013). Peats Ridge director Matt Grant accused of embezzling $1.3 million. Available online at http://musicfeeds.com.au/news/peats-ridge-director-matt-grant-accused-of-embezzling-1-3-million/ [accessed 24 July, 2014].

Rojek, C. (2013). Event management. In Blackshaw, T. (Ed.), *Routledge handbook of leisure studies*. Abingdon, Oxon: Routledge, pp. 493–505.

Shone, A. and Parry, B. (2010). *Successful event management: a practical handbook.* Andover, Hampshire: Cengage Publishing.

Silvers, J. R. (2007). *Risk management for meetings and events.* Abingdon, Oxon: Routledge.

Sled Island Festival (2013). Sled Island Festival cancellation. Available online at http://www.sledisland.com/slog/2013/6/21/sled-island-2013-cancellation [accessed 20 November, 2014].

Snow Reservation Centre (2013). Cool Summer Festival Cancelled. Available at http://snowreservations.com.au/news/cool-summer-festival-2013-cancelled [accessed 25 November, 2014].

Stocker, T. F., Qin, D., Plattner, G. K., Tignor, M., Allen, S. K., Boschung, J. and Vasconcellos de Menezes, V. (2013). *Climate change 2013. The physical science basis. Working Group I contribution to the Fifth Assessment Report of the Intergovernmental Panel on climate change: abstract for decision-makers*. Geneva, Switzerland: Intergovernmental Panel on Climate Change.

Taylor, A. (2013). Artists chase money from failed Peats Ridge Festival. *The Newcastle Herald* (online edition), 1 February. Available online at http://www.theherald.com.au/story/1273237/artists-chase-money-from-failed-peats-ridge-festival/ [accessed 25 November, 2014].

Taylor, T. and Toohey, K. (2005). Impacts of terrorism-related safety and security measures at a major sport event. *Event Management*, 9 (4), 199–209.

Chapter 11

The challenge of creating sustainable event legacies

Learning outcomes

After studying this chapter you should be able to:

- Understand what is meant by event legacies
- Analyse the legacies of past events
- Examine the challenge of developing sustainable event legacies
- Identify the implications from positive and negative legacies
- Identify lessons for future event legacy planning

Introduction

The enormous cost of mega-events, the long lead-in time and the lasting impact of the associated construction works means that legacy planning is an increasingly important part of bidding for and hosting a sustainable mega-event. A legacy is the longer-term outcomes or impacts associated with hosting any event. Positive legacies can include physical changes to the destination resulting from regeneration projects such as new venues or infrastructure; economic changes due to inward investment attracted by the event or upskilling of the local population resulting from training for the event; and psychological changes such as an increased sense of community and belonging as a result of being part of the event. This chapter follows on from Chapter 4 as urban regeneration is often a major part of event legacies.

In this chapter, the first of two about creating sustainable event legacies, we examine failed legacies and why they fail. By understanding what we should avoid, we can develop good practice for future event legacy planning and this is presented in Chapter 12. Legacy planning has become increasingly important since the cost of hosting mega-events has risen. While the term 'legacy' has long been associated with major events, the growing use of the term 'legacy' in Olympic bid documents has been in evidence since the 1980s. This is reflected in academic research on event legacies, which can be dated from 1992 (Preuss, 2007).

Failed or unsustainable legacies are bad for the host destination but also provide poor media coverage for the organising body, such as the International Olympic Committee (IOC), who need future destinations to bid to host their event. The International Olympic Committee in particular has directed attention on to the event legacy and rule 2, article 14 of the Olympic Charter states that an important role of the IOC is 'to promote a positive legacy from the Olympic Games to the host cities and host countries' (International Olympic Committee, 2013).

The challenges (or politics) of legacy planning

Firstly, the term 'legacy' is poorly defined and understood (Preuss, 2007). While the IOC has developed an understanding of what a planned legacy means, legacies can also be unplanned. Mega-events have a range of impacts, good and bad and these are not all planned by the organising committee, nor is the committee able to control all of these. The term 'legacy' must therefore be used with care and an awareness of its many meanings. Preuss argues that an event legacy can be presented as a three-dimensional cube with the following dimensions:

1 Planned/unplanned
2 Tangible/intangible
3 Positive/negative

Most mega-event organising committees focus on the planned, tangible and positive legacies.

Bidding for and hosting a mega-event is a political process. This is also the case for the associated legacy claims made during the bid and planning process for a mega-event. Often legacy claims sound like newspaper headlines, making broad claims rather than realistic strategies. While a mega-event may involve a whole nation, who may well be paying for it, legacies are felt most acutely immediately after the event and in close proximity to the venues (Cornelissen et al., 2011). The 2002 Manchester Commonwealth Games are often cited as an example of a successful legacy and Manchester City Council focussed on bringing benefits to the Greater Manchester area but specifically the deprived area of East Manchester, where the event was held.

Bramwell (1997) provides an early mega-event legacy analysis in his review of the 1991 Sheffield World Student Games. Sheffield City Council in the UK bid to host the World Student Games, the first mega-event to be held in the city at a time of social, economic and political change. The city was transitioning from an industrial to a service-based economy, the national government was promoting tourism as a means to redress industrial decline and cities across Europe were using flagship attractions to revitalise their centres. However, there was no formal planning prior to the event to link the event outcomes to any longer-term development strategy for the city. Rather, tourism regeneration plans were drawn up post-event to make use of the investment in new sporting facilities for the event.

More recent events are equally remiss in their longer-term planning. The 2010 Vancouver Winter Olympic Games was keen to deliver a volunteer legacy to the state of British Columbia and the city of Vancouver as a result of their volunteer programme, which trained and recruited 25,000 volunteers to assist at the event. In spite of the legacy claims, the training given to volunteers was focussed on preparing them for specific tasks at the event and no attention was given to how these volunteers might use these skills in other volunteer contexts post-event. Indeed, the Vancouver 2010 volunteer programme may even have reduced the pool of potential volunteers. Volunteering at the event was intense leading to burn out among some volunteers and others did not go back to their pre-event volunteer roles, so displacing rather than growing volunteering (Benson et al., 2014).

Box 11.1 Constraints for creating an employment legacy

Mega-events do create jobs and one sector which benefits from the preparations for the event is construction. However, the construction sector is typically male dominated, with seasonal work and only the large companies can afford to invest in their staff (Minnaert, 2014). Like events, construction firms usually have a small core and hire additional staff as needed. Firms want to reduce the recruitment costs involved in screening and training staff and typically rely on informal recruitment networks such as personal recommendation. The idea of construction as being an avenue through which skills, training and employment can be delivered to disadvantaged individuals, particularly those who are typically under-represented in the industry such as women and people with disabilities is perhaps unrealistic, particularly given the time pressure within which Olympic construction projects need to be completed.

What happens when legacy plans fail?

When legacy plans fail to materialise or there is a negative legacy for the destination following a major event, there are implications. Since both mega-events and their legacy plans are usually advocated and led by governments, there is the potential for a loss of political support. Various stakeholders such as local residents, businesses and the media can try to hold the government accountable for the failure. The negative outcomes associated with a failed legacy include:

- Economic cost to the community
- A failure to capitalise on the opportunities associated with hosting a mega-event
- Damaging media images of the post-event site
- Loss of political support for the presiding government

Mega-events receive much of their funding from taxation and/or diverting public money from other projects, which may have yielded greater benefit to the local community. Negative media coverage post-event will generate a poor image for the destination. This will only compound the legacy failure. Therefore, the implications of a failed legacy go beyond an immediate political loss for the government, which has failed to deliver on its promises to have wide-reaching and long-serving impacts on the destination and community.

Why do event legacies fail to deliver?

If sustainable legacy planning is a requirement of bid documents and is built into the planning stages for the event, why is it so hard for organising committees and governments to deliver?

The focus is on staging the event

The event itself has a definite start and end date. All of the organisation, venues, infrastructure and staff must be ready to go by the start of the event. The ramifications for failing to achieve this under the spotlight of global media are huge. This means that event organisers are focussed on the event and plans for the future can be an afterthought, something to worry about after the event has happened. Of course, by then it can be too late to consider alternative uses for an athlete's village, for example.

There is a lack of long-term legacy planning

A legacy, by definition, lasts for a long time. It is not simply what happens to the event site in the immediate aftermath of the event but how is it continued to be used for the next 20 years. Legacy planning is still in its infancy, taking over from regeneration planning as the proposed outcome for mega-events since the 2000s (Smith, 2012). Since most commentators agree that a legacy needs to be planned on the basis of a 20 year timeframe before it can be evaluated properly and that mega-events are just not that common and clearly situated with their unique economic, political and social contexts, there are few examples of good practice for host destinations to learn from.

After the event, the funding disappears

We have already established that mega-events are expensive and often run over budget. Given the pressure to deliver the event on time, money set aside for the legacy can end up being spent on the actual event. As mega-events frequently overrun their budget – Flyvbjerg and Stewart (2012) state that every Olympics Games since 1960 has overspent its original budget – the pressure to use up the budget on delivering the event is immense. After the event, it is harder to argue politically for even more money to be spent on the event. Since the event funds have frequently been diverted from other projects, there will also be pressure to prioritise these rather than invest even more in the event. It can take time to diversify venues for other use and even longer for that new use to generate an income and in the meantime they will require significant sums of money for maintenance. Minnaert (2014) analysed programmes designed to create more inclusive employment as part of the London Olympics and found that most programmes were expected to stop after the event, with the private sector to adopt the good practice spontaneously.

The benefits are over-inflated before the event

Given that bidding for mega-events is a competitive process and that legacy planning is part of the bid process, it is no surprise that bid documents can make grand claims about the longer-term benefits for the destination, if it is successful in winning the bid. On a national or local scale, governments need to 'sell' the event to their constituents, who will be paying for the event out of their taxes. Building up the benefits for them and their hometown is a way of gathering their support. Of course, when it becomes apparent that these over-inflated benefits will not be materialising, the event is usually well into the planning stages and it would be even more damaging to pull out. Sometimes, politicians and other event stakeholders simply get carried away in the excitement of the event and end up promising too much.

Regardless of over-inflating the potential benefits, forecasting is an inexact science. It is not surprising therefore that the figures predicted for the 2010 FIFA World Cup in South Africa were not achieved. The event attracted approximately one third fewer tourists than anticipated and generated substantially less tourist revenue – 3.64 billion rand instead of 8.9 billion rand (Cornelisson et al., 2011).

The intended benefits (and legacy) are vague

This is a problem with earlier legacy plans, where event organisers talked in general terms about how an event would place the destination on the tourist map, create jobs, attract visitors and investors and generally benefit the destination. The question is – what jobs, for whom and in what sectors? How will the event attract visitors and investors? From where and to do what? Legacy planning needs to be specific to the destination and the event and also needs to be realistic.

Box 11.2 The Sydney Olympic Park

The legacy plans for the Sydney 2000 Olympic Games have been criticised as being too vague. The plans for the Sydney Olympic Park (SOP) in particular were not well articulated. The park was envisioned as becoming a super sports precinct, a series of parklands for recreation and leisure and an environmental showcase. Yet after the event, the SOP was frequently empty, was only served by public transport to the specially constructed train station during a major event and was losing money. Recreation and leisure use of the SOP did not generate an income, which was needed to maintain the facility. The legacy plan had been vague and assumed rather than planned out (Cashman, 2009).

The SOP needed a plan and nine months after the games closed, the Sydney Olympic Park Authority was formed, with responsibility for developing a masterplan for the SOP's future. The masterplan included mixed-use developments next to the train station such as office space and residential units. This created an in situ community, making use of the facilities as well as a source of income for the longer-term sustainability of the SOP.

Unexpected changes in the global environment

The lead time from bidding for a mega-event, being awarded the event and delivering on the event is a long time. The legacy plans incorporated in the bid document may have been developed in a very different economic, social and political climate to that of the event itself. A recent example is the London 2012 Olympic Games. The event was awarded in 2005 before the Global Financial Crisis, which hit the UK hard during the planning stages. There was also a change in the national government from Labour to a Conservative–Liberal coalition and a change in the Mayor of London from a Labour incumbent to a Conservative.

The original legacy plans included building housing on the Olympic Park in East London. In 2004, the previous London Mayor promised that 50 per cent of the housing built on the Olympic Park would be affordable. This has been reduced to 30 per cent with 1,000 fewer homes being built in total (Donovan, 2014).

Methods of measuring legacies are flawed

The most common methods used for measuring an event's legacy are benchmarking, often used to forecast the legacy during the planning stage, and macro-economic indicators, used in post-hoc event evaluation (Preuss, 2007). Benchmarking against previous events is flawed as all events are unique and therefore so are all legacies. Even the same event hosted in the same city will take place at a different time and within a different economic, political and social context.

Economic indicators as evidence of an event's legacy are flawed. Firstly, they only measure the economic legacy, which provides a very limited picture of the event's outcomes. Secondly, the economic legacy of an event is likely to be relatively small compared to a city or country's overall economy, which makes this hard to track.

Box 11.3 A tourism legacy for the European Capital of Culture (ECoC)

Since 1985, the European Union (EU) has designated a specific European city, or more recently a pair of cities, as the cultural capitals of the EU for that year. Typically there is a lead-in period of 2 to 4 years and the city organises a wide range of cultural events throughout the year. This can extend to developing a city-wide cultural policy and refurbishing or developing new cultural venues. The ECoC is seen as an opportunity to revitalise the cultural landscape of a city and promote it as a place to live and visit. There is evidence that the ECoC events can boost tourism – Glasgow, reported a 50 per cent increase in international tourist arrivals in 1990, its ECoC year, compared with the previous year. However, Antwerp, found that although it enjoyed a boost in tour company brochure coverage in 1993, its ECoC, this went back to normal levels in 1994. Richards (2000) has analysed the impact of the ECoC on tourism and concluded that the largest impact is on day visitors rather than the more lucrative overnight market.

Legacy planning to avoid failure

It is clear that event legacies need to be planned, they will not happen automatically or without intervention. Sustainable legacy planning is an integral part of the planning for any mega-event and needs to be specific. Grand statements about legacy visions are not helpful in delivering results and can be detrimental by setting expectations too high. Sustainable legacy planning also needs to take into account possible unplanned negative legacies as these could easily detract from successful planned projects.

Legacies are complex and multi-faceted. Mega-events are frequently staged in deprived areas or locations within the host city with the aim of using the event to facilitate urban regeneration. The risk of regeneration, as identified in Chapter 4, is that the original residents can be either forcibly removed or priced out of their homes post-event as the area becomes gentrified. The gentrification can be good for tourism but bad for residents. An alternative is to accept that an area such as Stratford in East London, home to the London Olympic Park, is unlikely to become a major tourism drawcard. However, the event can be used to genuinely improve the lives of the people who live there, economically, socially and environmentally. In either example, the event is not able to deliver legacy outcomes to all the event stakeholders.

The Olympic Games is one of the financially riskiest projects for a destination to take on (Flyvbjerg and Stewart, 2012). The enormous pressure to deliver a world-class event in the gaze of the global media means that the event must be delivered at any cost. Hence, Flyvbjerg and Stewart (2012) discuss how an event budget is normally proposed as the maximum amount that can be committed to the project. However, in the case of the Olympic Games, they describe the proposed budget as 'a fictitious minimum that is consistently overspent' (2012: 11). As the expenditure increases, so too do calls for a longer-term outcome for the destination and its residents. However, unless the funds

Table 11.1 Cost overrun of the summer Olympic Games

Olympic games	Host country	Final cost US$ (billion)	% cost overrun
Beijing, 2008	China	40	4
Athens, 2004	Greece	15	60
Sydney, 2000	Australia	3.8	90
Atlanta, 1996	Usa	1.8	147
Barcelona, 1992	Spain	9.4	417

Source: Adapted from Flyvbjerg and Stewart, 2012, Table 1

are spent or committed beforehand, there is no guarantee that there will be anything left after the event for the legacy plans. The cost overruns for the summer Olympic Games, 1992–2008 are presented in Table 11.1.

An interesting point is that there does not appear to be a relationship between a successful event and a successful legacy. The 1996 Atlanta Olympic Games are viewed as having one of the strongest legacies, particularly as the event received considerable sponsorship, which allowed the event to break even. Yet the event itself was marred by transport problems, criticism of the over-commercialisation resulting from the sponsorship and a tragic bombing incident. In contrast, the 2004 Athens Olympic Games (see case study below) are now cited as having a failed legacy in spite of being considered a successful event.

Chapter summary

A key factor highlighted throughout this chapter is the importance of the political, economic and social context in creating a sustainable legacy. The lengthy lead-in time for the event means that there is a very real chance that the environment within which the legacy plans were devised will be quite different from that within which they need to be delivered. Governments change, economic crises and recessions arise, social problems emerge and trends for urban life evolve. Legacy planning needs to take into account the changing world within which the event is taking place.

This chapter has also identified a number of challenges in delivering legacies. There is a need to translate a broad legacy vision into specific programmes. Post-event venue use needs to be specific. Plans need to be realistic. Legacies are long term and have been criticised for failing to deliver immediate benefits. The money has been spent and after the initial euphoria surrounding the event has been forgotten, the media and residents want to see additional outcomes for the destination. Failed legacies make good headlines, when the real outcomes need to be assessed in decades rather than the months or years immediately following the event.

Legacy plans also need to be based on sound research both before and after the event. Before the event, methods can include cost–benefit analyses or feasibility studies but such forecasting techniques are imprecise. Current methods for measuring legacies have limitations but what are the alternatives? How long after the event should governments try to evaluate the legacy? How can the outcomes from the event be distinguished from other factors such as a global recession or economic boom? There remains a challenge of measuring and evaluating legacy outcomes.

Learning activities

1   Design a five-point legacy vision for the 2018 Commonwealth Games, which will be hosted on the Gold Coast, Australia.
2   Using the website for the 2012 London Olympic Park, devise a post-event use for three of the venues.
3   Suggest some ways of measuring the legacy outcomes for a host destination.

Case study: The 2004 Athens Olympic Games legacy

The 2004 Athens Olympic Games have become synonymous with the words 'failed legacy'. The event is most famous for creating white elephants, with new, state of the art sports venues left empty after the event. Post-event, media headlines at significant anniversary dates such as 2008 (the Beijing Olympics), 2012 (the London Olympics) and 2014 (ten years on) have focussed on the empty venues rather than the success of the event itself.

The cost of the Athens Olympics is debated, varying from 6 billion to 9 billion euros (although according to the official report, 8.6 billion euros) and estimated to have overrun by 60 per cent, although this is not unusual for a summer Olympic Games (Flyvbjerg and Stewart, 2012). Since the event, many of the venues have been left decaying and unused. Preparation for the event included construction and refurbishment of 36 venues; a 10,000 capacity Olympic village; the media centre; and a sea-facing restaurant. Some venues are being used, such as the main stadium, which is used by football teams but many are empty. Those that have found uses, did so a number of years after the event took place. Empty venues still incur considerable costs. The post-event maintenance of the venues and security at the site has been estimated at between 15 million and 74 million euros (Kissoudi, 2008).

The event itself was hailed as a success. Early media reports suggested that the venues would never be ready and the International Olympic Committee issued a warning to the organising committee in 2000, leading to claims that the organising committee had wasted three years of their seven year lead-in time. However, in spite of negative media reports leading up to the event, all the venues were ready on time for the games to return to the home of the Olympics. Although the last minute construction meant they had to pay workers for three shifts a day. The event also failed to attract as much sponsorship because major sponsors claimed that the market was too small and so withdrew (Panagiotopoulou, 2014).

A further unanticipated cost was that the security budget for the event had to be increased substantially, following the September 11 terrorist attacks in 2001. The event sparked national pride and showcased the city of Athens to the world. However, the subsequent recession has led to claims that the Olympics bankrupted the country. In 2009, Greece fell into a debt crisis that led to the Greek government twice asking the European Community to bail the country out with 240 billion euros. Over the past six years, following the Global Financial Crisis, Greece has experienced record unemployment, homelessness and poverty. Given the extent of the debt crisis, it is debateable whether the Olympic Games had any major impact.

Aside from delivering the event itself, the aim of hosting the Olympic Games was to transform Athens (Kissoudi, 2008). The often overlooked infrastructural legacy has led to longer-term improvements to the city. Prior to the event, Athens was a densely populated city experiencing congestion and pollution (Kissoudi, 2008). Infrastructure projects included:

- Extension of the Athens metro train system
- A new tramline connecting the city and the waterfront
- A new motorway and ring roads, which provided a faster route to the airport and reduced congestion in the city centre
- New footpaths connecting the major attractions
- New power stations and new telecommunications network

These projects benefit a large proportion of the city's residents and assist international tourists, on whom the Greek economy is dependent. These improvements have increased the standard of living for Athenians and the image of their city (Panagiotopoulou, 2014).

However, the Olympic Organising Committee failed to plan for both the upkeep and usage of the new venues after the event. In particular, they have been criticised for failing to develop a basic business plan for the venues post-event, let alone creating an environmental plan or conducting any economic feasibility studies for post-event uses. Many venues were built to specifications for sports with no strong base in Greece, such as softball and badminton. No plans were made for their use post-event and while some have been transferred into, for example, a convention centre or a cultural venue, many remain empty or unused. The venues were also constructed using heavy building rather than the prefabricated and temporary structures favoured by other mega-events, which enables more flexibility post-event.

Examples of post-event use for the Olympic venues include:

- Hellenikon Canoe/Kayak Slalom Centre – turned over to the private consortium who intend to develop it into a waterpark, although currently unused
- Hellenikon Baseball Stadium – converted to a football pitch, the home ground for Ethniko Piraeus Football Club
- Faliro Sports Centre (handball, taekwondo) – converted into the Athens International Convention Centre
- Ano Liosia Olympic Hall (judo, wrestling) – future home of the Hellenic Academy of Culture
- Goudi Olympic Complex (badminton, modern pentathlon) – converted into the Goudi Theatre, the largest in Greece

(Continued)

Case study (continued)

- The Olympic Village – 2,292 houses were given to beneficiaries of the Workers' Housing Organisation and the complex is now home to a community of 8,000 residents

Since the 2009 debt crisis, successive governments have sought to sell off as many of the venues as possible to reduce the ongoing costs and try to recoup some of the expenditure (Panagiotopoulou, 2014). The Organising Committee and the Greek government have also been criticised for failing to capitalise on the event by using it to further boost tourism, which may have reduced the impact of the debt crisis.

Discussion questions

1   The 2004 Athens Olympic Games is frequently criticised for its poor legacy but what went well, if anything?
2   Use the case study to draw up a list of legacy dos and don'ts for mega-event organisers.
3   What do you think are the major reasons why the 2004 Athens Olympic Games left such a negative legacy? Which of these could be avoided and which are outside the control of the Olympic Organising Committee and the Greek government?

Further reading and online resources

London citizens 'Olympic legacy guardians' march on City Hall. Available online at http://www.youtube.com/watch?v=w_XkiT3OPQM [accessed 20 November, 2014].

Olympics: Athens venues lie empty as tenth anniversary nears. Available online at http://www.bbc.com/sport/0/olympics/28693970 [accessed 20 November, 2014].

Rishe, B. (2011). How does London's Olympic bill compare to previous games? *Forbes*, available online at http://www.forbes.com/sites/sportsmoney/2011/08/05/how-does-londons-olympics-bill-compare-to-previous-games/ [accessed 20 November, 2014].

Storm, C. (2014). See what has become of 8 Olympic cities after the games left town. *Business Insider*. Available at http://www.businessinsider.com.au/olympic-games-sites-cities-ruins-abandoned-2014-8 [accessed 20 November, 2014].

The 2018 Commonwealth Games, Gold Coast, Australia. Available online at http://www.gc2018.com/ [accessed 20 November, 2014].

The London Olympic Park. Available online at http://queenelizabetholympicpark.co.uk/ [accessed 20 November, 2014].

The Olympic legacy. *Contemporary Social Science*, 2014, 9 (2), 137–284, special journal issue on event legacies.

The Sydney Olympic Park. Available online at http://www.sydneyolympicpark.com.au/ [accessed 20 November, 2014].

Usborne, S. (2008). After the party: what happens when the Olympics leave town. *The Independent*. Available at http://www.independent.co.uk/sport/olympics/after-the-party-what-happens-when-the-olympics-leave-town-901629.html [accessed 20 November, 2014].

References

Benson, A., Dickson, T., Terwiel, A. and Blackman, D. (2014). Training of Vancouver 2010 volunteers: a legacy opportunity? *Contemporary Social Science*, 9 (2), 201–26.

Bramwell, B. (1997). Strategic planning before and after a mega-event. *Tourism Management*, 18 (3), 167–76.

Cashman, R. (2009). Regenerating Sydney's West: framing and adapting an Olympic vision. In Poynter, I. and McRury, G. (Eds), *Olympic cities: 2012 and the remaking of London*. Farnham: Ashgate.

Cornelissen, S., Bob, U. and Swart, K. (2011). Towards redefining the concept of legacy in relation to sport mega-events: insights from the 2010 FIFA World Cup. *Development Southern Africa*, 28 (3), 307–18.

Donovan, T. (2014). Olympic park affordable housing 'trade-off'. BBC News. Available online at http://www.bbc.com/news/uk-england-london-25749691 [accessed 20 November, 2014].

Flyvbjerg, B. and Stewart, A. (2012). *Olympic proportions: cost and cost-overrun at the Olympics 1960–2012*. Said Business School Working Papers. Oxford: Said Business School, University of Oxford.

International Olympic Committee (2013). *Olympic charter*. Lausanne: IOC.

Kissoudi, P. (2008). The Athens Olympics: optimistic legacies – post Olympic assets and the struggle for their realisation. *The International Journal of the History of Sport*, 25 (14), 1972–90.

Minnaert, L. (2014). Making the Olympics work: interpreting diversity and inclusivity in employment and skills development pre-London 2012. *Contemporary Social Science*, 9 (2), 196–209.

Panagiotopoulou, R. (2014). The legacies of the Athens 2004 Olympic Games: a bittersweet burden. *Contemporary Social Science*, 9 (2), 173–95.

Preuss, H. (2007). The conceptualisation and measurement of mega-sport event legacies. *Journal of Sport and Tourism*, 12 (3), 207–28.

Richards, G. (2000). The European cultural capital event: strategic weapon in the cultural arms race? *International Journal of Cultural Policy*, 6 (2), 159–81.

Smith, A. (2012). *Events and urban regeneration*. London: Routledge.

Chapter 12

Creating sustainable legacies from events

Learning outcomes

After studying this chapter you should be able to:

- Review different types of legacies
- Discuss the difference between hard and soft legacies
- Analyse the reasons why legacies are successful
- Identify good practice in legacy planning
- Examine the legacy plans for future events

Introduction

Legacies are the long-term post-event impacts and Chapter 11 set the scene for event legacies by examining the challenges for events in delivering on their planned legacies. Event legacies are planned or unplanned within specific economic, political and social contexts, which are ever-changing over the long lead-in time for a mega-event.

Chapter 11 raised a number of challenges for creating a sustainable legacy from an event. The legacy plans need to be specific, realistic and based on sound research and planning. The event organisers need to ensure there are funds to deliver the legacy and that these are not spent on the actual event when the budget is inevitably exceeded. Legacy plans also need to be long term and this needs to be communicated to the media, so that legacy claims are not challenged immediately following the event.

Legacies are complex, and positive outcomes are not necessarily planned. For example, the host community may feel much more positive about hosting an Olympic Games where their national team has performed well. This chapter seeks to identify good practice in event legacy planning and delivery.

Different types of legacy

We have seen that legacies are complex and can include physical changes to the host destination as well as economic and psychological changes. The complexity of mega-event legacies creates challenges in trying to achieve such multi-faceted event outcomes but that does not stop event organisers making big claims. The International Olympic Committee (IOC, 2013) lists the possible legacies of hosting the Olympic Games as:

- *A sporting legacy* – through the venues that are built or refurbished and through increased interest in sport which can be leveraged to increase participation at both the elite and community levels.
- *A social legacy* – by showcasing the host nation's culture to the world through the cultural Olympiad and the opening and closing ceremonies; building friendship and respect through the volunteer programme; and creating new ways of working, which involve all the stakeholders in a destination in the planning for the event and its legacies.
- *An environmental legacy* – through improvements to the urban landscape; host governments investing in more renewable energy sources to make the event more sustainable.
- *An urban legacy* – through urban renewal and improvements to the host city and infrastructure improvements.
- *An economic legacy* – due to increased economic activity both in the planning and construction phases and in tourism during the post-event period.

These legacies provide a good overview of the diversity of potential outcomes from a mega-event and it is easy to see how complicated delivering outcomes against all of these criteria can be. These legacies can also be classified into the hard and soft legacy.

Box 12.1 Social legacies of Manchester 2002 Commonwealth Games

As part to of the urban renewal of post-industrial Manchester, the Commonwealth Games (CG) was considered to provide a catalyst for the persistent problems of economic stagnation, unemployment, low education levels and social tensions. Other post-industrial cities in the United Kingdom were confronting the same problems and were watching Manchester's strategies in relation to redevelopment of the inner city and waterfront, attraction of mega-events and tourism and the associated investment, employment, income and image that flows from these initiatives. Indeed, a UK Urban Renewal Policy was in place to support the programmes and policies of post-industrial cities across the UK and also across Europe.

In particular, the social legacy of the Manchester CG was explicitly planned and formed one of the key objectives of the corporate plan, as follows:

To create a social legacy of benefits through culture and educational programmes associated with the Commonwealth Games.

Three strategic objectives were identified as follows:

- To improve skills and education within the target area, as well as in the CG communities and young people.
- To improve community health development to create cohesion and improve skills among the disadvantaged through health improvement programmes linked with the CG.
- To enhance business competitiveness and commercial opportunities generated by the CG to improve the competitiveness of target sectors and ethnic businesses.

These objectives were supported by a host of organisations associated with the CG including:

- Manchester Investment and Development Agency Service (MIDAS)
- The UK government
- Manchester City Council
- Manchester 2002 Limited
- East Manchester Limited

In achieving these objectives, the agencies were looking to enhance employment prospects through education skills of local people, address social exclusion, support and promote growth in local economies.

The main emphasis for the urban renewal programme of the north west was in line with UK government policy, which was the establishment of a large skills base in the population and to increase skills of the unemployed. This was done through gaining work experience, qualifications, and skills that led to employment through the volunteer programme.

The programme was targeted at the 25 most disadvantaged areas in the region where an average of 120 people from ethnic minorities, aged 16–25 years, and long-term unemployed were to be recruited. The social and economic renewal programme was limited by available funding. Due to the scarce resources available for the social programmes, they could not be fully adapted to address all the problems faced by the city. Allocating available resources to areas that would most benefit from the programme could provide opportunities for urban renewal to take place.

The CG in Manchester facilitated not only economic renewal but also established a social and cultural legacy. Manchester has large communities from other Commonwealth countries and the cultural programmes created awareness of these communities and promoted understanding throughout the Commonwealth. The social and cultural policies were implemented through the cultural programme 'Let's Celebrate'. Education programmes were established within schools to raise awareness and understanding of the various Commonwealth countries. Social and community development took place through cultural activities within the Commonwealth communities to increase mutual understanding of cultural diversity (Manchester 2002 Ltd., 2000).

The hard legacy

The hard legacy refers to material gains such as jobs, houses and infrastructure. This includes all of the urban regeneration projects described in Chapter 4, with the focus on the physical and economic benefits. The hard legacy is the most visible, the most easily quantified and has typically been the focus of most regeneration programmes. The hard legacy makes good headlines and provides politicians with good sound bites and is the easiest to 'sell' to the electorate. The hard legacy is encapsulated in the Barcelona model, described in Box 12.2.

Box 12.2 The Barcelona model

The 1992 Barcelona Olympic Games are hailed as an enormous success due to the urban regeneration programme, which was built around the event and in terms of the legacy. What was the Barcelona model, described as 'an outstanding example of a certain way of improving cities' (Marshall, 2004: 1) and why was it such a success?

In addition to new sporting venues built on Montjuic, the Olympic Village was situated on industrial land and used to open up the formerly industrial seafront to create a beach area; the rail network was restructured and the lines that divided the city from the newly regenerated seafront were eliminated. Traffic was improved through the construction of new ring roads; the airport was upgraded with new terminals; new hotels were built and existing hotels

(Continued)

The Barcelona model (continued)

refurbished alongside cultural facilities. Today, Barcelona is a major tourist centre and this is seen as evidence of the city's successful redevelopment.

Smith describes Barcelona as a 'good example of event-themed regeneration' (2010: 125) and this tells us that the regeneration was not solely focused around delivering the Olympic Games. In fact, the projects associated with the Olympic Games were part of a long-term plan for urban renewal, which was accelerated and made bolder by the opportunity to host the mega-event (Monclus, 2007).

Key success points to be learnt from Barcelona are that urban plans were developed from the bottom up rather than imposed through a city masterplan and that the regeneration was not limited to one location within the city but used to revitalise a series of new 'centres'.

While there is much discussion of the 'Barcelona model', the ideas were borrowed from other cities and brought together effectively in Barcelona (Smith, 2012). As with other legacy plans, the political context of the redevelopment was important. Barcelona is the capital of Catalonia region in Spain, which has a strong regional identity and indeed its own language. Up until 1975, regional identities had been repressed under the Franco regime. Barcelona's redevelopment took place at a time of Catalan nationalist resurgence. The economic context was also important as Barcelona had suffered a dramatic fall in its manufacturing industry and was ready for change. When Spain joined the European Union in 1986, this opened up new funds for redevelopment.

The inspirational (or soft) legacy

The inspirational legacy refers to moral, affective or spiritual gains. These include psychological legacies, where hosting the event creates a sense of pride within the local community. For example, while the 2004 Athens Olympic Games have been described as a failed legacy, the event did create considerable national pride in the country's ability to deliver the event (Panagiotopoulou, 2014).

Box 12.3 The FIFA World Cup 2010 and reconciliation in South Africa

Hosting the 2010 FIFA World Cup in South Africa was controversial given the expenditure required from a developing country. The government heavily invested in new stadia and while football is popular, even Premier Soccer League (PSL) games do not draw the crowds that top level games in Europe attract, leaving additional post-event costs in maintaining these new stadia. However, this event was about reconciliation both within South Africa and across the continent. The South African government used slogans and images, which emphasised the pan-African theme of the event, and efforts were made to extend the benefits beyond the host country (Cornelissen et al., 2011).

Other soft legacies include knowledge, networks and cultural goods (Preuss, 2007). Knowledge can be both event specific or more general – for example, the host destination may improve its knowledge of large-scale security operations. Networks include the partnerships between varied stakeholders, which are needed to bring about a mega-event that can have longer-term outcomes for a destination. These partnerships can include formal networks such as sport federations or informal networks created through, for example, the volunteer programme. Cultural goods may be new cultural ideas or shared memories of the event.

Different types of events, different legacy opportunities

While legacies are multidimensional, so are events and the opportunities for the delivery of positive event outcomes will depend on the scope and scale of the event. Events can be mono-site or multi-site and the event legacy is most acutely felt within close proximity of the event site. This means that a multi-site event has the potential to spread the legacy more widely but at the risk of diluting the benefits. A multi-theme event will have a broader appeal and therefore could be more effective at generating a longer-term legacy for the host community and attracting wider media coverage potentially leading to increased tourism and investment. The legacy opportunity matrix (Figure 12.1) differentiates between mono/multi-theme and mono/multi-site events to identify the potential legacies, which could be derived from the event.

The matrix shows that criticism is hard to avoid for legacy planners. Legacy plans will have the greatest impact if they are concentrated in specific programmes within geographical limitations – such as Glasgow's plans for using the 2014 Commonwealth

	Mono-theme	*Multi-theme*
Multi-site	Broader geographical spread but concentrated within a specific group of stakeholders Risk: some stakeholders feel excluded Example: Rugby World Cup	Greatest number of opportunities to spread the benefits geographically and across the largest number of stakeholders Risk: legacy benefits are too widely dispersed to have any significant impact Example: Live Earth
Mono-site	Most concentrated – one geographical area and limited stakeholder groups – which can lead to maximum impact Risk: criticism that benefits are too narrowly focussed Example: International Sailing Federation World Championships	Geographically concentrated but across a broader range of stakeholders within the destination Risk: critics from outside the destination; hard to meet all stakeholders' needs Example: European Capital of Culture

Figure 12.1 The legacy opportunity matrix

Games to boost sports participation, leading to a healthier population in the longer term. However, this can attract criticism from people who are outside the immediate beneficiary groups. An event that offers opportunities to spread the benefits more widely, can equally be criticised if these become too diluted.

Sustainable legacy planning

What makes a successful and sustainably legacy? It is clear that legacy plans need to be based on sound research as to what long-term goals would best meet the host destination's needs. This research also needs to take into account the available resources for delivering these goals and the viability of the intended legacy outcomes.

As was noted in Chapter 11, mega-events, which are the events most likely to be associated with legacy planning, tend to overrun their budget (Flyvbjerg and Stewart, 2012) and with the pressure to ensure that event is staged on time, money can be borrowed from the legacy budget. This means that to ensure sustainability, the delivery of the legacy needs to take place substantially before the event is held (Minnaert, 2014) while there are still funds and political and public support for the event.

The venues

The design and construction of new venues needs to take into account alternative post-event uses. It can be difficult to devise new uses for some of the more specialist venues in the case of the Olympic or Commonwealth Games but having these plans and contracts in place before the event saves the poor publicity and ongoing upkeep costs that have been associated with the 2004 Athens Olympic Games. The 2012 London Olympic Games, for example, made use of temporary venues to avoid post-event claims of white elephants. These have since been dismantled in order to make the venues more usable. For example, the aquatic centre had temporary seating areas attached to each side to allow for an Olympic sized audience. These have now been removed. The basketball arena has also had its seating removed and relocated to another sporting venue in another part of London. The venue is for sale, but if it is not sold, it will be dismantled and the materials recycled. There is a contingency plan in place.

Employability and volunteer programmes

Many events seek to create an employability legacy as a means to improve the lives of the host community (see Chapter 9). An example from the 2012 London Olympics was a programme to employ disadvantaged local people in construction projects for the event (Minnaert, 2014). If this is going to become a reality, there need to be contractual requirements to ensure that the target group are employed in the run up to the event. People from disadvantaged backgrounds and the long-term unemployed can be difficult for recruiters to reach and may need persuading of the benefit of participating in the programme. The event organisers may need to draw up a partnership agreement with the contractors to share the burden of identifying and recruiting these people, providing appropriate training programmes, particularly given that contractors' priority is to get their job completed to time and to budget.

An event's volunteer programme is frequently promoted as a means for creating a volunteer legacy, as with Manchester Event Volunteers (see Chapter 9). A volunteer legacy involves introducing thousands of people to a culture of volunteering and providing them with the necessary training and skills to take on volunteer roles both within the event and afterwards within the community. However, most mega-event volunteer programmes are focussed on delivering the event and not the volunteer legacy. The volunteer programme needs to involve training individuals with a broad set of skills to develop a post-event volunteer sector not just for the event but for afterwards (Benson et al., 2014). Participants of both employability and volunteer programmes are also likely to need further assistance post-event to learn how to translate their new skills and experience into other contexts so that the longer-term outcomes can be realised.

Long-term planning and media management

The general view is that legacies should be evaluated up to 20 years post-event (Cornelissen et al., 2011). A legacy is about long-term benefits, not short-term outcomes. Mega-event planning is part of the broader planning for a destination (Bramwell, 1997). The legacy plan needs to communicate this to residents and the media, both in the present and continuing into the future. A challenge is that both the host community and the media have seen the possibly monumental changes to the urban environment that have taken place over the preceding few years. These changes will have to be paid for, most likely out of taxation. The benefits, such as higher employment and standards of living, take substantially longer to come to fruition. Sustainable legacy planning needs to include a communications strategy, which might, for example, include releasing regular positive news stories to keep the focus on the positive outcomes.

A viable legacy

A legacy plan needs to distinguish between short-term economic impacts and long-term economic growth (Preuss, 2007). Tourism, for example, is identified as a positive benefit from hosting an event. However, increased tourism is derived from two sources: firstly, the event itself can attract substantially more tourists but secondly, and more importantly, the enhanced image of the host destination, displayed on global media, can increase tourism in the longer term.

Sustainable legacy planning therefore needs to use the event to improve the city's profile by piggy-backing structural changes to the city's locational factors, i.e. the factors that attract tourists to that location such as proximity to natural resources or cultural attractions. Examples include investing in the city's tourism infrastructure such as improving transport to and around the city, upgrading hotels, refurbishing historic buildings and redeveloping run down areas. Barcelona's regeneration associated with the 1992 Olympic Games is a good example of how investments in transport, museums and opening up and revitalising the beaches has helped turn the city into a major tourist destination in the long term.

Monitoring and measuring the legacy

Legacy planning should involve substantial research and monitoring both before and after the event. Pre-event research should involve consultation with host communities to identify how far proposed legacy outcomes will actually meet their needs. This echoes principles of sustainable event regeneration, which emphasise the importance of community consultation (Smith, 2012), including the often hard to reach most vulnerable residents of the host destination.

The challenge is how to measure the impact of legacy outcomes, particularly as this can involve assessing the impact an event had on a destination a number of years after the event has taken place. For example, the defence of the America's Cup, which took place in the port city of Fremantle in 1987–8 (see Chapter 4), is often cited as having significantly revitalised the city. Macbeth, Selwood and Veitch (2012), however, query the actual impact of the event. They argue that, at the most, it simply accelerated the process of gentrification, which was a global trend at this time in waterside former industrial zones.

Preuss (2007) suggests that one method for measuring how much the legacy outcomes are due to the event and not due to other factors is to use a 'control' city. Clearly, given the uniqueness of mega-event host cities, this is a difficult task. Preuss also calls for a bottom-up approach to event evaluation, that is, examining how the event has made a difference to the overall development plans for the city, although he acknowledges the challenge of achieving this.

Stages of the legacy planning process

This section has placed the emphasis for sustainable event legacy planning on the pre-event planning stage. This is partly so that funds are spent and plans put into action before everyone loses momentum after the event. However, legacy planning is also for the long term. Figure 12.2 presents a timeline for sustainable legacy planning, which incorporates the different stages involved in planning and delivering the legacy.

The legacy needs to be part of the original plans for the event and encapsulated in the bid document. This is increasingly a requirement for client organisations but is also essential practice. However, the plans do need to be specific, for example, how will new venues be used post-event? The planning phase for the event legacy needs to take place alongside the planning for the event and all the majority of legacy funds must be spent or at least committed at this stage. The event itself will be the culmination of years of preparation so the legacy may be put on hold during this brief period.

The biggest challenge for legacy planning is the transition phase, immediately following the event. As soon as the event is over, the media and other stakeholders will start to ask questions about the legacy. This is the transition phase and may take a few months to a few years before legacy plans begin to show outcomes. For example, it will take time to convert an athlete's village into any other sort of accommodation. At this stage the media communication strategy is essential to manage negative press. The final stage sees the legacy start to generate outcomes and ideally this stage will continue for several years, with ongoing monitoring so that the destination can learn for subsequent events.

Chapter summary

This chapter has examined the ways in which mega-event organising committees can deliver a planned and sustainable long-term legacy from the event. Delivering a sustainable legacy presents a number of challenges. Legacies are complex and

Bid document prepared	Event planning phase	The event	Transition phase	Legacy phase
Legacy vision and post-event plans for site and venue developed

Feasibility studies conducted | Planning for legacy takes place during this phase

Contracts for post-event programmes and venue uses put in place

Funds for legacy must be spent or committed now | The legacy is temporarily on hold while the focus is on the staging of the event | In the immediate aftermath of the event, legacy plans begin to be put into process but it will take time to yield results. A media communication plan is needed to prevent premature negative press. | The legacy plan is put into action

Ongoing research and monitoring of event impacts |

Figure 12.2 The sustainable legacy timeline

many-faceted and not all legacy outcomes will be planned or even anticipated. In particular, legacies can be categorised as the 'hard', visible and more easily evaluated urban regeneration programmes or economic outcomes, or the softer, more subjective social and psychological outcomes. As identified in Chapter 11, the context for both planning the legacy and delivering it post-event can have a significant impact if the political, economic or social conditions change substantially between the planning and the delivery phases.

To be successful, legacies need to be planned and largely delivered (or firm plans put into place) prior to the event. This will reduce the risk of funds running out, political support evaporating or event organising staff being redeployed to new projects post-event. Immediately post-event is a period of transition, where the event legacy plans are put into place and at this stage, host community opinion and media reports need to be carefully managed as sustainable legacies take time to achieve their intended outcomes. Finally, legacy planning is a process, which needs to be based on sound research and regularly monitored.

Learning activities

1   Choose a pre-2000 Olympic city. What can you find out about the Olympic legacy in that city? Do you find more positive or negative stories about the event's legacy?
2   The London 2012 Olympic Games, only months after the event, began to receive negative publicity questioning whether the promised legacies would be delivered. Design a media campaign for managing media expectations about the 2012 legacy.
3   Using Figure 12.2, devise a sustainable legacy plan for a future planned mega-event of your choice.

Case study: Legacy planning for Brazil 2016

Rio de Janeiro, Brazil, is hosting the 2016 Olympic Games and has been planning the event and its legacy prior to being awarded the event in 2009. This is the first time the event will be staged in South America. The host city has been a controversial choice because of the enormous cost associated with staging the event for a developing country and a city with significant social problems. Achieving a positive legacy from the event is therefore essential. There are early signs of problems with event planning, as the IOC chair reportedly intervened in 2014 to try to speed up preparations, with alternative 'fall back' host cities (Linden, 2013) being considered elsewhere if the event organisers are not ready in 2016. A further controversy is that the main Olympic Park will be built on the site of one of Rio's favelas (slum settlements), currently home to approximately 4,000 people who will be relocated under a state law that allows the Government to forcibly seize property.

The plans for the 2016 Olympics will involve using three main sites around the city, which has the potential to spread the benefits of the event more widely. According to the city's bid document, the legacy planning has been incorporated into the city and country's long-term strategy. The legacy plans include:

Urban renewal

- Improvements to the city's infrastructure and the port area 'will deliver a more connected community, creating new opportunities for employment and other benefits' (Rio de Janeiro, 2016: 21).
- Greater emissions controls for industry and mass transport to improve air quality.
- Improved public transport through the development of the High Performance Transport Ring.
- Planting 24 million trees by 2016 as part of an urban forest preservation programme.
- Redevelopment of the harbour area into a mixed-use development with residential and tourist accommodation, businesses and entertainment.
- New infrastructure developments in the Barra da Tijuca zone of the city.
- New housing and retail developments in the Maracana and Deodoro zones of the city.

Social inclusion

- Four legacy villages will be built, which will create new apartments with 24,000 rooms across the different venues.
- A Rio-2016 funded programme of Professional and Volunteer Training, delivered in partnership between the government, universities and training institutions, will be available to 48,000 adults to increase their employability after the event.
- The event will create 50,000 temporary and 15,000 permanent jobs in the fields of events, sport management, tourism and venues as well as additional employment in construction projects associated with the event.
- The event organising committee aims to procure services and equipment from local communities.

A sporting legacy

- Scholarships will be made available to 11,000 Brazilian athletes up to 2018.
- The Brazilian Government will invest US$210 million to help the Brazilian Olympic and Paralympic Teams prepare for the event.
- The event will create 14 Olympic training facilities, which will be used by local communities after the event.

Unlike the London 2012 Olympics, which developed their Olympic Park in a deprived and rundown area of East London, the locations that are targeted for the new developments are relatively well-off. The Barra da Tijuca suburb (Flueckiger, 2013) is one of the wealthier parts of the city and Deodoro is the home of a large military barracks. Maracana is not a poor area either but does at least have a strong sporting culture due to the famous Maracana stadium.

Two groups will oversee the legacy planning: a Rio 2016 Legacy Committee – a coalition of government, businesses, the Brazilian Olympic Committee, community and policy groups, who will oversee the legacy planning from 2009 to 2020 and an Urban Legacy Committee, led by the city government. The Urban Legacy Committee will focus on the venue locations to 'ensure full alignment of the Games Master Plan with the long-term city objectives, optimizing the benefits to all' (Rio de Janeiro, 2016: 21). The IOC's Olympic Games Impact study will be used to monitor the games. The local organising committee has subcontracted the OGI research to an academic institution – the Alberto de Luiz Institute Graduate School and Research in Engineering – who will produce four reports monitoring the period 2007–19, examining the economic, environmental and socio-cultural effects of the event, with a focus on impacts in areas including:

- Education
- Health
- Security
- Sports
- Infrastructure

Sources: Rio2016.com and Rio de Janeiro 2016 candidature document

Discussion questions

1   Look at the bid document for Rio 2016, how well do you think this meets good practice in sustainable legacy planning?
2   Which stakeholders will benefit from the legacy of Rio 2016? Will this create the best legacy outcomes for the International Olympic Committee and the host community?
3   How effective are the plans for monitoring and evaluating the event legacy outcomes?

Further reading and online resources

Carlsen, J. and Taylor, A. (2003) Mega-events and urban renewal: the case of the Manchester 2002 Commonwealth Games. *Event Management*, 8 (1) 15–22.

Games Monitor – a blog dedicated to exposing Olympic myths. Available online at http://www.gamesmonitor.org.uk/ [accessed 20 November, 2014].

Garcia, B. and Cox, T. (2013). *European capitals of culture: success strategies and long term effects.* Brussels: European Union. Available online at http://www.europarl. europa.eu/RegData/etudes/etudes/join/2013/513985/IPOL-CULT_ET(2013)513985_ EN.pdf [accessed 20 November, 2014].

Gratton, C. and Preuss, H. (2008). Maximising Olympic impacts by building up legacies. *The International Journal of the History of Sport*, 25 (14) 1922–38.

References

Benson, A., Dickson, T., Terwiel, A. and Blackman, D. (2014). Training of Vancouver 2010 volunteers: a legacy opportunity? *Contemporary Social Science*, 9 (2), 2010–226.

Bramwell, B. (1997). Strategic planning before and after a mega-event. *Tourism Management*, 18 (3), 167–76.

Cornelissen, S., Bob, U. and Swart, K. (2011). Towards redefining the concept of legacy in relation to sport mega-events: insights from the 2010 FIFA World Cup. *Development Southern Africa*, 28 (3), 307–18.

Flueckiger, L. (2013). Barra de Tijuca: upmarket Rio suburbs. *The Rio Times*, available online at http://riotimesonline.com/brazil-news/rio-real-estate/barra-da-tijuca-the-rio-suburbs/# [accessed 20 November, 2014].

Flyvbjerg, B. and Stewart, A. (2012). *Olympic proportions: cost and cost-overrun at the Olympics 1960–2012.* Said Business School Working Papers. Oxford: Said Business School, University of Oxford.

International Olympic Committee (2013). Olympic Legacies. Lausanne: IOC. Available online at http://www.olympic.org/Documents/Olympism_in_action/Legacy/2013_ Booklet_Legacy.pdf [accessed 20 November, 2014].

Linden, J. (2013). Rio tells IOC they will be ready for 2016. *Reuters*, available online at *http://www.reuters.com/article/2013/09/08/us-olympics-rio-idUSBRE9870GQ20130908* [accessed 20 November, 2014].

Macbeth, J., Selwood, J. and Veitch, S. (2012). Paradigm shift or drop in the ocean? The America's Cup impact on Fremantle. *Tourism Geographies*, 14 (1), 162–82.

Manchester 2002 Ltd (2000). *Manchester 2002: the XVII Commonwealth Games factsheet.* Manchester City Council, unpublished document.

Marshall, L. (Ed.) (2004). *Transforming Barcelona*. London: Routledge.

Minnaert, L. (2014). Making the Olympics work: interpreting diversity and inclusivity in employment and skills development pre-London 2012. *Contemporary Social Science*, 9 (2), 196–209.

Monclus, F. (2007). Barcelona 1992. In Gold, J. and Gold, M. (Eds), *Olympic cities*. London: Routledge, pp. 218–36.

Panagiotopoulou, R. (2014). The legacies of the Athens 2004 Olympic Games: a bittersweet burden. *Contemporary Social Science*, 9 (2), 173–95.

Preuss, H. (2007). The conceptualisation and measurement of mega sport event legacies. *Journal of Sport and Tourism*, 12 (3), 207–28.

Rio2016.com. Available online at http://www.rio2016.com/en/tags/legacy [accessed 20 November, 2014].

Rio de Janeiro 2016 candidature document. Available online at http://www.rio2016.com/sites/default/files/parceiros/candidature_file_v1.pdf [accessed 20 November, 2014].

Smith, A. (2012). *Events and urban regeneration*. London: Routledge.

PART IV

Conclusion

Chapter 13

Developing sustainable events: summary and future directions

Learning outcomes

After studying this chapter you should be able to:

- Review and reflect on the key concepts of sustainable event development
- Summarise the economic, social and environmental impacts of sustainable events
- Understand the roles and responsibilities of all sustainable event stakeholders
- Consider the future of sustainable events in all of their forms

Introduction

This book is one of the first to provide detailed insights into the inextricable and complex inter-relationships between events management and sustainable development. It has demonstrated that there are multiple stakeholders in the transformation of events towards sustainability, with each having an integral role in the process. It is axiomatic that in order to manage, it must be possible to measure, and a substantial section of the book provides instruction as to how to identify and measure the economic, social and environmental impacts of events – both positive and negative. Systems thinking for event management is recommended as the means to overcome partial or compartmentalised approaches and introduce a holistic and integrated platform for developing sustainable events. There is no doubt that the challenges of developing sustainable events and creating sustainable legacies will grow in the future, and so too should community support and political will to confront and overcome these challenges.

Summary and review

The book begins by analysing the internal and external operating environment as the first step in developing more sustainable events. The environment for events is analogous to an ecosystem, where each part is dependent on other parts for survival and success. Just as ecosystems are sensitive and subject to both internal and external forces of change, so too is the operating environment for events. The internal resources that event managers have available were identified and typically include people, information technology, equipment, materials, physical space, transport and time. The specific resources that are available to individual events will vary according to their scope and scale, but all event organisers and managers are subject to the constraints of time as all events have a defined start and end date.

Extending the ecosystem analogy, the specific internal resources could be considered as species and sub-species (it is interesting that the words specific and species have the same root word) that all have defined needs if the ecosystem is to thrive. Hence the people involved in events and the physical, technological and temporal needs required to stage a sustainable event are the focus of subsequent chapters. Techniques for identifying and analysing the operating environment for events were described and both PESTLE and strategic SWOT analysis could be used to understand and manage the complex external event environment.

Chapter 3 examined the relationship between events and public policy. Governments at all levels have a key role to play in sustainable events. Governments are involved in events for many reasons, including provision of public good, pursuing social equity, confirming ideology and avoiding market failure. The range of involvement from the 'hands-off' laissez-faire approach to a regulatory and interventionist approach were identified and the need for sustainable events policies was emphasised.

The nexus between mega-events and urban renewal was explored in Chapter 4. Two overall approaches – event-led or event-themed – were compared and contrasted with event-themed urban renewal found to deliver longer-term benefits to the destination and local residents. The chapter also appraised the physical, economic and social benefits which are derived from regeneration programmes and recognised that they are not always successful or particularly sustainable; with the risk of creating white elephant venues identified and the challenges of spreading the regeneration benefits across the destination discussed. Some regeneration projects were found to have a dark side, with residents forcibly displaced from their homes, communities and livelihoods, or even unintentionally priced out as an area becomes gentrified and housing more expensive. Finally, the chapter reviewed principles for sustainable event regeneration.

Chapter 5 described the positive and negative economic impacts associated with events. Proper evaluation of the net economic benefits using a range of techniques for measuring those effects, as well as the relative strengths and limitations of each was also described. The net economic benefits of events is an important determinant of the future government and community support for the event and therefore, sustainability in the future.

Chapter 6 defined the environment and identified the positive and negative environmental impacts of planned events and then discussed the different scales at which these exist. This was followed by a discussion of impact measurement and management, citing carbon emissions as an example. The chapter exemplifies the various management techniques used to minimise negative and enhance positive environmental impacts using the example of the Peats Ridge Festival.

Chapter 7 examined the socio-cultural impacts of events and identified both positive and negative impacts. It discussed how socio-cultural impacts can be measured and demonstrated the difficulties associated with understanding the relationship between events and the community. Social capital was identified as one theory that would be helpful in achieving this understanding. Finally, the chapter considered the meanings and perceptions of events to communities, and highlighted the issues that can arise when there are multiple, or conflicting meanings associated with events.

Chapter 8 demonstrated the requirements for delivering the sustainable event. Event organisers must consider the practical ways in which they can work towards creating an economically, socio-culturally and environmentally sustainable event. It introduced the need for event organisers and planners to take a systematic approach to delivering a sustainable event by considering all aspects of sustainability – economic, social and environmental – in a holistic and integrated way.

Chapter 9 examined staffing issues and how staffing models can be developed which ensure that events are able to staff the event by using an event staffing agency or volunteers. However, volunteer management key concerns include avoiding exploiting volunteers and ensuring they are properly trained, managed and rewarded. The chapter used examples to illustrate efforts to create more sustainable approaches to event staffing and whether legacy plans are unrealistic given the economic and time pressures to deliver the event. This was explored further in Chapters 11 and 12.

Chapter 10 emphasised the importance of risk management and introduced the risk management process for sustainable events that identifies a range of potential risks that may be faced by event organisers. It also discussed the relationship between risk and sustainability and examined how event managers and organisers can deal with crisis and disaster management through risk management planning processes.

Finally, Chapters 11 and 12 identified a number of challenges and opportunities in delivering sustainable event legacies. Legacy planning must take into account the changing world within which the event is taking place. There is a need to translate a broad legacy vision into specific programmes. Legacies are long term and many of the criticisms are that they have failed to deliver immediate benefits. Legacy plans also need to be based on sound research both before and after the event. Before the event, methods can include cost–benefit analyses or feasibility studies (see also Chapter 5) but such forecasting techniques can be imprecise.

Impact		
	Economic	**Social**	**Environmental**
Positive	• Employment • Event income • Increased business/ trade • Increased tourism expenditure • Funds supporting ongoing community development	• Urban renewal • Nature conservation • Pro-environmental behaviour • Enhanced environmental awareness	• Community pride/ prestige • Community cohesion/ networks • Skills and capacity building • Entertainment opportunities • Volunteering opportunities • Increased commercial activity • Improved destination image • Revitalisation of traditions • Increased tolerance of diversity • Employment
Negative	• Short-term employment • Economic leakage • Inflation • Opportunity cost • Externalities (environmental costs)	• Air pollution • Water pollution • Litter and waste • Overcrowding • Trampling	• Increased noise • Increased traffic • Overcrowding • Antisocial behaviour • Loss of amenity • Social dislocation • Opportunity cost • Develop negative community image • Community alienation • Loss of authenticity of traditions

Figure 13.1 Summary of economic, environmental and social impacts described in this book

The future of sustainable events

The level of academic and public interest in events has burgeoned over the last three decades and that trend is set to continue well into the future. Kim et al. (2013) examined the trends in event studies since the 1980s based on publications in three leading tourism journals and found that the number of papers published increased from just 18 between 1980 and 1989 to 118 between 2000 and 2010. Topics expanded from a narrow focus on administration, strategy, research and development of events in the 1980s to include finance, control/operation, marketing and human resources in the

2000s (Kim et al., 2013). Of particular note is the growth in research into the motivations, perceptions and satisfaction of event participants as well as their demographic profiles. From the organiser's perspective, topics such as event coordination, marketing, risk management, administration, evaluation, tourism, risk management and destination development have emerged in the academic literature, reflecting the increased diversity of disciplinary interest in the field. However, of all topics of interest to emerge, studies of event impacts have shown the most dramatic increase over the last three years, from just four in the 1980s to 45 in the 2000s. Extrapolating this trend into the future further underlines the aims of this book to encourage a more holistic and systematic approach to understanding, managing and monitoring the positive and negative economic, social and environmental impacts of events in the future.

Developing sustainable events will not be without its challenges, as this book clearly recognises and explains. This is in accordance with a list of ten global challenges (see Box 13.1) for the events sector proposed in Getz (2007), five of which relate directly to sustainability, namely:

- All events must become green and environmentally sustainable
- Events have to equally benefit residents as well as guests
- Event planning should be fully integrated with other forms of environmental, community, economic, tourism and leisure planning
- Events must be valued and evaluated equally in social, cultural, environmental and economic terms in order to be sustainable
- The event sector will continue to grow and diversify to the point where the supply of events in many areas threatens to exceed resources or demand

Box 13.1 Global challenges for the events sector

1   Terrorism threatens events more than most forms of business, leisure and tourism.
2   All events must become green and environmentally sustainable.
3   Events have to equally benefit residents as well as guests.
4   Professionalism in event management must be globally implemented.
5   Event planning should be fully integrated with other forms of environmental, community, economic, tourism and leisure planning.
6   Governments at all levels should adopt comprehensive policies and support programmes for the event sector.
7   Events must be valued and evaluated equally in social, cultural, environmental and economic terms in order to be sustainable.
8   Event design, production and management education has to be embedded in Event Studies.
9   The event sector will continue to grow and diversify to the point where the supply of events in many areas threatens to exceed resources or demand.
10 New event types will continue to merge, giving rise to unexpected challenges and opportunities for policy-makers, planners and managers.

Source: Getz, 2007

Conclusion

There are many other points that could be added to the list of global challenges confronting sustainable events that emerge from this book, including:

● Event managers must adopt environmental guidelines and toolkits as an integral part of planning, managing and evaluating their events
● Event managers need to analyse the internal and external environment in which their event operates
● Governments need to develop and implement sustainable event policies and programmes
● Green and sustainable events should form the basis of urban renewal and regeneration policies and programmes
● A standardised and rigorous approach to the economic evaluation of event impacts should be taken by all levels of government
● Sustainable events should be considered as central to the mitigation of environmental impacts from climate change and severe weather events
● Social capital should be used as the metric for maximising the positive socio-cultural impacts of sustainable events
● Systems thinking should be considered a prerequisite in delivering sustainable events
● The models for staff and volunteer management need to be based on inclusivity, skills development and future opportunities as legacies of sustainable events
● Risk management will become increasingly important to sustainable events
● The potential legacies, both positive and negative, of sustainable events must be measured and monitored
● Future legacies of sustainable events must be planned and implemented to ensure that they are realised

Sustainable development is essential in our world today. Event organisers may experience increasing pressure from stakeholders, needing to meet their corporate social responsibility commitments, to improve the sustainability of their event and this could become a major factor in funding agreements with sponsors and other partners. Ideally, we will see a move away from the triple bottom line approach towards integrating additional factors including community, governance or climate, for example, which can only be incorporated by using systems thinking.

Specific issues that are likely to impact on event sustainability into the future are:

● Increasing urbanisation
● Economic development/poverty reduction
● Economic uncertainty/growing economic inequity
● Climate change
● Changes in environmental regulations
● Technological developments

As the world becomes increasingly urbanised, some rural festivals may fail to attract audiences or be able to recruit volunteers. Urban festivals may experience problems with crowding, traffic and managing capacity. Urban areas are likely to continue to use events and festivals to brand themselves and attract tourism. Events still offer an opportunity to extend the tourist season and bring economic benefits but these must be weighed up against potential problems associated with crowding. The combination of more people moving to bigger cities, the growing gap between rich and poor may see more displacement of poor and undesirable communities for mega-events, as governments seek to present their city in the best light. There will be ever greater pressure for governments to justify hosting expensive mega-events, when the host community needs other, more urgent facilities. Mega-events will need to deliver better and more durable legacies.

Climate change poses a risk to events destinations, particularly if international air travel becomes cost prohibitive. Major airline hubs such as Doha and Singapore have positioned themselves as events destinations based on their location and if air travel decreases in the future, their viability will be brought into question. Events destinations will have to carefully consider the advantages and disadvantages of hosting events such as the Formula 1 Grand Prix, which generates substantial income but is hardly environmentally sustainable.

Changes in environmental regulations within destinations will demand that event organisers make better use of resources, more efficient use of energy and water and demand easier and wider access to green power. New venues will aspire to meet environmental measures and be more efficient both to save costs and promote themselves to event organisers and audiences. Developments in technology will lead to more energy efficient venues, wide access to green power for event organisers using green-field sites and improved technology will also enable easier and more effective online attendance at events (particularly business events, but also other types of events) (Mair, 2014).

In summary, sustainability is now ingrained in society and the economy and is set to assume an even more important position in building awareness of natural processes that sustain all life on Earth in the future. All stakeholders in events – governments, event organisers, hosts, participants and attendees – play a role and interest in the transformation of events towards sustainability and the knowledge, tools and techniques provided in this book should contribute to a better understanding of the responsibilities of event stakeholders in this process of transformation.

Final thoughts

There are many ways of conceptualising the future of sustainable events depending on the perspective of those whose future is being projected. From a public perspective several questions arise:

- How will governing bodies' and event clients' requirements evolve?
- In what ways will governments seek to use events and festivals for political leverage and/or the benefit of their town, city or region?
- What role will events play in future regeneration plans?

From the event participants' and audience's perspectives, the following questions arise:

- How will event participants' expectations change?
- How far will event participants embrace the sustainability agenda?

From the event sponsors' and partners' perspectives, the following questions could be posed:

- What is the role of sponsors and partners in ensuring that events become sustainable?
- How far will sponsors be driven to impose sustainability requirements on event organisers by their own corporate social responsibility agendas?

Conclusion

From the event staff and volunteers' perspective:

- What management models work best for event staff and volunteers?
- As the events sector is expected to continue to become more sophisticated, how will this impact on career opportunities?

Finally, from an event organiser's perspective, the following questions are crucial to the future:

- How can we incorporate the principles and practices of sustainability into all aspects of event management?
- How can event organisers engage with stakeholders to ensure that sustainability goals are shared?

Learning activities

1   Choose an event in your own country. How could systems thinking be applied to this event to make it more sustainable?
2   Look at the websites of some future events (for example, the Rio de Janeiro 2016 Olympic Games, the 2015 Cricket World Cup or the Qatar 2022 FIFA World Cup or similar) and identify any sustainability innovations that the event organisers are using to make their event more sustainable.
3   Which of these issues – increased urbanisation, economic uncertainty, technological change, climate change – do you think is most likely to have the biggest impact of the future of events and festivals in your town? To what changes do you think this will lead?

Further reading and online resources

Carlsen, J. C., Andersson, T. D., Ali-Knight, J., Jaeger, K. and Taylor, R. (2010). Festival management innovation and failure. *International Journal of Event and Festival Management*, 1 (2), 120–31.

Getz, D. (2008). Event tourism: definition, evolution and research. *Tourism Management*, 29, 403–28.

Greenpeace protest at the Belgian Formula 1 Grand Prix. Video available online at http://www.theguardian.com/environment/video/2013/aug/27/shell-belgian-f-1-grand-prix-greenpeace-protest [accessed 20 November, 2014].

Yeoman, I., Robertson, M., Smith, K., Backer, E. and McMahon-Beattie, U. (Eds). (2014). *The future of events and festivals*. London: Routledge.

References

Getz, D. (2007). *Event studies: theory, research and policy for planed events*. Oxford: Butterworth-Heinemann.

Kim, J., Boo, S. and Kim, Y. (2013). Patterns and trends in event tourism study topics over 30 years. *International Journal of Event and Festival Management*, 4 (1), 66–83.

Mair, J. (2014). *Conferences and conventions: a research perspective*. Abingdon, Oxon: Routledge.

Glossary

AU$ Australian dollars

BSI British Standards Institute

Carbon footprint The total amount of carbon emitted by an event

Civic pride Residents' positive attitudes towards their local area

Computerised general equilibrium models CGE models are sophisticated input–output models (see below), which are able to incorporate more complex economic effects and relationships

Congestion Overcrowding caused when an event is attended by a greater number of people than the venue is physically able to cater for within a given time period

Cost–benefit analysis A method for estimating the net benefits of a project in comparison with alternative projects

Crisis A situation where the root cause of an event is, to some extent, self-inflicted

Demonstration effect The impact of the event on behaviour and attitudes of attendees and the wider community

Disaster A situation where an event is confronted with sudden unpredictable catastrophic changes over which it has little control

Displacement Forcible or unintentional relocation of people and communities from their homes

Economic impacts The outcomes of an event that potentially have an impact on the local, regional or national economy

Employability legacy A legacy which uses the event to increase the opportunities for local residents to gain employment during and after the event

Environmental impacts Any change to the environment, whether damaging or beneficial, that results from the planned event taking place

Environmental management system (EMS) Voluntary, internal, formalised procedures that can help ensure compliance with legal requirements

Event-led regeneration Redevelopment that is designed simply to meet the needs of the event, without any broader or longer-term impacts

Event-themed regeneration Using the event to create longer term regeneration benefits for the host destination

Event stakeholder Any group or individual who may be affected by an event

GBP Great British Pounds (Sterling)

Glossary

Green-field festival   A festival that takes place on undeveloped land, requiring all facilities to be brought in for the event

Hard legacy   The material gains from hosting an event

Ideology   The fundamental philosophies that guide political parties

Identity   The meaning and significance that a country or place has for an individual or a group

Infrastructure   The physical and organisational structures that support the events sector, such as transport and power supply

Input–output model   Input–output models make broad assumptions about economic structure and sectoral relationships in order to model economic impact

Intangible   Not able to be directly observed

Interventionism   The political belief that governments should intervene to fund and regulate various aspects of economic and social life

ISO   International Standards Organisation

Laissez-faire   The political belief that government should not get involved in the private and business decisions of their constituents

Legacy   The longer term outcomes or impacts associated with hosting an event

Market failure   Where an event that would otherwise not be profitable is supported by government because it brings social benefits

Multiplier   A ratio used to calculate the sum total of direct, indirect and induced effects of event-related expenditure

Nature conservation   Actions focussed on maintaining the endemic plant and animal species and/or essential ecological processes in a given area

Nature rehabilitation   The restoration of nature in an ecologically degraded area

PESTLE analysis   Analysis of the political, economic, social, technological, legal and environmental factors in the external environment may have an impact on the event

Public good   Tangible and intangible benefits that accrue to society

Regulatory approach   The political belief that governments should step in and regulate in order to prevent negative outcomes of the free market system

Resilience   The ability of a system to absorb sudden as well as gradual changes without shifting into an alternate system state

Sense of community   Feeling that one belongs in a community, shares values with that community and has a shared understanding of the community

Sense of place   Historical and current forces which have shaped the image and identity of a place for those living there

Social capital   The various features of social organisation, such as networks, norms and trust that facilitate human interaction and cooperation

Social equity   Refers to equality of access to events for all members of a community

Socio-cultural impacts   The outcomes of an event that potentially have an impact on the quality of life for local residents

Soft legacy   The moral, affective or spiritual gains from hosting an event

Subvention   A financial and/or non-financial incentive designed to attract international business events

Succession planning   Making plans as to who will take over an organisation when the current leadership leaves or retires

Sustainable development   Sustainable development is a process that results in the goal of sustainability

Sustainability   The ability to exist in perpetuity without depleting the resources necessary for continuation into the future

SWOT analysis   Identifying the Strengths, Weaknesses, Opportunities and Threats relevant to organisation or destination

Systems thinking   Understanding relationships between the parts of a system and how they influence each other and the whole system over time

Tangible   Able to be directly observed

TPB (triple bottom line)   Economic, socio-cultural and environmental impacts

Trampling   Vegetation loss and soil compaction as plants (including lawn) are crushed by repeated foot or vehicle traffic

Urban regeneration   A comprehensive and integrated vision and action, which leads to the resolution of urban problems and leads to lasting improvements

USD   United States Dollar

Volunteer   An individual who gives their time free of charge

White elephant venues   Venues that are expensive to upkeep but have no viable use

Index

9/11 events 170

air pollution: airborne smoke particles (particulates) 85; carbon monoxide/dioxide (CO/CO_2) 85; methane (CH_4) 85; nitrogen oxides (NOx) 85; sulphur oxides (SOx) 85
Al Jazeera 49
Australia Day 107
Australian Bureau of Statistics 71

Barcelona model 177–8
BluesFest Blues and Roots Festival, Byron Bay, Australia 108–10
book summary 8–9, 192–3
Boston, US Marathon bombing 156–7
Bread Not Circuses 42
British Standards Institute (BSI) 120
Brundtland, Gro Harlem 3
BS8901 (sustainability) 6–7, 120
Business Events, Sydney 21

carbon dioxide (CO_2) emissions 85, 90–1
carbon offsetting 121
Carson, Rachel 2
Centre for Housing Rights and Eviction (COHRE) 55–6
climate change 197
Coachella Valley Music and Arts Festival, Indio, California 118–19; environmental guides/checklists 120–1
Commonwealth Games: Delhi, India, 2010 49, 57–9; Glasgow, UK, 2014 143; Gold Coast, Australia, 2018 142; Manchester, UK, 2002 144, 164, 176; national identity 105; staging 6

Commonwealth Heads of Government Meeting (CHOGM), Perth, Australia, 2011, 140–1
community festivals in NSW, Australia 105
computable general equilibrium (CGE) models 72
concept of sustainability 3
corporate social responsibility (CSR) policies 109
cost-benefit analysis (CBA): description 67–71; FIFA World Cup 2022 69–70
'crisis' term 149
Crystal Palace, London, UK 88
Culture and Creative Sector Skills Council, UK 136

death/injury at festivals/events 152
definition: risk, crisis and disaster management 149; sustainable development 2, 4
delivery of sustainable events: carbon offsetting 121; Coachella Valley Music/Arts Festival 118–19; economic sustainability 114–16; environmental management systems 119–20; environmental sustainability 119–20; holistically sustainable event 122–3; infrastructure gains 115–16; introduction 114–15; Olympic Games, London 2012 127–9; resilience 125–6; socio-cultural sustainability 117–18; Splendour in the Grass music festival 121–2; systems thinking 123–4, 124–5
development of sustainable events: description 2–3; why? 2

development of sustainable events (conclusions): final thoughts 197–8; future 194–7; global challenges 195; introduction 192; summary/review 192–4

direct in-scope expenditure (DISE) 71, 73

'disaster' term 149

economic impacts (sustainable events): computable general equilibrium models 72; cost-benefit analysis 67–71; estimation 66–7; evaluation 72–3; FIFA World Cup 2022 CBA 69–70; Indy 500 64–5; input–output models 71–2; introduction 64–5; meta–analysis of 18 major events in New Zealand 74–7

economic impacts (sustainable events, positive/negative): employment 65; externalities 66; income 65; inflation 65; legacy 66; opportunity/cost 66

economic issues: description 5; regeneration 53; sustainability 4, 114–15

Edinburgh, Scotland, Hogmanay (risk management) 157–8

Ehrlich, Paul R. 2

Eiffel Tower, Paris, France 49, 88

employment legacy constraints 164

employment, volunteering and sustainable events: bring your own 141; Commonwealth Games, Glasgow, 2014 legacy 143; community events 138; employment/employability legacies 142–3; event workers 141; introduction 136; management of event volunteer programmes 139–40; Manchester Event Volunteers 144–5; membership management 141; Olympic Games, Vancouver, 2010 137; outsourcing 140–1; staffing 136–7; volunteers and sustainable events 138–9; volunteer programme (CHOGM) 140–1

ENCORE Festival and Evaluation Kit 73

environment: issues 5; sustainability 4

environmental impacts of events: 'environmental impact' meaning 80–1; Event Impacts Project 82; geographical/temporal scale 81; introduction 77; management 92; measurement 90–1; Peats Ridge Festival, Australia 93–5;

types 82–4; what is 'the environment'? 78–9

environmental impacts of events (negative impacts): air pollution 85–6, 86; congestion/crowding 87–8; litter/waste 86–7; vegetation trampling 87

environmental impacts of events (positive impacts): demonstration effects 89–90; nature conservation/rehabilitation 89; urban renewal 88–9

environmental management systems (EMS) 119–20

European Capital of Culture (ECoC) tourism legacy 168, 179

European Union (EU) culture capitals 168

event environment: internal/external: description 21–2; PESTLE analysis 21–2; scope 21; stakeholders 24–5, 25–6; strategy 23–4; SWOT analysis 22–4

event environment (internal): equipment 18, 19; information 18; information technology 18, 19; materials 18, 19; Moscone Centre, San Francisco, US 20; people 18, 19; space 18, 19–20; time 18, 21; vehicles 18, 20

event environment (sustainability constraints): audience 28; bid process 26; FIFA World Cup bidding 27; funding 26–7; infrastructure 28; International Sailing Federation World Championships 29–31; political support 27–8

event impact standards and guides 6

Event Impacts Project 82

events and economic, social and environmental impacts 5–6

event volunteers 139–41, 144–5

Festival of Britain, 1951 49

Festival Social Impact Attitude Scale (FSIAS) 101

Football Federation Australia 26

Fremantle, Australia and the America's Cup 50, 54

Games Makers (volunteers) 128

Gay/Lesbian Mardi Gras, Sydney, Australia 107

Glasgow City Council (games contracts) 143

Global Financial Crisis 55

glossary 199–201
'Green Event' 5
greenhouse gases (GHGs) 85
greening a music festival 10–12
Guardian (newspaper) 138
guides, toolkits and standards (sustainable
events) 7

Heysel stadium disaster, Brussels,
Belgium 152
Hillsborough stadium, Sheffield,
UK 152

Indianapolis 500 Festival 64–5
'induced tourism' 74
International Olympic Committee (IOC):
athletes' village 49; event location 51;
Olympic Games, Athens, 2004 170;
Olympic Games Impact study 185;
Olympic Games organisation 24;
unsustainable legacies 163
International Sailing Federation World
Championships, Fremantle, 2011
29–31, 179
International Standards Organisation
(ISO) 120
ISO 31000 (risk management) 149
ISO 20121 (event sustainability) 6–7,
120, 129

legacies *see* sustainable event legacies
Legacy 2014 Young People's Fund,
Scotland 143
'Legacy for Change' report (LOCOG) 128–9
'legacy' term 163
Live Earth (music festival) 10–12
London Organising Committee for the
Olympic Games (LOCOG) 25, 127–9
Love Parade Festival, Druisberg,
Germany 152

Malaysia convention industry 43–4
Malthus, Thomas 2
Manchester Event Volunteers (MEV) 145
Moscone Centre, San Francisco 20

New Zealand: Major Events Development
Fund 74–5; meta-analysis of 18 major
events 74–7

NewhamVolunteers (London
Olympics) 141
Notting Hill Carnival, London, UK 107

Olympic Games: Athens, Greece, 2004 51,
137, 169, 170–2; Atlanta, US, 1996 169;
Barcelona, Spain, 1992 49, 50, 143, 169,
177–8; Beijing, China, 2008 42, 51, 137,
151, 169; Rio de Janeiro, Brazil, 2016
184–5; budgets 166; cost overruns 169;
financial risks 168; Lilliehammer,
Norway, 1994 20; Los Angeles, US, 1984
49; Munich, Germany 1972 156;
national identity 105; 'one city' principle 51; politics 41–3; post-event use 52;
redevelopment 89; Rome, Italy, 1960
49; Seoul, South Korea, 1988 49; Sochi,
Russia, 2014 42, 137; staffing 136;
Sydney, Australia, 2000 49, 167, 169;
Tokyo, Japan, 1964 49; urban regeneration 6, 49, 88; Vancouver, Canada
2010 137, 164
Olympic Games (Rio de Janeiro, Brazil,
2016): social inclusion 184; sporting
legacy 185; urban renewal 184
Olympic Games (London, UK, 2012):
employment legacy 142, 166; employ-
ment/skills strategy 128; GDP contribution 127–8; ISO 20121 6; labour force
contribution 127–8; national identity
105; Newham Volunteers 141; one site
policy 51; physical legacy 128;
stakeholders 24–5; sustainable event
delivery 128–30; tourism contribution
127–8; UK GDP contribution 127–8;
volunteers 138
Our Common Future (Brundtland report)
3, 9

Parkes Elvis Music Festival, NSW,
Australia 73, 88, 107–8
Peats Ridge Festival, Glenworth Valley,
Australia: case study 20, 92, 93–5;
collapse 151; conclusions 95; description 93; energy 94; green procurement
94; sustainability capacity building
94–5; transport 95; waste management
93–4
People and Power (TV programme) 49

Political, Economic, Social, Technological, Legal and Ecological (PESTLE) analysis 21–2
Pre-Volunteer programme (PVP) in Manchester 144–5
public policy (sustainable events): community involvement 38–9; description 41; governments 34–6, 36–8; introduction 33–4; politics 41–2; politics and the Olympics 42
public policy (sustainable events, government involvement): ideology 35; intangible benefits 35–6; interventionist approach 37–8; laissez–faire 36–7; Malaysia convention industry 43–4; market failures 35; public good 34; regulatory approach 37; Singapore F1 Grand Prix 38; social equity 34–5; VMEC 36
public policy (sustainable events, government policy): cultural policy 39–40; economic development 39; environmental policy 40–1; social policy 40

resilience concept: description 125; ecological 125–6; engineering 126
risk, crisis and disaster management definition 149
risk/crisis management for sustainable events: Boston, US Marathon bombing 156–7; crisis/disaster management 156–7; death/injury at festivals/events 152; definitions of risk, crisis and disaster management 149; Edinburgh, Scotland, Hogmanay 157–8; introduction 149; Peats Ridge Festival collapse 151; risk types 149–51; risks and event sustainability 151–2; weather 153, 154
risk/crisis management for sustainable events – management process: 1. context 154; 2. risk identification 154; 3. risk analysis/evaluation 154–5; 4. options assessment 154–5; 5. options implementation 156

Singapore F1 Grand Prix 38
Skills Development Scotland 143

'social capital' term 103
Social Impact Perception (SIP) scale 101
social issues: events 5; regeneration 53; sustainability 4
social legacies of Commonwealth Games in Manchester 176–7
socio-cultural impacts of events: civic pride 106; community perception 104–5; FIFA World Cup, South Africa 102–3; identity 105–6; introduction 99–101; measurements 101–3; positive/negative 100; sense of community 105, 106; social capital 103–4; what do events mean to communities? 106–7
socio-cultural sustainability: consumption 117; education 118; engagement 118; production 118; social interaction 118
Special Event Volunteer Motivation Scale (SEVMS) 139
Splendour in the Grass (music festival) Byron Bay, NSW, Australia 121–2
staffing 136–7
stakeholders: community perception of events 104, 106–7; events 24–5, 25–6; public policy 33; sustainable events 6–7
stakeholders (theory): legitimacy 25; power 25; urgency 25
sustainability concept 3
sustainable development definition 2, 4
sustainable event legacies: Barcelona model 177–8; Commonwealth Games, Manchester, UK, 2002 176–7; description 175; employment legacy constraints 164; European Capital of Culture (ECoC) tourism legacy 168; events/opportunities 179–80; hard legacy 177; inspirational (soft) legacy 178–9; intended benefits (and legacy) are vague 166–7; introduction 163; legacy measurements are flawed 167–8; Olympic Games, Athens, Greece, 2004 170–2; Sydney Olympic Park 167; types 175–6; World Cup, South Africa 178
sustainable event legacies (challenges): failure to deliver 165–7; legacy planning 163–4; legacy planning to avoid failure 168–9; what happens when legacy plans fail? 165

sustainable event legacies (challenges, failure to deliver): after the event funding disappears 166; benefits (and legacy) are vague 166; benefits are over-inflated 166; global environment 167; legacy measurements are flawed 167–8; long-term legacy planning 165–6; staging 165; Sydney Olympic Park 167

sustainable event legacies (planning): employability /volunteer programmes 180–1; long-term planning and media management 181; monitoring/ measurement 181–2; Olympic Games, Rio de Janeiro 2016 184–5; process 182; venues 180; viable legacy 181

sustainable events: description 5; development 2; stakeholders 6–7

'sustainable' term 2

SWOT (strengths, weaknesses, opportunities and threats) analysis 22–3

Sydney Olympic Park (SOP) 167

Tamworth Country Music Festival, NSW, Australia 115

Taylor Report (Hillsborough disaster) 152

The Sage, Gateshead, UK 19

United Nations (UN): Brundtland report 9; environment summit 3; human activity/negative impacts 81; sustainable development definition 2

urban regeneration (sustainable events): beyond the venues 52; Commonwealth Games, Delhi, 2010 57–9; dark side of event-led regeneration 55–6; description 53–5; event venues 51–2; event-led and event-themed 50–1; Fremantle and America's Cup 50; governments 49–50; introduction 49; outside physical regeneration 52–3; post-event use of Olympic villages 52; principles 54–5

Vancouver Organising Committee for Olympic Games (VANOC) 137

Verified Emission Reductions 121

Victoria Major Events Company (VMEC) 36

Wembley Stadium, London, UK 89

World Commission on Environment and Development (WCED) 2, 4

World Cup (FIFA, Football): 2022 cost-benefit analysis 69–70; bidding 26–7; Brazil, 2014 138; Germany, 2006 102; Japan/South Korea, 2002 102; locations 51; Qatar, 2022 137–8; South Africa, 2010 102–3, 166, 178; staging 6

World Cup (Rugby): locations 51, 179

World Student Games, Sheffield, UK, 1991 164

Zuma, Jacob 102